The Power of
Countertransference

The Power of Countertransference

Innovations in Analytic Technique

KAREN J. MARODA

JASON ARONSON INC.
Northvale, New Jersey
London

First softcover edition 1994

Copyright © 1991 by John Wiley & Sons Ltd.
Baffins Lane, Chichester,
West Sussex PO19 1UD, England

A hardcover edition of this book is published by John Wiley & Sons, Ltd.
It is here reprinted by arrangement with John Wiley & Sons, Ltd.

Library of Congress Cataloging-in-Publication Data

Maroda, Karen J.
The power of countertransference : innovations in analytic
technique / by Karen J. Maroda.
p.   cm.
Originally published: Chichester : New York : Wiley, c1991
Includes bibliographical references and index.
ISBN 1-56821-431-6
1. Countertransference (Psychology)   2. Psychoanalysis.
I. Title.
[DNLM: 1. Countertransference (Psychology)   2. Psychoanalytic
Therapy—methods.   WM 62 M354p 1991a]
RC489.C68M37   1995
616.89'17—dc20
DNLM/DLC
for Library of Congress   94-23505

Manufactured in the United States of America. Jason Aronson Inc. offers books and cassettes. For information and catalog write to Jason Aronson Inc., 230 Livingston Street, Northvale, New Jersey 07647.

To

EJH

Contents

Foreword

There are very many books on the subject of countertransference but not many like this. A psychoanalytic therapist has, in the best tradition, learnt from her clinical experience and presented us with the fruits of the experiment. Dr Maroda shows how the therapist's neutrality, a hallmark of much psychoanalytic teaching, can in practice be used as a place for the therapist to hide from the patient. The analytic stance does not require a wooden, detached and unresponsive therapist calmly and compassionately battling with the patient's "psychopathology". This only fosters omnipotence and authoritarianism in the therapist and can frustrate and harm the patient. Dr Maroda shows how one can willingly enter into the reciprocal role assigned by the patient then, through reflective disclosure, help the patient to find an alternative to the closed and repetitive patterns of the past.

Of course, this is not simple, as many have found to their (and their patients') cost. Dr Maroda takes a range of complex issues and explores them through scholarship and reflective clinical practice. She also draws out the general principles underlying and guiding disclosure of the countertransference so that it is not a sanction for therapists unloading their own problems and burdening the patient. In doing this, she clarifies a number of specific aspects of technique which commonly cause difficulty or discomfort to clinicians.

Dr Maroda does not claim that she is the first to use the counter-transference therapeutically, indeed she links her points well to other writers' work. As she points out, however, there is immense resistance to hearing this message within psychoanalytic culture.

It seems to me that some psychoanalytic practitioners will never relinquish the illusion of a safe hiding place that Dr Maroda describes, whereas therapists from other schools may wonder what the fuss is about, but without understanding why, when and how to disclose feelings. Both groups would find reading this book a stimulating challenge.

A large and growing body of psychoanalytically oriented practitioners within psychiatry, psychology and social work are aware that the psychotherapeutic process has two participants in mutual interaction and that both parties bring to the relationship their own human needs, feelings and aspirations. I believe this book has a great deal to tell us about how to use this truth without fear and for the patient's benefit.

GLENYS PARRY
Formerly Co-Editor of Wiley Series
on Psychotherapy and Counselling

Acknowledgments

I have always believed that any significant accomplishment by any individual was made possible by the avid support of one, or many, friends, family members or colleagues. Unquestionably this book would not exist without the contributions of the fine people I have worked with and loved over the years. In addition to all of my patients I would like to thank the following people.

Johanna Krout Tabin, PhD for her reading and critique of the first draft of the manuscript, and for her continuing support and friendship. Her keen eye helped maintain the focus of the book and her clinical expertise served to let me know when points needed to be elucidated and when clinical examples were needed. In addition to her professional skills, I am grateful for the great care and time she took from a busy schedule to help make this book all that it could be.

L. David Levi, MD, who for the past ten years has challenged and debated my ideas with me, helping to forge the strong convictions I now have. He continues to enrich my personal and professional life in a way that few have.

Mary Alice Houghton, MD, for her careful reading and critique of the first draft of the manuscript, and for her friendship and enthusiasm.

Also, John Gilligan, PhD, Michael Osborn, PhD, Gale Graubart-Roman, MA, and my loving family for their support and encouragement.

Finally, I would like to thank Glenys Parry, PhD, the previous European editor of the Wiley series in which this book appears, who discovered me when I presented a paper on countertransference at an APA convention. She immediately suggested that I write this book and initiated the steps leading to a contract. Without her there would be no book. So I am deeply grateful for her faith in my talent and hope that this book proves worthy of the confidence that she and all of the others mentioned here have placed in me.

KJM

Introduction

This book is the culmination of a decade of struggling to implement the psychoanalytic method. At different times I have struggled for different reasons. Initially, of course, I struggled with the basics—trying to understand what my patients were saying to me, trying to fit that with general diagnostic categories and typical clinical portraits, trying to listen without attempting to mold or fashion someone else's life to my own liking, and ultimately trying to intervene in a manner that would facilitate my patients' often valiant attempts at self-healing. Toward this end, I studied the analytic literature, completed a personal analysis, and consulted regularly with psychoanalysts and psychoanalytic psychologists.

I had faith that this effort would not go unrewarded, that I would come to master a method of inquiry and treatment that I believed in and admired, that my own analysis would be successful, and that I would concurrently and subsequently treat others successfully. To some extent this turned out to be true.

However, I felt stalemated, both as patient and therapist, in many areas. I was plagued by feelings of restraint and artificiality. I felt as though my analyst was trying too hard to contain my emotional experience and that I, too, was restraining my patients' expression of their emotions. There seemed to be something inherent in the analytic approach that was stifling, especially as it applied to the expression of the deepest and most primitive feelings.

I had been taught to be sympathetic in the face of my patients' intense feelings but unyielding in my professional stance. All of my training and everything I read in the literature told me that my patients would naturally try to influence me, and that this influence would be in the direction of furthering their psychopathology. Although it was never actually stated this way, I was left with the impression that a certain duality existed within a patient that consisted of the part of him that wanted to get better and the part of him that did not. This sense of duality originated in the concept of resistance, but in practice it came out more primitively, the rough idea being that there was an innocent, suffering patient who was more or less at odds with his demonic-like psychopathology. It was the job of the therapist to turn a deaf ear and refuse to be swayed by the voice of pathology. The splitting had its appeal for me and other clinicians in that it allowed us to maintain positive feelings toward the "good" patient and negative feelings toward the "bad" psychopathology.

The obvious weakness in this formulation is that it never really permits integration of the whole person. If I feel hatred when my borderline patient hurls insults at me, yet also feel compassion and understanding because I know he is afraid of intimacy, what am I left with? The easy way out is to say I care about him but hate his pathology. Viewed from this perspective, the therapist takes on a priestlike role in which he heroically tries to exorcise the pathological demons from the innocent patient.

The exorcism strategy meant that I had to resist the temptation to be swayed from my stance of neutrality by my patient's emotional storms or periods of emptiness and hopelessness. In fact, I strongly believed that one of the hallmarks of a courageous and competent therapist was the ability to compassionately maintain one's position during such difficult times. Though I never literally subscribed to the notion of separating the patient from his pathology, nor do I believe that most clinicians do, it is evident in any scan of the analytic literature that subtle as well as not-so-subtle variations on the demon theme are still quite common.

What presented the greatest difficulty for me was that I found myself being moved by many of my patients' pleas to respond more emotionally to them. I had been taught to respond to their rage with understanding and forbearance, to their pain and desire for comfort with a compassionate distance, to their love and admiration with neither rejection nor reciprocity, and to their loneliness and hopelessness with a stoic understanding of the human condition. I also believed that anything the patient implored me to do was probably an invitation to the dance of the past, and to accept was to doom the patient and abdicate my responsibility to insure that the past was not repeated with me.

Wanting very much to be a good analytic therapist and to do right by the people who gave me both their trust and their money, I followed the rules. I felt that the strong emotional pull that certain patients elicited in me was the very siren song that I was duty-bound to resist. Knowing how important limit-setting and self-discipline are to a sane and satisfying life, I took on the challenge of holding my ground. I did so with the assurance from my supervisors that to do so was correct and that someday my patients would understand the benefits of my behavior.

As a neophyte much of this was difficult and I knew that at times I appeared quite rigid or wooden to my patients. I told myself that my discomfort with accepted technique was a function of my lack of experience and expertise. I believed that in time I would be more comfortable in my role and would cease to feel so clumsy and non-responsive. And to some extent, this proved to be true.

Yet even when I had lost the new therapist's self-consciousness and awkwardness, I still felt there was either something I had not yet mastered or something missing in the way I was practicing, because at the most crucial and deeply emotional moments in treatment, everything I did seemed inadequate. Somehow, even if partially effective, my interventions seemed to fall short of the mark, to not do justice to the awesome task of responding to the patient's most heartfelt expressions.

Worse still, patients I worked with over several years began to confirm my fears by telling me how unsatisfying, or demeaning, or frustrating, or lonely it was for them to receive such a minimal response from me. Why couldn't I show more emotion? Why couldn't I reveal what I honestly thought and felt? The only answer I could give myself was that I really believed it would thwart the therapeutic process, that it somehow would interfere with or diminish their own emotional experience and ability to contain it. And I would be guilty of "acting-out"—finding relief for myself at the expense of my patients. So when my patients implored me for a more personal response, I told myself, and sometimes them, that it was perfectly understandable for them to want it and equally understandable that they suffered in not getting it, but that the success of the treatment depended on both of us tolerating this state of deprivation.

What happened over time, however, was that certain patients pushed me beyond my ability to contain myself. These were the most emotionally intense and demanding patients, usually those with the diagnosis of borderline personality disorder. I discovered, during the occasional episodes when I expressed my anger or frustration at these patients, that rather than being disastrous, such shows of emotion were indeed quite therapeutic. In fact, they led to dramatic breakthroughs, both with patients who had previously shown little sign of progress, and with those who had rather poor prognoses from the outset of treatment.

Seeing the positive results of being more emotionally responsive to my narcissistic and borderline patients led me to experiment with this approach in situations other than those in which I could no longer contain myself. I tried using it in a more deliberate and controlled way, with the consideration that it might prove to be quite valuable if used at appropriate times rather than only when I felt pinned against the wall.

I began these experiments with *countertransference* committed to the idea that my immediate emotional reaction to the patient was the most important thing to reveal, and that I would not disclose personal information about my life unless it was clearly necessary for understanding the transference–countertransference interaction at the moment. At all times the objective was to use my feelings for the purpose of illuminating and understanding the patient's experience in the therapeutic relationship, and to integrate it as much as possible with the patient's past.

My work has led me to two major conclusions about the use of countertransference in psychoanalytic psychotherapy. First, countertransference disclosure can be valuable and effective in working with *all* patients, not just those with personality disorders. Second, countertransference can be incorporated into the analytic position without diminishing it. Concomitantly, I also believe that changes in the basic analytic stance are necessary and desirable. The changes I consider to be beneficial include shifting from an authoritarian to a more mutual and reciprocal relationship between patient and therapist. I think we also need to acknowledge that patients not only come to treatment prepared to relive the past but, also, that this reliving—with the therapist taking the role assigned by the patient—is critical to the therapeutic process and, as such, it needs to be encouraged rather than discouraged. However, the script needs to change: the therapist needs to behave differently from the original characters in the patient's life drama. Disclosure and analysis of the countertransference are essential aspects of this redramatization, as is analysis of the transference. When used correctly, these changes in basic technique enhance the psychoanalytic method. (No distinction is made in this book between psychoanalysis and psychoanalytic psychotherapy because they are not absolutely distinct and because they share the same basic principles and techniques.)

The key elements of transference and resistance are not only retained but expanded to acknowledge that these phenomena are expressed not only by patients, but also by their therapists. Psychoanalytic treatment is re-defined in the sense that it is viewed as mutual and interpersonal, and the emotional responses of the therapist are viewed as an integral part of the process, rather than something to be stifled, overcome, or analyzed away. Further, I think that failure to actively use and express the countertransference can lead to negative outcomes such as stalemates, premature or forced terminations, and even sexual acting-out.

If psychoanalysis is to grow and thrive, meeting the needs of the people it attempts to serve, it must have both greater flexibility and a stronger basic core. Endless parameters and exceptions to traditional analytic practice demonstrate the weakness of global principles that once presumed to cover all treatment situations and threaten to render all but the basic tenets inadequate.

In preparing this manuscript, I felt some sadness as I read the insights of analysts like Little (1951) and Gitelson (1952), both of whom understood the importance of actively using the countertransference. They poignantly wrote of this more than thirty years ago, yet they failed to have a significant impact on analytic technique. Given the current avid interest in and abundance of writing about countertransference, particularly in Britain, I hope that those of us who write and advocate its disclosure and analysis will not suffer the fate of those who came before us. Clinicians must come to believe that there is not only no place to hide, but also no reason to.

CHAPTER 1

The Myth of Authority:
On Building a Working Relationship

The focus of this chapter is on the value of establishing a mutual, reciprocal, and non-authoritarian relationship between therapist and patient to facilitate an optimal treatment outcome. A more egalitarian treatment relationship maximizes individual freedom and promotes and encourages a working partnership. Conversely, authoritarian and autocratic approaches are stifling, infantilizing, and adversarial. Before use can be made of the countertransference, a tone that promotes disclosure of both the transference and the countertransference needs to be established in the treatment relationship, and this should be addressed from the moment the patient arrives for the first appointment. This is important for a variety of reasons. First, because of a desire for consistency and stability, or because of a fear of losing face or seeming indecisive to the patient, most therapists will not shift from their original positions. Second, while the texture and color of the transference and countertransference are determined in large part by the personalities of both parties and by the initial attitudes each brings to the therapeutic endeavor, the therapist controls the amount and degree of progress in the treatment. It is only in the most unusual circumstances that a patient can surpass his therapist. Although the question of which professional attitude serves to best promote and resolve the most significant aspects of the transference is not a new one, it remains vitally important.

Clinging to the Past

Issues such as how much power and control the therapist should have and what feelings toward patients are "healthy" or therapeutic remain controversial. The therapist who believes in the necessity of absolute authority will naturally set a different tone from the therapist who believes in a more mutual and non-authoritarian relationship. Similarly, the therapist who finds only compassionate or loving feelings to be acceptable and professional is certainly in a different position from the therapist who feels free to hate his patients.

Hirsch (1980–81), in his discussion of the psychoanalytic relationship, points out that the authoritarian position stems not just from the medical model, but also from the authoritarian society in which Freud lived. The anachronistic character of classical analysis is no doubt what produces discomfort and even disorientation in some patients, as they struggle to adapt to a situation so different from anything they know. Walking into some analysts' offices, where turn-of-the-century fainting couches, heavy draperies, oriental rugs, and busts of Freud prevail, can be like entering a time machine.

Wallerstein (1988) bemoans the tendency for psychoanalysis to be weighed down by its sense of history and its loyalty to its founder. He points out that even though Freud died over fifty years ago, we have still not come to terms with his death:

> What this persisting feeling, of course, adds up to is that, unlike other sciences, psychoanalysis has not yet been able really to accept Whitehead's famous dictum: "A science that hesitates to forget its founders is lost." (p. 9)

The psychoanalytic institutes in America, in contrast to those in Europe, have proven to be particularly dogmatic, citing the *Standard Edition* as though it were scripture and viewing deviations from the classical approach as heresy. Though Freud continually reworked his views, occasionally altering major aspects of his theory and admitting failure in some of his experiments, this same evolution through maturation and trial and error has not been an accepted part of American psychoanalysis.

The tendency to cling to an idealized past has ramifications for every aspect of theory and practice in psychoanalysis. Clearly, an authoritarian stance is not compatible with establishing a cooperative partnership in therapy. It is worth considering that perhaps the Victorian medical model simply is outdated and not as effective as other approaches. Even Freud did not hold to this stance as fervently as American psychoanalysts do today. In fact, Freud wrote about his patients in a much warmer and more humane way than is evident in the current literature, and he was not above providing reassurance or even a small loan.

Another important point to consider is that psychoanalysis at the turn of the century was not only developed in a culture much different from our own, it was also conducted over a shorter period of time. Psychoanalysis in Freud's day was typically a six- to eighteen-month event. It seems only natural that a certain reserve in both parties would be maintained during that period. Analytic treatments today, however, typically last a minimum of five years, and frequently as long as seven to fourteen years. How on earth can a formal, unilateral relationship possibly survive that long? And why have our ideas about the nature and quality of the relationship not changed to keep pace with the dramatic change in treatment duration?

The most obvious area for rethinking and redefining analytic treatment is acknowledging the different stages and the greater intensity that are often the consequences of a very long-term treatment. It seems logical that, at least for those patients capable of participating, deeper and longer regressions will result, as well as longer terminations, so that both parties are able to come to terms with the end of a relationship that has been such an integral part of their lives for so long. It also seems likely that increasingly long treatments are more varied and complex, commanding a greater repertoire on the therapist's part.

This point might seem less critical in a worldwide mental health delivery system that emphasizes, if not imposes, increasingly shorter treatments that often consist of not more than ten sessions. Since few people have the resources required for a long psychoanalysis, brief dynamic treatments are more common, and techniques are needed to respond to these changes. Given this state of affairs, how relevant is use of the counter-transference? Even though using the countertransference is seemingly easier and less risky in longer treatments, I believe that it is still of great value in shorter treatments. In such treatments, the therapist needs to be actively engaged with and responsive to the patient early in the treatment. And, it seems to me that patients who know from the start that they will only be in treatment for a short time tend to ask for more feedback earlier in the treatment process. They are just as in need of emotional responses as patients who are in longer treatments, but they do not have the luxury of easing their way into the transference–countertransference relationship. Unfortunately, because patients in briefer treatments do not have the opportunity to establish the complex and emotionally diverse relationships with their therapists that analytic patients do, both the transference and countertransference are less rich. But the patient's need for insight and understanding of his emotional impact on others remains the same. For these reasons, countertransference can be used to benefit patients in both short and long treatments.

The Optimal Therapeutic Stance

Before discussing the nature of the therapist's repertoire, we must first decide the issue of the optimal therapeutic stance. The basic authoritarian position is defined, not as one in which the analytic therapist is cold, hostile or domineering, but rather as one in which the therapist maintains a certain personal distance throughout the treatment. He believes that self-revelation pollutes, distorts, or inhibits the transference; that "acting-out" is likely to permanently bury an issue that needs to surface; that the traditional "blank screen" is the appropriate analytic stance; that important decisions affecting the course, circumstances and duration of the treatment are primarily the therapist's responsibility; that a decision made cannot be recanted; that information that reveals the therapist's affective state or details of his personal life is usually a burden to the patient and, as such, constitute irresponsible and inappropriate disclosures in most cases; that the therapist is emotionally healthier than the patient; and that the patient is likely to try to influence the therapist in the direction of repeating the patient's past pathological episodes or relationships. This final point is commonly labeled the "resistance" and represents the dragon to be slain by the authoritarian, yet benevolent, analytic practitioner.

In discussing these points with Dr R, a traditional yet open-minded colleague, I found myself up against a wall of resistance when I suggested that she might have something to gain from behaving differently with her patients. She told me that many of her patients were quite angry with her because she extended her planned three-week vacation to four weeks, owing to her mother's sudden illness and hospitalization. Upon returning from her "vacation" several of Dr R's patients felt that she had been unfair and even abusive to them in staying away an extra week. They all shared similar fantasies that she, on a whim, had merely decided that she didn't feel like returning to work and wanted an additional week off.

This left them feeling unimportant, hurt and angry, as well as confused regarding her professionalism and commitment to them. She said that she found their reactions particularly hard to take, especially after a grueling week at the hospital with her mother. She admitted to feeling a bit martyred, but said that this was all in a therapist's day.

I asked her if it bothered her that her patients honestly believed that she had abandoned them in pursuit of a good time. She said of course it did, but, after all, how could they possibly know or suspect that something like a family emergency had occurred precisely at the end of her vacation, requiring her to fly out again as soon as she had arrived home? What else were they to think other than that she had decided to vacation a bit longer?

I asked Dr R if she had thought about telling them the truth, particularly after they had revealed and explored their own fantasies and feelings about the situation. She said, oh no, she couldn't do that. I asked her why not. She said that she wouldn't want to burden them that way, that they would only feel guilty and terrible about being angry with her, and she naturally didn't want that to happen.

I pointed out to her that, as things stand now, they are disappointed and resentful, questioning her ethics and involvement with them, and that the working relationship seemed pretty strained. And if that wasn't a burden to them, what was? Could knowing the truth be worse? She argued that it was, that they would feel foolish and asinine if they knew the truth.

I counterpointed, saying that she had admitted to me that she had had to withdraw emotionally during some sessions in which she was severely criticized by her patients because it had been too much to take on top of her mother's illness. Knowing that she was innocent of the crime of which she was accused made it even more difficult. I told Dr R that it seemed to me that if she had told them the truth she would not have had to withdraw from them and, just as important, they would not have reason to question her professionalism. Telling the truth would serve both sides by maintaining rather than weakening the therapeutic alliance.

She responded by saying that she did not want her patients to feel guilty about their anger—what about that? I said that she could simply tell them that she understood how they could think and feel that way, that all she had to do was convey the natural empathy that she was feeling for them already. It was just a matter of verbalizing her thoughts to them.

She had to admit that it sounded good but, if it really works, why does everyone say that you are "burdening" the patient if you tell them the truth? And why don't people practice this way if it really works? After a minute or two of cognitive dissonance she shook her head and decided that she had done the right thing after all. My ideas were interesting, she said, but that is just not the way analytic therapy is done.

As a final note, I asked her how she would feel and how it would affect her practice if her mother died soon. She said she would be terribly upset and would definitely have to take time off from her patients. I asked how she would confront this situation with them. She said that, of course, she would have to tell them that her mother had died. There simply would be no reasonable explanation for another absence and, besides, they would be able to tell that she was very upset. Then *she would have to tell them the truth*.

I tried to show her that this was somewhat hypocritical, as well as destructive to her patients, because many of them would probably accurately surmise that her mother's death was connected to her earlier absence and that they had been wrong all along in what they thought. I also thought that Dr R's patients would not only feel extremely guilty about having punished her for her prior absence, but they would also feel newly abandoned, having to deal with their guilt and anguish alone as Dr R left town to bury her mother. But Dr R felt that life crises of this type, as often illustrated in the literature, legitimately call for the therapist to come clean. She said that she thought this would qualify as one of those times when an exception needed to be made.

This anecdote illustrates many of the characteristics of the typical authoritarian stance as I outlined it. Dr R declined to tell her patients the truth concerning her extended vacation and, as a result, stimulated reactions of hurt and anger in her patients. They felt unimportant and Dr R ended up feeling like a martyr, exposing herself to needless confrontations with her patients. In some cases, her patients were so enraged that Dr R had to withdraw from them emotionally. To her way of thinking, being honest with her patients was a "burden" that she could not expose them to, so rather than be truthful, she decided to test, unnecessarily in my view, the strength of the therapeutic alliances with her patients. I also believe that her effectiveness will be seriously compromised if and when her mother dies, at which point she will have to tell her patients the truth.

I think this anecdote also illustrates not only how difficult it is for therapists to change the way they practice, or even to conceive of practicing differently, but also how accepted analytic practice can break down at the most critical times in the lives of patient and therapist. It seems that at the junctures where all that is truly important is what the person is feeling, and all that is therapeutic is a human response to that feeling, traditional psychoanalytic technique often fails.

Giving up power and authority is not easy for anyone, which makes it easy to understand why many analytic therapists are reluctant to do so. Yet at the same time the negative aspects of authoritarianism cannot be ignored. Balint, in *The Basic Fault* (1968), said:

> The more the analyst's technique and behavior are suggestive of omniscience and omnipotence, the greater is the danger of a malignant form of regression. On the other hand, the more the analyst can reduce the inequality between the patient and himself, and the more unobtrusive and ordinary he can remain in his patient's eyes, the better are the chances of a benign form of regression. (p. 173)

Though most therapists might agree with Balint's statement, conveying this sense of humanness so that the patient does not forever remain the imperfect child in relation to the perfect parent is difficult. How does the non-traumatic de-idealization of the therapist occur without the admission of human weakness and failure? And when this hurdle is successfully jumped in an analytic treatment, is it because classical technique was followed down the line, or because the "parameter" of admitting to a mistake and apologizing was used? And if all of us regularly do this, why is it considered to be a "parameter" rather than accepted technique?

It can be argued that we should not admit to our mistakes because a patient who had a parent who would never admit that he was wrong will lose the opportunity to confront the therapist on the same grounds. In other words, too quick an apology will bury that aspect of the transference. Though this has always been the "party" line, most of us know from experience that it simply is not true. In fact, most of our patients tend to accuse us over and over again, no matter what our response, until they can resolve an issue in some meaningful way.

For example, a patient I came to care about very deeply insisted that she was unlovable and, as she became more attached to me, grieved terribly over the thought that I could never reciprocate her feeling. Finally, one day when she was particularly depressed, she asked me how I felt about her, and I said that I cared very much about her. Though I believe that she accepted my response at the time and that it confirmed what she had perceived but dared not believe, it certainly did not settle the issue of her feeling unlovable. It came up over and over again, regardless of my feelings for her, simply because it was still a problem for her. I believe that my admission of feeling for her helped to validate her own perceptions and perhaps give her hope, but it naturally could not wipe out her deep feelings of unworthiness. What is more critical, it also did not in any way suppress or repress this important aspect of her treatment. In fact, it helped clarify for her the difference between *feeling* unloved and actually being unloved. She had always believed that no-one had loved her because she could not sustain the feeling of being loved and lovable. Gradually she began to realize that many other people had cared deeply for her, and that her inability to sustain those relationships was based on her feeling unworthy, and not because no-one wanted her.

The idea that many of the same issues appear and reappear over the course of every individual's treatment is addressed by Hirsch (1980-81):

> . . . one trend of thought suggests that a conflict, once resolved via acting-out, will never again emerge and present itself for healthy resolution. The analysis is tainted and incomplete at best. An alternative position is that issues appear and reappear repeatedly. The beauty of analysis is that one rarely loses an issue by missing it the first time or by seeing it handled through acting-out. (p. 110)

Hirsch also believes that an authoritarian relationship only serves to further the patient's pathology. As he says, "Fromm (1956) summarizes the whole course of therapy as the patient freeing and curing himself of attachment to irrational authority" (p. 105). And Hirsch argues convincingly for a therapeutic relationship that breaks this irrational tie to authority rather than encouraging it.

Defining a New Relationship

The problem, of course, is to define a new position that does not discourage or inhibit a patient's growth and emancipation. Gill (1982) makes it clear that he favors a more mutual and humane relationship, yet does not clearly state what this entails. Schafer (1983) provides the most comprehensive definition of an appropriate "attitude," but I think that his position is untenable because it requires self-discipline and a ritual of personal psychological hygiene that seem humanly impossible to maintain. Perhaps this accounts for his rather pessimistic conclusion that

> . . . one way or another, the analyst's temptation is to use the analytic work to get otherwise unavailable gratifications, support faltering defenses, enhance grandiose fantasies, and, in the end, to *use* the analysand rather than to *work for* him or her. (p. 25)

The basic point is that the more hidden, removed, and authoritarian the analytic therapist is, the more likely Schafer's worst-case scenario is to be true. The reality seems to be that the therapist needs to be monitored by the patient almost as much as the patient needs to be monitored by the therapist. The authoritarian approach is not only infantilizing and unnecessarily depriving for the patient, it is also dependent on too great a state of perfection in the therapist. As Schafer implies, no-one is up to this task. What has not been evident in the past is that the patient is perfectly capable of helping the therapist to stay on track and, as such, is an untapped source of strength and stability in the analytic relationship. For example, when I first started doing analytic therapy I was concerned about being able to discern when I had overwhelmed a patient, either by being too strong in my choice of words or by making a premature intervention. Later, I had the same concern regarding disclosure of the countertransference. I worried about missing my patient's subtle negative reactions that would let me know if I had erred in some way. I quickly discovered that my fears were quite unfounded; whenever I overwhelmed them, they responded immediately with anxiety, often leaving their sessions feeling physically ill, or being disoriented, having nightmares, raging at a spouse or friend, or reporting some other obvious symptom of intense distress. Sometimes they were capable of directly telling me that these untoward reactions were my fault. At other times they would deny this, for fear of making me feel guilty, but their distress told me all that I needed to know. I soon realized that I didn't need to be a detective to know when I had made a significant error. All I had to do was open my eyes and ears.

To tap this valuable resource we must change our ideas about the basic nature of the therapeutic relationship. As Racker (1968) says, "the first

distortion of truth in the myth of the analytic situation is that analysis
is an interaction between a sick person and a healthy one" (p. 132). Many
of our patients will be healthier in some respects than we are, and even
our sickest patients will understand parts of ourselves better than we do
and will be strong where we are weak. Though Gill (1982) does not
provide a blueprint for the therapist's role, he certainly advocates a more
humane attitude in the therapeutic relationship. Building on the contributions of others, he states:

> Lipton (1977a) has suggested that the unresponsive analyst may be
> responsible for making the patient appear more narcissistic than he is,
> because the patient has not really been given the opportunity for an object
> relationship. Namnum (1976) takes a similar view. He insists: "A transference
> can only develop in the climate of a human and to some degree reciprocal
> relationship" (p. 11). In his opinion, Freud did not intend to prohibit any
> "spontaneous participation" on the analyst's side. In fact, Namnum
> contends, the attempt at complete anonymity or total abstinence may even
> interfere with the analysis of transference. (p. 87)

If Gill, Lipton and Namnum are right, then the old notions of neutrality,
which demand the maintenance of a "professional distance" and
adherence to the aforementioned definition of an authoritarian
relationship, may actually *distort and inhibit* the transference that would
have developed in a more reciprocal relationship. For example, unless
a patient has grown up in a very formal and authoritarian household, in
which case he may actually prefer the authoritarian therapist, it seems
unlikely that a strict environment could stimulate the variety of transferences that could be formed in a more mutual relationship. It seems
reasonable to ask whether the authoritarian relationship biases the
transference in the direction of stimulating the most negative transferences
or reaction formations, which are manifested as intense idealizations or
sexual preoccupations with the therapist, as a response to a patient's
intense frustration and deprivation. That is, does the patient who has been
intimidated by his authoritarian analyst have to repress the anger and
frustration that authoritarianism provokes, because he wants his analyst's
approval? And is this repression characterized by the reaction formation
of over-idealization or an excess of being in love with the analyst? (This
it not to deny that true positive transferences also develop. But the issue
at hand is whether *any* approach to treatment is genuinely neutral and,
if not, which approach is likely to be most effective in stimulating and
resolving the most important conflicts.)

Some clinicians might argue that even if bias is created, the traditional
approach promotes a deeper and more primitive transference by
frustrating the patient at superficial levels. They might say that for the
treatment relationship to more closely resemble other social and business

relationships is to strip it of the characteristics that make it work. If we relate to our patients similarly to other people in their lives, then how will the therapeutic relationship differ in a way that promotes deeper revelation, understanding and change? The obvious answer is that, in being less opaque and more responsive to our patients, we need not in any way dilute our aim of making the unconscious conscious, experiencing it in an emotional way, and accepting and integrating it.

For example, traditional psychoanalytic thought says that if a patient asks you a question and you answer it, you will inhibit the patient from expressing anything that is at odds with your answer. Some practitioners have amended this so that at certain times the therapist may answer, but only after the patient has given his associations and fantasies. In my practice, however, I have found these maneuvers to be totally unnecessary. I find that most patients do not ask many, if any, personal questions in the early phases of treatment. Later, once the relationship has been established for some time, they tend to ask more questions, but they are also subtly offended and demeaned by refusals or deferred answers. Since I agree that it is important that the patient reveal and explore his or her fantasies, I simply strike the bargain with my patients that I will answer their questions if I am comfortable doing so—provided that they reveal their fantasies about the subject of their inquiry. And I have never found this to be at all inhibiting. If the patient's fantasy is the opposite of the answer I give, he feels free to say it, probably because the atmosphere of a non-authoritarian treatment supports and encourages spontaneity and straightforwardness. Conversely, in an authoritarian relationship, in which such exchanges are not possible, patients are guarded and more restrained, with the possible exception of expressions of frustration, rage and defenses against these affects. The patient who never knows what his therapist really thinks is afraid of disapproval. If on the couch, he listens intently for changes in voice tone or manner of speaking—anything that will tell him how his therapist is feeling. If face-to-face, he watches body posture and facial expression in an attempt to get a "fix" on the ever-elusive analytic practitioner. Though patients can certainly be pathologically over-concerned with the person of the therapist, it seems more common that they are not very concerned at all, and I think that in many ways these are the least healthy patients. In treating narcissistic, schizoid, or obsessive compulsive personality disorders, for example, it is a red-letter day indeed when they discover that I exist and that I have feelings, too. Not surprisingly, this is normally coincident with discovering the rest of the human race in the same way.

There is no question that the classical stance of neutrality promotes affect, but it often seems, as stated above, that what it does best is to promote frustration and rage or intense sexual preoccupations with the therapist. This would be acceptable if the method produced results that justified the typically long bouts of futility, anger, or silence that are often reported in the literature. But does it? If not, then how can the terms of psychoanalytic treatment be justified?

Lomas (1987) points out that the very real limits of the therapy relationship, including that the therapist will never be a lover or a parent and must someday be left, provide more than enough grist for the anguish mill. Contradicting fundamental psychoanalytic thought, he states:

> . . . projections and transference are bound to appear in the course of therapy—such is the power of the unconscious. One could not stop them if one tried. Secondly, every stance invites its own selection of the fantasies that are available. The so-called blank screen approach (even if it were possible) would not necessarily attract those most useful therapeutically. And thirdly, if the therapist does reveal himself openly and honestly, if he tries to avoid evasions, hypocrisies, confusions and concealments, which are so readily a part of social life, then the patient is in a better position to understand where her projections depart from reality. It can therefore be argued that the most fruitful therapeutic stance in relation to the patient's fantasies is strikingly different from that advocated by Freud. (p. 66)

As Lomas says, an authentic relationship between patient and therapist allows for the possibility of the former getting "real" reactions from the latter, something that is not usually available in normal living. Few people will admit to angry feelings, let alone express them, even in intimate relationships. Even fewer will admit to envy, boredom, hatred, or a desire to be relieved of the presence of another person. Though the manner in which this might be done productively in treatment will be taken up in another chapter, it is worth noting here that the socialized difficulty in being authentic, particularly regarding negative feelings, means that it would be no small task to train therapists to do this well. And many therapists would no doubt be less than excited over the possibility of adopting a role that, at some point in the treatment, could make such heavy personal demands on them.

This brings us to the discussion of the following question: *"If the psychoanalytic method is so restricting, unnecessarily depriving, and impersonal and, as such, is less effective than a more reciprocal approach, why have people been doing it this way for fifty years?"* Two basic answers readily come to mind. First, they haven't. From discussions with colleagues and from reading the literature, it seems evident to me that most practitioners deviate occasionally, if not consistently, from the classical approach. Some of the deviations have gained acceptance as emergency measures only to be used with difficult patients and have been labeled as parameters. Other deviations are often hidden or discussed only with a close colleague, leaving most analytic practitioners either feeling guilty or questioning the unyielding efficacy of classical analysis, or both. Second, many of those who basically adhere to the classical method may very well do so because it serves as a protective shield for the therapist. One of the basic tenets of psychoanalytic treatment is that patients have great difficulty tolerating the intense, primitive affects that are felt and expressed during regression. If this is so, it must be equally true for the therapist. Formerly, it was thought that the analytic therapist's personal analysis served as a kind of inoculation for problems of this sort. But very few of us still believe this.

As essential and helpful as a successful personal analysis is, it does not guarantee that the therapist can tolerate the patient's intense affects. (This is especially true when the therapist is also regressed—for example, caught up in an intense countertransference reaction.) A personal analysis cannot eliminate a therapist's internal struggle or the fact that sometimes he will fail in his struggle. Strachey (1934), Money-Kyrle (1956), and Brenman-Pick (1985), among others, have noted that an analyst will naturally avoid anything that stirs his own fears and threatens to reveal what he wishes to keep hidden from himself. What is distinctive about psychoanalysis is that the defenses used by the therapist to protect himself are highly intellectualized and that this protection was built into the system at its conception.

The Limits of Neutrality and Interpretation

There is a fine line between using the intellect to organize emotional experience and to make it understandable, and using the intellect to defend against affect that is in some way threatening or undesirable. Psychoanalysis aspires to the former, but readily and easily slips into the latter. The problem is the difficulty, for either the patient or the therapist, in knowing absolutely when this slip occurs. If the patient rails against the therapist for being too intellectual or having absurd ideas, is it because the therapist has fled to his intellect for cover or because the patient is resisting knowing the truth? Far too often, the patient's behavior is written off as resistance.

The analytic literature is certainly permeated with intellectualization. Stein (1988) recently noted that many analysts are reluctant to write about their methods and that the literature has become stale and lifeless. Is this because too many psychoanalytic practitioners have removed themselves from any true emotional connection to their patients and even themselves? Schafer (1983) says "... how many competent analysts come across as paragons of normality to those who know them best in their private lives?" (p. 38) and adds later, "The time is likely to come when you ask yourself 'To whom would I refer someone I love?' or 'To whom would I go for a second analysis?' All too often, these are not easy questions to answer" (p. 38). It seems to me that at least some of Schafer's observations about his colleagues are the result of the aforementioned institutionalized emotional isolation. Because psychoanalysis *is* intellectual (in the best sense of the word), accusing it of being overly-intellectual can easily be dismissed as the scurrilous complaint of untreatable patients and hysterical or insufficiently intelligent therapists. With this armament in place, psychoanalysis in many ways defies both criticism and reform.

In my opinion, the defenses of the institution have become "characterological" and the consequences for technique are considerable: emotional exchanges between therapist and patient are undesirable and anything that cannot be *thought* or rationally explained is devalued. For example, interpretation is an "intellectual" therapeutic intervention that has long been the bread and butter of psychoanalytic treatment, though it has been acknowledged for some time that interpretation cannot be the *only* therapeutic tool (Lomas, 1987). A bias toward repackaging other kinds of therapeutic responses and selling them as interpretations remains.

For example, it is difficult to find an analytic therapist who does not use clarification, questioning, confrontation, empathy, self-disclosure and silence, as well as interpretation. (See Compton (1975) for a study that shows that most analytic interventions are *not* interpretations.) No doubt other types of interventions could be added to this list, and what is needed is a discussion of creative and effective uses of all of them. To take one example, "empathy" has certainly received its share of attention lately, yet it, too, has suffered from the aforementioned problems. The word is now used to describe both a therapeutic stance and a particular type of intervention, resulting in some confusion when it is used. For example, a favorite story about Kohut that is frequently recounted is the time when a resident he was treating came to a session bragging about his daredevil driving on the freeway. Kohut listened to him intently and then responded with, "You idiot!", which the patient took well because he knew Kohut was upset with him for his self-destructive behavior and cared about whether he killed himself or not. This intervention is highlighted as an example of an empathic stance, achieved through confrontation. A direct empathic response to what the resident was feeling, however, would have been something on the order of, "Sometimes you must feel so frustrated and angry that you want to cut loose and don't care about the consequences." A dichotomy exists between an empathic *stance*, which could conceivably be reflected in any type of intervention, and an empathic *response*, which typically means that the therapist communicates to the patient what he believes the patient is feeling at the time. Some are even now insisting that empathy is a kind of interpretation, adding further confusion to an already existing mess. "Interpretation" should refer to a specific intervention generally distinct from other interventions. To relabel everything as interpretation renders the term meaningless and dilutes the value of the language we use.

Of course, to merely reject authoritarianism and excessive intellectualization is not enough. Something must take their place, and that something must be more than an interesting and esoteric philosophy of relationships or a novel method for therapists to obtain gratification from their patients. Like Schafer (1983), Abend (1989) cautions that any approach, attitude, or technique may be used defensively by the therapist or for his gratification. Mindful of this, he is cautious regarding any new trends away from authoritarianism:

> . . . it would be entirely contrary to what analysis has taught us about the human psyche to think that authoritarianism is the sole pitfall of which analysts must be leery. It is hardly necessary to dwell on the familiar knowledge that an analyst's characterological need to be kind, or therapeutic, or understanding, empathic and accepting, is not necessarily always or exclusively beneficial to his or her patients. All of those qualities may be part of advantageous compromise formations, and hence of qualifications to do analytic work, but like any compromise formation, they can assume disadvantageous forms as well. Countertransference potentials are as infinitely varied as the mind. (p. 390)

Though the self-psychology movement has been a breath of fresh air in the analytic world, self-psychology's emphasis on empathy has the potential for being misused in just this way. Moses (1988), in response to the considerable confusion regarding the definition and use of empathy, warns against therapists becoming too all-knowing and all-accepting of their patients' behaviors, and remaining too passive. He says that too much emphasis is placed on what amounts to tiptoeing around the patient's narcissistic vulnerabilities, for fear of stimulating the patient's flight from treatment. In this way, he suggests, the psychoanalytic ideal of seeking and knowing the truth is sabotaged, not by personal aloofness and authoritarianism, but by the therapist's misguided efforts to help the patient to feel safe and understood. He says:

> The fears of being intrusive in the therapy may lead the therapist to sit with enormous amounts of information without engaging the patient in meaningful inquiry; the therapy often takes place only in the therapist's mind rather than the patient's. (p. 590)

In addition to Moses' ideas about the misuse of empathy one could add that to assume that the patient wants and needs nothing more than to be understood is not only limiting but also infantilizing. Yet the heavy emphasis on empathy continues, particularly among self-psychologists.

Perhaps many clinicians responded so strongly to Kohut's (1971) ideas concerning empathy because he identified something that they felt but that had never been overtly discussed in the analytic world: analysts were not alert and responsive enough to their patients' vulnerabilities. Traditional analysts criticized Kohut on the grounds that empathy was not a new idea, that a fully-functioning analyst would naturally be empathic. Yet in reality, too often this was not the case. The over-emphasis on intellectualization often resulted in analysts who focused inappropriately on thoughts when it would have been more therapeutic to understand and communicate how their patients were feeling. So when Kohut encouraged analytic therapists to allow themselves to feel what their patients felt, therapists themselves felt emancipated by his dictum. The emotional relief and positive results experienced by so many therapists are no doubt responsible for the idealization of Kohut both before and since his death.

But, no single idea, no matter how good, is without its limitations. And a good idea, when pushed beyond its limits, quickly becomes a bad idea. For example, the notion of empathy, even though it is one aspect of self-psychology, has been over-used and over-applied. Empathy is of tremendous value in the early stages of treatment, particularly in the first six to twelve months when the patient is often in acute distress and needs to know that the therapist understands him before proceeding to other analytic tasks. But it can become anti-therapeutic if it is *the* major focus in later stages of treatment. The patient who needs to be confronted, to receive a direct answer from his therapist, or to know that it is normal for both him and his therapist to feel anger or even hatred, can be hindered in his emotional growth by the presumption that all he needs is to be understood. Though not all self-psychologists adhere to such a simplistic application of Kohut's ideas, the over-emphasis on empathy seems quite evident in the literature.

Just as no-one can be truly neutral all the time, no-one can be truly empathic all the time, either. Luckily, there are also no patients who really need either response consistently, so we are in a good position to give up these roles. The problem for clinicians anxious to relinquish the authoritarian position is finding a new role that is compatible with analytic principles. For some, this means continuing the struggle to remain as neutral as possible, yet doing so from a more humane and empathic position. As I previously indicated, however, a stance of neutrality may very well lead to distortions or inhibitions in the transference, as well as to stimulation of only certain affects, such as frustration or rage. Wachtel (1986) argues persuasively for abandoning the clinical notion of neutrality which, as Greenberg (1986) points out, has become a "burdened term." Discussing the issue in a symposium, he asserted that the concept of neutrality needs to be maintained, purportedly because it has fallen prey to the same linguistic mutilation as the term "interpretation." That is, it has been over-used and over-applied in the same way as interpretation, with neutrality becoming synonymous with providing a safe and non-judgmental environment. Greenberg's statements seem to reflect a fear that the importance and necessity of providing the appropriate analytic environment may be lost if the term "neutrality" is abandoned. Wachtel, however, humorously chides the advocates of neutrality who fear that responsible professional decorum will be the baby thrown out with the neutrality bathwater:

> Usually the influence of the analyst is recognized and acknowledged by advocates of neutrality, but the claim is made that one can and should strive to minimize that influence as much as possible. . . . Thus while strict neutrality is admitted to be impossible, relative neutrality is put forth as a valid and salutary ideal. This seemingly sophisticated and realistic position seems to me much like describing someone as a little bit pregnant. (pp. 61–62)

However, if we accept Wachtel's position that neutrality is truly impossible, and further agree that attempts to hide from the patient behind a veil of authority are untenable and even deleterious to the treatment, while acknowledging that *any* position, even the more humanistic empathic stance, can be misused, then what position is viable? Are we not left merely with the existential argument that the only true therapeutic stance is no stance at all—that flexibility and adaptation to the patient's immediate need are everything? In a way, yes, but the optimal stance is not totally without definition. It's more than just "going with the flow" in that it is based on a certain theory about what needs to happen in therapy, and how the personal limitations of patient and therapist serve to circumscribe this experience.

It seems to me that the only tenable position for us to adopt is to focus on the nature of the interaction and the emotional states of the therapist and the patient *at the moment* to determine what approach is most helpful within the realm of what is genuine and humanly possible. The idea is to approach treatment with no absolute rules about how it should be done and no assumptions about what a given individual needs. This is done in the interest of being optimally responsive rather than fixing on a specific stance, like neutrality or empathy, that may have enormous value at a given moment with a given patient, yet may be equally detracting at another moment or with another patient. *The critical guiding factor for the therapist is the patient. The patient will tell you everything that you need to know, if you will only listen to him and consult with him*. This removes the burden from the therapist of having to make decisions that are really not his to make in the first place, and involves the patient directly in taking responsibility for the course of treatment.

Is the Patient Our Adversary?

This approach also means giving up the notion that the patient is out to destroy the treatment. I believe that anyone who stays in therapy and makes a commitment desperately wants the treatment to be successful. I find that patients who want to be gratified more than they want to change will leave treatment within the first year, usually in response to achieving symptom relief.

I think that the only workable position for a therapist to take is that the patient wants to change, but does not know how to and is afraid. People naturally cling to the familiar when they are most fearful, which is why our patients seem to vehemently insist on remaining the same just as they are about to change. One patient told me that he felt I was asking him to take a boat out into the middle of a large lake, then jump overboard, trusting that he would be strong enough to swim to shore. He noted that this was a great deal to ask from someone who was not known for either his confidence or his courage. I agreed.

Other patients make similar comparisons related to trust, such as jumping off a diving board blindfolded, or taking a long free-fall from a plane. The organizing principle, regardless of metaphor, is that changing is difficult and terrifying, and to do so requires trust in oneself and one's therapist, as well as courage. And all of us who are therapists know that a great deal of time and effort is demanded from both parties to make such moments possible.

The difficulties inherent in the therapeutic process make the notion of resistance an obvious one. We easily talk about resistance, both in the literature and among ourselves. When therapists get together they are most likely to vent about the patient who is not getting better, despite their best efforts, or about the patient who is driving them crazy with his provocative or intrusive behavior.

I think that this has led to an unfortunate over-emphasis on the patient's desire *not* to change, and to an erroneous conclusion that the patient's aim is to get us to behave in a manner that serves as a re-enactment of past pathological relationships. As stated in the Introduction, this can only lead us to distrust the patient and to create an adversarial relationship with him. We cannot split the patient into the part of himself that is innocent and suffering—the part with which we ally ourselves—and the part of him that diabolically tries to lure us into repeating the past—the part that we must fight to the death. For one thing, how can we at any given time know which is which? And how can we communicate to the patient that we trust him and want to work *with* him, yet at the next moment take the attitude that he is trying to lead us down the proverbial road to hell? It seems to me that the most that can be achieved this way is a relationship consisting of alternating alliances and misalliances, which can only last or succeed to the degree that both patient and therapist perceive each other to be well-intentioned.

The perception of the patient as a person who attempts to derail the therapist is, I believe, *the single most faulty aspect of the psychoanalytic approach*. Paradoxically, it's an erroneous conclusion based on two *accurate* perceptions: first, that the patient resists change out of fear, and second, that the patient attempts to recreate the past in the therapeutic relationship. The critical information ignored in this formulation is that, while the patient is in fact *actively* seeking to set the scene from the past, he is trying to do it this time to create a new and healthier outcome. It has long been recognized that the past is repeated for the purpose of gaining mastery of the traumatic or conflicted situation. But, operationally, this has been defined by some as the patient unwittingly forcing the same pathological outcome. Though this is viewed as tragic and regrettable, it is the accepted state of affairs. Pity the poor patient, or for that matter, pity us all, that we constantly bring down upon our own heads the very misery we were seeking to escape.

It would be foolish not to acknowledge the element of truth in this. Obviously there is a reason why we all seem to expertly arrange for the same situations to recur in our lives over and over again. There is a certain role that every person has learned and tends to act out over and over again, like a long-running play. Because our scripts also contain lines for all the other actors, who usually acquiesce under pressure and end up saying what we coach them to say, the past is easily repeated.

When a person comes for analytic treatment, he seeks to set the stage anew, and invites the therapist to become one or many of the major characters. And the lines he spontaneously delivers, along with the way he delivers them, cue the therapist to behave in a certain way, often very much like past figures. Traditional psychoanalytic thought says that the patient sabotages himself and the treatment through this method. Rules of technique say that interpretations must be made at this point, that the patient must be made aware of what he is trying to do. The belief is that armed with this insight, he will be less inclined to persist in pursuing these repetitions. Conventional wisdom says the greatest error on the part of the therapist consists of *accepting* the role assigned by the patient and acting it out. So the therapist steadfastly refuses this role, knowing full well that frustration, rage, depression, silent withdrawal, and all other manner of negative behavior, as well as the patient's protestations, may be stimulated by this act. But the therapist must withstand this onslaught, *for the patient's own good.*

At this point I find that conventional wisdom breaks down, and I must make a major departure from standard clinical practice. Rather than remaining on the outside and interpreting, I believe that the situation demands that the analytic therapist cooperate with the patient and accept the role being offered to him. Re-enactment becomes the goal of treatment rather than something to be assiduously avoided. The caveat, however, is that this time the patient must succeed in making something different happen. And the role of the therapist is to facilitate a new, more positive outcome while helping the patient to understand how and why it is different from what happened in the past. Sandler (1976) made the point succinctly when he said that the therapist, in responding to the patient, establishes "a compromise between his own tendencies or propensities and the role-relationship which the patient is unconsciously seeking to establish" (p. 47).

If the reader wonders if "role-responsiveness" in the context in which I am applying it refers to "re-parenting," or a similar approach that focuses primarily on easing the patient's pain and providing the love that he did not receive from his parents, believe me it does not. In fact, it has been my experience that accepting the role assigned by the patient, but changing the script so that the dynamic exchange and outcome are different, usually means that the therapist will have to say some difficult and painful things to his patient. This is not a love cure. If anything, it more often consists of illuminating the dark side of life.

An example of recreating the past productively is illustrated in the case of Barbara, who came to treatment with a history of failed relationships, combining a certain haughtiness and demandingness with believing that she was unlovable and obnoxious. This combination became a self-fulfilling prophecy in that her intense and unrelenting demands to be compensated for past losses and neglect often resulted in her behaving in a manner that was truly unbearable. Then, when people sought emotional distance from her, she said, "Aha! I knew it. I knew I was unlovable and that no one wants me, and no one will ever want me." She then proceeded to cry pitifully and produced a litany of self-pitying remarks that fueled her bout of martyred grief. Even though Barbara is very intelligent, capable, attractive and able to be quite charming and even playful when she is in the mood, these attributes could not make up for the terrible tantrums just described. So people did eventually get fed up and leave her.

After about the first year of analytic therapy, coming four times a week, she began to make these demands on me. She desperately wanted me to rescue her from her lifetime of loneliness and despair, and to love her the way her mother could not. In pursuit of this goal, she would ask me to provide comfort for her whenever she came to a session in pain. This included overt and covert demands for me to say soothing things, provide reassurance, and hug or hold her. When I explained to her that this was not my role, she erupted in tirades, bitterly complaining that I was not helping her. When I interpreted to her that she had difficulty tolerating my inability to compensate her for past losses and be the mother she had always wanted, she replied, "That's right. I want this and I want it from you, and I can't accept that you can't give it to me."

For a while I tolerated this behavior, trying to help Barbara deal with her hurt and rage that I could not be the person in her life that she wanted me to be. Though she would sometimes deal with these feelings, and even have long spells of sobbing over the love that she felt she had never received, she would always return at some point to her tantrums. And these tantrums were not short-lived. She could sustain one for as long as a week or two, which would stress both of us to the limit.

Not surprisingly, one of these long and difficult bouts occurred just prior to a vacation I was taking. As the week was coming to an end, Barbara exhausted herself, criticizing and raging at me, and finally breaking down sobbing. This is how these bouts would usually end, with me responding empathically to her tremendous frustration and grief. But on this particular occasion I had had it. I was overdue for a vacation and I was tired, irritable, and quite alienated from Barbara after her week-long, going-away tirade. This time when she cried I was noticeably less tender and understanding, and she correctly perceived and commented that I seemed distant, cold, and unmoved by her pain.

The next day she returned for her final session prior to my leaving, and accused me of being fed up with her. She said that she thought I would be relieved to be away from her and wondered if I wished she would terminate so that I would never have to deal with her again. After saying these things she cried copiously and told me how much it hurt and scared her to think she was doing the same thing with me that she did with everyone else, and that the thought of losing me too was cataclysmic. She said that if she couldn't make it work with me, then surely she was doomed.

As promising as this insight of Barbara's sounds, you may or may not be surprised to hear that her "solution" to this problem was still to get me to respond the way she wanted and provide loving words and comfort. In her mind, she had to succeed in this or all would be lost. It's at this point that I think traditional approaches do not work. An interpretation would have been superfluous—she already had an intellectual grasp of the situation and this had little effect on her emotional position. I believe that an interpretation would have merely fueled her rage at me, upping the emotional ante to still another level and leading to yet another uncontrolled outburst. An empathic response would have provided some relief for her (and for me), but momentary relief was not going to benefit her in the long run. And I certainly was not going to gratify her wish. Barbara did not get the love that she wanted as a child, but she was obviously successful in getting her way as a "good enough" substitute. She made it difficult for anyone not to act "as if" they loved her. So she settled for this victory. And a therapist who would give in to her would be doing so for the same reason her family did—to get this extremely strong-willed, unrelenting person off your back. Though this would constitute accepting the role assigned by the patient, it would also constitute a failure to confront the situation in the interests of positively transforming a bad situation into a better one.

So, instead of replaying the old drama or refusing to take the role that was offered, I responded to her provocative behavior by using the countertransference in a focused and dynamic way to create a new and more authentic drama. When Barbara looked me in the eye and said, "You *are* glad to be leaving me, aren't you? Admit it, I'm a pain in the ass and you're happy that your vacation will give you a break away from me, right?", I said, "Yes, I have to admit that's true. I'm exhausted from all I've been through with you the past week or two, and I *will* be glad to have this respite. I have pulled away from you because of how stressful it's been to deal with you lately, and I just don't have the energy to do it anymore right now."

She responded to this by crying and asking me if I hated her and wanted to be rid of her permanently. My honest response was that I didn't want to get rid of her, I just needed a break. And, after all, didn't she know how difficult she could be? She smiled and said that, yes, she did know, and told me that it was relieving to have someone admit the truth about how hard it was to stay close to her when she behaved this way.

And when I spoke to her the frustration and exasperation that I felt were clear in my voice and facial expression. Though I believe that it is essential for the therapist to be in control when revealing strong feelings to a patient, I do not subscribe to the theory that it should be done in a calm, cool, and intellectual way. Showing genuine feeling in response to a patient's implied request is part of being a real participant in his drama, and it facilitates a deeper emotional experience for him as well. Once this emotion has been tapped, the way is clear for discussion and understanding of what took place and how it was both like and unlike what happened in the past.

It is not uncommon for discrepancies to exist between what a patient thinks he is asking his therapist for and what he stimulates at an emotional level. Barbara, for example, overtly demanded gratification and affection from me, yet covertly she inspired frustration and irritation. But, the therapist must trust himself and his patient by *responding to the power of the stimulated affect*. If you listen primarily to a patient's overt requests you will sometimes be left with no choice but to take an adversarial position, fighting off the patient's attempts to persuade or even coerce you into some kind of past role. *However, if you believe that the guiding force is the emotion that your patient stimulates in you, then he can be viewed as facilitating the therapeutic process.*

The case of Barbara illustrates this principle of the therapist responding to stimulated affect rather than to the patient's words or responding by attempting to mirror the patient's affect. Barbara's intense feelings of hurt and frustration, along with her pleas for me to be soothing and comforting to her, stimulated anger in me as well as a desire to distance from her. Giving in to her demands to be soothed would have been destructive, just as conventional analytic wisdom dictates. Providing empathy only encouraged her tantrums, and perhaps even gave her the illusion that she would be placated. And she experienced interpretation as distancing and alienating. Only my show of intense countertransference affect reached her and served to change this frequently played-out scenario in her life.

I believe it is worse than useless to hide from patients and to refuse to let them know that they have "gotten to you." Therapists should convey the feelings that provocative patients stimulate in them. This means having therapists show anger rather than sitting white-knuckled in their chairs while appearing to remain unmoved. Or it may mean shedding a tear, or expressing affection or respect. The idea is for therapists to respond to their patients' affect on a regular basis, rather than trying to remain impervious to them. There are no rules, except to let the patient be the guide. When the patient consciously knows and experiences his emotions he will spontaneously express them, and subsequently stir emotion in his therapist. If he cannot tolerate his own affect, he will still find a way to communicate those feelings so that the therapist can understand and help him to deal with them.

Using Projective Identification

This leads to discussion of how to recognize the patient's method of communicating disavowed affect, which is vital to the process of following his affective path. To the extent that the patient is circumscribed overtly by his old script and invites only a repetition of the past, how does the therapist know how to facilitate a new interaction that will lead to greater understanding? Again, the patient will provide the clues. At an unconscious level the patient communicates with us by stimulating his disavowed affect in us, with the hope that we will be able not only to tolerate his affect, but also to respond to it. This, of course, is projective identification. It was initially defined by Klein as an intrapsychic process through which the child fantasized ridding himself of unwanted feelings by assigning them to someone else. This early notion of projective identification was purely intrapsychic and did not include the stimulation of feelings in another person. Subsequent definitions (Bion, 1959; Malin and Grotstein, 1966) have broadened the term to refer to the feelings experienced by the therapist, as stimulated by the patient, usually those the patient either could not acknowledge having or could not tolerate experiencing. Fury, rage, and hopelessness projected by borderline patients on to their therapists are prime examples.

But, again, this phenomenon is commonly viewed in a negative way. Therapists, sometimes as unable to tolerate these feelings as their patients, often blame them for providing unwanted stimulation. For example, Kernberg (1975) provided the first in-depth discussion of the typical emotions elicited by certain patients with personality disorders in *Narcissistic and Borderline Conditions*, which was very popular with clinicians. His descriptions of these difficult patients and the primitive affect that they regularly, and sometimes assaultingly, stimulated in their therapists, helped therapists to understand their patients better and be more empathic toward themselves for their negative countertransference. However, while Kernberg's work may have released us from our guilt over hating our borderline patients, it failed to adequately address the problem of constructively using our emotions to help them.

There are a number of different views regarding the purpose and use of projective identification in the analytic process. Finell (1986) objects to the term because therapists use it too often for the purpose of relinquishing responsibility for their own feelings, and denying the importance of their idiosyncratic responses:

> The interaction between two personalities communicating on a projective–introjective level is open to many different influences. No two analysts will react identically to the same patient. . . . I believe it is an oversimplification to propose that *any* therapist would react identically to a particular patient. Neat theoretical conceptualizations may satisfy the analyst's need for intellectualized closure, but the richness and nuances of the therapeutic interaction are lost. The ultimate value of a clinical concept lies in the degree to which it fosters accurate understanding and analytic skill. Projective identification runs the risk of shutting down rather than opening up the therapist's attitude to the patient and the clinical material. (p. 106)

In discussing Finell's ideas, Whipple (1986) wishes to retain the concept of projective identification as potentially useful, yet admits that

. . . the concept of projective identification has tended to exonerate the analyst, that is, it has helped him or her avoid the real issue of countertransference. Instead, the patient can be blamed for our untoward reactions. (p. 121)

In all fairness to Kernberg, he has more recently (1987) tempered his emphasis, citing an instance of self-revelation as therapeutic. Like many others, he has broadened his views regarding the usefulness of projective identification, stating that it is "a fundamental source of information about the patient and requires an active utilization of the analyst's countertransference responses in order to elaborate the interpretation of this mechanism in the transference" (p. 818).

Stolorow, Brandchaft and Atwood (1987) echo the cry for therapists to take responsibility for their own feelings, while acknowledging the frequency with which patients stimulate certain categories of reactions. In other words, just because borderline patients are very likely to stimulate rage and hopelessness in their therapists, it does not mean that the therapist's individual tolerance for this experience and the depth and frequency of his response will not reflect his emotional make-up. It is ironic that when patients blame others for their feelings, we characterize them as personality disorders who are unable to take appropriate responsibility for their feelings and behavior. Yet we consider it perfectly acceptable to blame our difficult patients for the emotions that they stir in us.

Bion (1959) and Malin and Grotstein (1966) expanded the definition of projective identification in that they were able to see beyond its use as mere defense mechanism, emphasizing its functional value as a way of establishing object relationships. They believe that the patient learns to contain and integrate his emotional experience as the therapist "beams it back" to him. This is a prime example of a truly useful and productive way of conceiving of patient–therapist communication. Yes, the patient is trying to protect himself, but he is also trying to find a way to tell his therapist (or anyone who will listen) what he needs help with.

Tansey and Burke (1989), in the interests of improving communication and helping therapists to deal with their countertransference, built on existing constructive approaches to projective identification. Emphasizing interpersonal aspects, they discuss the need for the therapist to receive the patient's communication through projective identification. Toward this end they coined a new term, "introjective identification," which refers to "the reception of a projective identification from the patient" (p. 49). Tansey and Burke's approach is useful, but I take issue with their subsequent determination regarding what the therapist does once he has received the patient's communication. Like many analysts writing about countertransference, they subscribe to the notion that the therapist should not typically respond with emotion. Rather, he should experience his emotion silently and use it as a guide to interpreting the patient's experience. No doubt this would sometimes be the best course of action but, in my experience, certainly not always, or even usually.

Again, we see an emphasis on intellectual activity as the exclusive acceptable domain for analytic activity. Why can the analytic therapist not acknowledge feeling, in addition to interpreting and offering intellectual understanding? To me it defies reason that what is unquestionably an affective event, aimed at communication at an affective level, should ultimately be reduced to an intellectual statement, no matter how accurate that statement might be.

I would like to take this argument one step further and discuss the idea that a great deal of what gets communicated between therapist and patient goes unacknowledged by either party. The writings of Bion (1962), whose conceptualizations of the treatment situation have influenced therapists worldwide, lead many clinicians to conclude that at least some of what goes on in a treatment remains outside conscious experience. In other words, an "underground" relationship, so to speak, exists, with the extent of this relationship varying with the astuteness of both therapist and patient. But it will always exist to some extent. For example, Bollas (1987) speaks of the "unthought known," which he defines as

> . . . a form of knowledge that has not yet been mentally realized, it has not become known via dreams or phantasy, and yet it may permeate a person's being, and is articulated through assumptions about the nature of being and relating. (p. 213)

Of course, in the best of all possible worlds, there would not be any major psychodynamic interplay between therapist and patient that would not be addressed by both at some time during the treatment. But this does not always happen. Stern (1989) discusses the problems in trying to reach this material and, in an earlier work (1988), he says:

> . . . Even when we are in the midst of understanding one interaction, we are blindly carrying out another. . . . We must cultivate a tolerance for the possibility of continuous unknown participation. We are just in no position to trust our experience to be transparent to our own scrutiny. (p. 609)

If we acknowledge that this "subterranean" relationship exists, then we must also conclude that at least some of what is communicated back and forth in treatment is never consciously known, let alone stated. We must probably also conclude that at least some of what goes on between therapist and patient is pre-verbal or non-verbal. So we, as therapists, are left with the challenge of finding a way to confront these phenomena that *is* verbal, because that's how we acknowledge that communication of any sort has taken place. The task is to find the best way to do this. How do we tap an experience that we cannot consciously know about—and how can we relay information that we don't have to the patient?

I think the only viable solution to this problem is through the therapist's emotional experience, *and communication of this experience*, to the patient. We use our minds to defend against threatening thoughts, but, simply put, our emotions do not lie. In this sense the emotional reality between patient and therapist is the only reality. Anything else has the potential for being little more than so much rationalization. And even if it is not, even if what we and our patients come to through the normal process is accurate and true, we run the risk of burying something that was even more important if we do not pursue the relationship at an affective level.

Addressing the affective components of the relationship, in partnership with the patient, is achieved through believing that the patient is trying to communicate what is needed, and this is accomplished through projective identification, which may or may not jibe with the patient's overt verbal message. The therapist can follow the patient's lead, accepting the role offered to him, but helping to create a new script by responding out of his genuine emotional reaction to the patient. What enables the therapist to react in this way that is so different from others in the patient's life is not only the intellectual understanding resulting from the therapist's years of formal education, but also the insight and capacity for managing difficult feelings achieved during his or her personal analysis.

This brings me to the issue of therapist responsibility. Does a non-authoritarian therapeutic relationship, based on a belief in the expressive use of the countertransference and the notion of mutuality, mean that the therapist equally shares control and responsibility with the patient? No. The therapist is responsible for being in control and preserving the necessary limits and restrictions that constructively define the therapeutic relationship. Understanding what is happening when the patient experiences chaos or confusion, and having the discipline to say "no" to the patient's intense desires to be rescued, are all in the province of the therapist's legitimate power. The theme of mutuality concerns itself with preserving a respectful, healthy emotional equilibrium in the relationship that allows the patient to guide the therapist in, and make significant active contributions to, determining the course of treatment.

Patients come to us because they believe that we have sufficient knowledge, skill, and self-awareness to enable us to guide them through their own self-discovery. They rely on us to make the best decisions possible and to protect them from abuse and unnecessary pain as they make their journey. They give us the power not to presume to know what is right for them but to listen to them, invite their cooperation, and then make the best decisions we possibly can about what is most therapeutic. It is toward this end that the concept of a non-authoritarian mutual relationship is proposed, to facilitate the active use of the countertransference.

CHAPTER 2

Motivations for Treatment: The Pursuit of Transformation

If we are to use our responses to our patients constructively, we need to understand not only what they are seeking when they come to us, but what we are seeking in making ourselves available to them. In this chapter, the issue of motivation—especially that of the therapist—is discussed. Active use of the countertransference depends on the therapist's awareness of the needs she brings to the treatment setting. Within this context, the mutual needs of the therapist and the patient for transformation and regression are presented, for it seems to me that to some extent the analytic therapist must "go mad" with her patients in order to promote their independence and growth.

People come to long-term psychotherapy or psychoanalysis with certain expectations, sometimes great ones. Obviously, no-one expects to leave in the same state in which he arrived, and many expect that they will leave as entirely different persons. I think that most patients, at some level, share the desire to be transformed or to be rescued. They want to be magically healed in a way that they believe is possible yet insist they have never experienced. In my own clinical work I find few patients who realize that a pivotal point in the treatment will be the acceptance that the wished-for degree of transformation will not occur. Some seem to accept this grudgingly, struggling with feelings of betrayal. Others seem to accept it too easily, slipping quickly into resignation. Yet most eventually accept the loss and the necessary grieving, in part because they have discovered that transformation in the way they had imagined it is not so important after all. For these patients the realization that transformation means changing how they feel about themselves, rather than who they are, is something they can live with.

In my opinion, as much as people want to change they also want to stay the same, even if they are destroying themselves in the process. Freud thought that this was the essence of the death instinct, but the idea has never been widely accepted. Resistance is born out of fear and distrust, both of self and others. I don't think people actually resist change so much as they resist penetration, submission and vulnerability. No matter how maladaptive their behavior might seem to an outside observer, from their perspective they are at least alive. Many patients express the fear that they will be killed in the treatment. I have had many patients say directly to me, "Do you know that you could kill me?" This question is usually asked as they are about to relinquish the last line of defense. Before becoming so defenselessly vulnerable, they ask me if I truly understand the magnitude of the responsibility that I am undertaking.

When adult patients speak of death, they do not mean physical death, of course. They are referring to an emotional death through repetition of past traumas, irreparable breach of trust, or some act of interpersonal violence that they might experience as annihilation. And most patients say that this emotional death is certainly worse than the prospect of physical death, which is over quickly. To be abandoned and betrayed, for example, and then be left to live out one's life is considered by many to be a fate worse than death. (For many patients, they are referring to what has already happened to them, whether they realize this or not.) This may sound melodramatic, but these patients could not be more serious. They fear, and *resist*, not change, but the death of the person they have managed to salvage over the years. Many fear that they will be traumatized in the therapeutic relationship, just as they were when they were very young. Patients often tell me that tolerating this trauma as an adult will be far more difficult than the original trauma. I think this might well be true because as infants and small children our cognitive limitations forced us quickly into repression. But as adults in treatment, it is not so easy to deny reality. The potential for extreme pain, even trauma, in the therapeutic relationship, naturally produces intense fear. For some patients, the notion of re-experiencing past injuries without the benefit of repression seems a little like going into major surgery without the benefit of anesthesia. Viewed in this light, resistance is a matter of survival, not self-sabotage.

Though the patient comes to treatment with the dual motivations of seeking transformation yet also wanting to remain the same, another motivation springs forth as the treatment relationship is established. Once the person of the therapist becomes real and present in the patient's life, the desire to transform, or heal, the therapist often emerges. For the patient this arises from a desire for equality and reciprocity in the relationship, as well as from genuine concern or caring for the therapist, who is often the most important person in his life. Concern for the therapist becomes more evident, of course, if the patient sees the therapist as vulnerable or hurting in some way.

I remember my shock a few years ago when my patients expressed concern that I had *not* taken a vacation in a while. I had been going through a difficult period in my personal life and did not particularly feel like playing. My patients were accustomed to my vacations at regular intervals and had come to expect them, and I was waiting slightly longer than usual to schedule my next absence. The disruption in my routine, no doubt combined with their awareness of some depression on my part, led many of them to say to me, "When are you going to take a vacation, anyway? Don't you think you need a rest?" These comments became truly remarkable when they came from some of my most narcissistic and schizoid, withdrawn patients. My internal response was one of shock, yet I was also touched by their tender concern. Like most therapists, I was much more familiar with my patients protesting any absence, sometimes vehemently. I was very much taken aback by their comments suggesting that I leave, but also impressed with how much they had "silently" monitored me and depended on me to take good care of myself. When the therapist is quite obviously vulnerable, either physically or emotionally, this "caretaking" behavior by patients can quickly surface.

Searles (1973) writes poignantly of the patient's need to heal the "afflicted mother," noting that emergence of this attitude is indicative of a blossoming transference:

> The more ill a patient is, the more deeply indispensable does he need to become, at this pre-individuation level of ego-functioning, to his transference-mother, the analyst. This necessary transference evolution is made all but impossible by the traditional view of the analyst as the healthy one, the one with the intact ego, who is endeavoring to give help to the ill one, the patient. . . . The latter is thus "afflicted," indeed, but to some real degree, so . . . is the analyst. Without this "affliction," in fact, he could not hope to function effectively as the analyst in the therapeutically symbiotic phase of the patient's treatment.
>
> No one becomes so fully an individual, so fully "mature," as to have lost his previously achieved capacity for symbiotic relatedness. (pp. 249–250)

According to Searles, once an attachment is made to the therapist and a strong transference (or, if you prefer, transference neurosis) develops, the patient will recreate his original need to heal his "afflicted mother." Searles notes that our vulnerability as therapists is necessary so that the patient can, in fact, re-invoke these feelings and work them through in the treatment.

In addition, his reference to never losing the ability to relate at a symbiotic level is linked to our own need to be healed by our patients. We are always prepared, whether we can admit it or not, to merge with the proper person, someone who might provide a measure of healing that has not occurred before. Perhaps it is a reaction to this buried, intractable desire that results in our over-emphasis on *not* using the therapeutic situation for our own benefit. I think many therapists fear that their own need to be transformed will inevitably lead to abuse of patients, instead of using this knowledge to become engaged in a relationship that could be ultimately beneficial to both parties.

Therapeutic Symbiosis

In spite of the prominence of Searles and his writing, his references to necessary therapeutic symbiosis are generally left within the realm of treating severe borderline personality disorders and psychotics. This strikes me as both a significant oversight and an unfortunate underestimation of the importance of Searles' clinical observations. Granted, the degree of regression is certainly far greater when treating more severely disturbed patients, as is the case with the complementary regression in the therapist. But I think we are deluding ourselves if we believe that a similar type of mutual regression and symbiosis does not take place in any successful analytic treatment. As with everything, it is a question of degree. And once the notion of a symbiotic phase of treatment is accepted, then the core personality of the therapist and her capacity to function while partially regressed become critical factors in the therapeutic process. If the concept of therapist regression is accepted as not only unavoidable, but also desirable, then the therapist's capacity for merging and separating become vitally important to her ability to treat patients. I think it has been long-accepted that the therapist should have stable, firm boundaries, particularly if treating patients who do not. What we don't talk about is the desirability of the therapist having *permeable* boundaries that allow for reasonably controlled regressive experiences. What I mean by this is that the therapist is able to share in her patient's experience of his primitive affective states rather than simply observing them. Sharing in the patient's affect means that the therapist must be relatively undefended and open to experiencing potentially uncomfortable feelings, such as her patient's sense of confusion, anxiety, craziness, hopelessness, or anger. Little (1981) cites the importance of the therapist's openness to regression with seriously disturbed patients:

> Just as we need to enable psychotic or borderline patients to tolerate repeated temporary breakdowns, rather than encouraging them to expect to reach a stage where breakdown does not happen again, so we need to allow ourselves to regress, or break down. (p. 251)

Little's statements also apply to less disturbed patients, in that they need to repeatedly "dip down" into the reservoir of their own pain and confusion so that order may be made of this chaos. Our ability to help them to achieve insight and integration depends on our expertise in accompanying them on their journey into their own primitive souls. To make this journey with the patient, the therapist needs experience with knowing and managing *her* undefended and primitive self, something we hope has occurred during the course of a personal analysis. The therapist who can function well only when her defensive system is intact fears the experience of regression, and will need to strenuously fend off any patient who clamors for a mutually regressive moment in treatment. (I think this is why patients who constantly try to break through their therapists' defenses are so frequently the object of their therapists' negative countertransferences.)

Naturally, if we accept that our patients will inevitably know us as we know them, at the deepest and most primitive levels, then it is incumbent upon us to understand ourselves at these levels, particularly in regard to what we are seeking in making ourselves available as therapists. I do not think we can continue to delude ourselves that simply by remaining well-defended we can treat our patients well. As necessary and appropriate as self-restraint can be, it certainly isn't everything, and can do as much harm as anything else. We cannot avoid doing harm to our patients by playing it safe. I think we can only avoid abusing them, or not seeking excessive gratification from them, if we thoroughly understand and accept what we want from particular patients at particular times. Though specific countertransferences can be attributed to an immediate situation with a patient, or to the past history of the therapist, all responses and attitudes of the therapist can be viewed within the larger scope of why we are therapists in the first place. What we want from our patients, and ourselves, in the therapeutic situation colors everything we do—or do not do.

The Therapist's Motivation for Doing Treatment

It is not enough to say that we wish to help troubled people make their lives better, even though we do. It is not enough to say that we want meaningful work that is emotionally and intellectually stimulating, even though we do. And it is not enough to say that we are proud to make a contribution to society, even though we are. To be effective I think we need to acknowledge that there is no such thing as therapist "neutrality" (recall from Chapter 1, that this is comparable to declaring yourself "a little bit pregnant") and that we each have our own personal axes to grind as we undertake each treatment. We are there because we want something that goes beyond earning a living and beyond a commitment to social service or intellectual inquiry.

We seek to be healed ourselves and we heal our old "afflicted" caretakers as we heal our patients. I think we choose to do this as therapists, rather than randomly forming relationships out in the world, because of our need for control. As children, we were limited in our healing capacity because we were not in control of the situation. Our parents were. This lack of control contributed both to our failure to heal and to our fears that intimacy will be frustrating, defeating, and hurtful. As therapists we are allowed the control that eluded us as children. This control offers the legitimate possibility for facilitating a better outcome, yet also proffers a situation where our frustrated needs for intimacy are gratified while minimizing the interpersonal risks we must take. Perhaps our own vulnerability to frustration, hurt, and feelings of powerlessness lead us to a position of over-control as therapists.

Further, is the desire to be so defended and in control within the therapeutic relationship at odds with the necessary symbiotic phase that occurs during an analytic treatment? I think that it is. Our desire to re-do the past while remaining safe and emotionally insulated from our patients is at odds with the involvement and vulnerability our patients need from us. In order to function well we must admit to ourselves and to our patients that our ability to control the situation is dependent on our ability to acknowledge the interpersonal realities that exist between patient and therapist, and on our ability to maintain the appropriate boundaries that define the analytic setting.

If we cannot admit to ourselves that we wish to be transformed by our patients, then we are in a poor position to deal with the feelings that arise from this. And we will be incapable of accepting our patients' curative moves toward us. Bollas (1987) speaks of every person's desire to be transformed and the regularity with which this is expressed in the pursuit of religion, transcendent aesthetic experiences, and, of course, relationships. (On a more mundane note, we could add beauty make-overs, cosmetic surgery, body-building, obsessions with healthfoods, and pop psychology.) He also addresses the primitive, ontogenetic origin of this desire, which is born out of early experience and characterized by intense affect.

Bollas points out that one of the ways in which the need for transformation is gratified is through becoming the "transformational facilitator." In this way vicarious pleasure is received from helping to transform someone else, which is one of the ways in which we, as therapists, make constructive use of our own desire to be transformed. Since our role and responsibilities cannot allow for any direct pursuit of our own transformation when we do therapy, we must channel this desire through our attempts to facilitate *our patients' transformation*. To do this well, however, we must be realistic about the limits of transformation.

Bollas notes that the desire to transform, just as the desire to be transformed, easily slips into the realm of grandiose fantasy and magical thinking. Therapists who become absorbed in the tragedy of a patient's life and become consumed with "saving" that patient have obviously slipped into a joint delusion that "magical" healing is possible. It is surprising how many therapists believe that such cures are possible, and are unable to acknowledge that they are trying to save themselves by saving their patients, even though this is quite evident to any outside observer. Perhaps if we paid more attention to this phenomenon in the training of therapists, helping them to understand and to deal with this experience, there would be less denial on their part when these kinds of situations arise. I think it desirable for us to be aware of the degree to which we are seeking to reclaim ourselves by reclaiming our patients, and to realize when we have lost our capacity to be realistic because we have joined our patients in romantic, idealistic imagining.

The extent to which we want or need to do this will vary greatly from patient to patient and therapist to therapist, because the need for transformation logically depends on the extent of early loss or conflict. But it seems likely that, as with most things in life, there is an optimal degree of desire for transformation. The therapist who insists that her personal analysis and social relationships have rendered her invulnerable to needing her patients is unlikely to deal effectively with the inevitable wishes for transformation that she will have, albeit unconsciously for the most part. Similarly, the therapist who is all too willing to be transformed will engage in rescue operations that protect both her and her patients from the difficult and painful moments that are required for growth and change. This is illustrated in the following example.

Dr C, a therapist who had just completed her doctorate, was seeing a female law student in her private practice. They shared a certain propensity for depression, low self-esteem, and a need to be nurtured. Dr C's completion of her doctorate had been the occasion for a month-long break in the treatment, which coincidentally preceded a month-long break that her young patient had taken to do legal research in another city. Upon being reunited, Dr C found her somewhat schizoid patient feeling depressed, agitated, and hopeless. Her patient said that she felt abandoned by the long breaks in the relationship, even though she knew they were unavoidable. No matter what she told herself, she felt unwanted by Dr C, and desperately alone.

Dr C felt great sadness at seeing her patient in such bad shape, and provided appropriate empathy and more frequent sessions in an attempt to address her despair. However, as time went on and Dr C discussed this patient with me at regular intervals, two things became evident. One, the patient was getting worse instead of better, which was not what

I had expected. Second, Dr C was becoming quite depressed, too. As these two phenomena converged Dr C became increasingly solicitous toward her patient, particularly as she began making references to suicide. The issues of medication and hospitalization were raised with the patient, and it was ultimately decided that medication was appropriate. During the course of the next week, Dr C's patient asked if she should be hospitalized. At these times Dr C became unsure, saying that she wanted what was best for her patient, and that she didn't want her to commit suicide. If hospitalization was necessary to accomplish this, then she wanted her to be hospitalized.

These conversations continued for another week, with Dr C seeming less and less sure of herself as the therapist. She became very motherly toward her patient, making unsolicited phone calls to her, "just to make sure she was alright." The patient subsequently decompensated further and was hospitalized by the consulting psychiatrist who was handling her medication. I saw Dr C shortly after this occurred, and she was obviously clinically depressed herself. I asked her what was going on and why she was so depressed. All she could say was that she found completing her doctorate to be anticlimactic and that she was also terminating with her analyst, which was difficult for her. She told me about her patient, and she was clearly feeling defeated and worried. She then told me of her plans to call her patient in the hospital because she had not heard from her regarding setting up sessions following her discharge. I urged her not to do this, saying that I thought she was continuing to be intrusive and overly solicitous to her patient, both of which undermined her autonomy and self-esteem, but to no avail.

Even though I was not privy to all of the psychodynamics, both individually and between Dr C and her patient, it became obvious that *their* depression was exactly that—a shared event. It seems likely that the depression reflected the early deprivation of each and the current life events with which each was struggling as well. Dr C was only partially aware of her intense identification with her young patient and, in spite of her analysis, was still caught up in the misguided notion that she could "nurture" away her patient's sadness and hopelessness. With her strong need to nurture her patient, she lost sight of her patient's need for her to be more decisive and "in charge" of the treatment. Needless to say, it was beyond Dr C's tolerance to consider that her own feelings of sadness and helplessness may have been projected on to her patient, that she was inadvertently making her worse. Another colleague, also generally familiar with Dr C's crisis with her hospitalized patient, suggested sarcastically that perhaps they should have arranged for adjoining rooms.

Dr C's difficulties with this case were no doubt worsened by her relative lack of experience in the field. Neophyte therapists are quite vulnerable to over-identification with their patients, in addition to not having the confidence and skill that comes with greater experience. Yet similar incidents can be seen with more experienced therapists as well. In Dr C's case, she could not seriously consider that she might have been making her patient worse, because this idea had never been presented to her as "normal," as something that is bound to happen to any therapist at some time or another. (However, Dr C's depression, which seems to a large extent to be unrelated to her patient, may have been too great for Dr C to continue treating this patient. Dr C could have acknowledged her countertransference, but this is only a starting point—it certainly does not guarantee that success will result, particularly when the patient is not the primary stimulus for the therapist's emotions in the sessions. Had Dr C admitted to her own disabling depression, she may well have had to refer her patient elsewhere, which to my mind would have led to a more productive outcome, rather than simply allowing the patient to linger for months in depression and finally to terminate in a demoralized state.) To Dr C, acknowledging that her own personal crisis was being "transferred" to her patient could only increase her feelings of guilt, shame and inadequacy. But had this idea been introduced to her when she was receiving her training, she conceivably could have been more open to her patient's experience, and to consultation that pointed in this direction. As it was, she was lost in a symbiotic merger that resulted in intolerable depression for both her and her patient, with Dr C desperately attempting to be the "good mother" instead of the analytic therapist who could help her patient (and herself) understand and contain their experience.

Like most therapists, Dr C wanted very much to be a healing presence in her patient's life. Approached realistically, there is plenty of room for these sentiments. After all, saying that we believe in transformation is another way of saying that we believe in the possibility of change. It is a wonderful thing to sustain this kind of belief in the ability of the human spirit to be inspired to transcend itself, even though this happens in reality far less than in our imagination. Yet at the same time, if we hold out unrealistic expectations for ourselves and our patients, the heroic, quixotic vision of ourselves can quickly and traumatically be destroyed by disillusioned patients who come to understand that their dreams of perfection or salvation can never become reality. And those patients will come to hate us and feel betrayed by us if we encourage them to want what cannot be.

Though maintaining the appropriate balance between illusion and reality is always a challenge, the therapist who is too cynical and the therapist who is too naive or too much of a Pollyanna are in trouble. To work effectively with the symbiotic phase of treatment the therapist must be willing to lose herself to a certain extent—something that the cynic would disdain. On the other hand, becoming lost with the patient—and remaining lost—can only lead to grandiose fantasies of "love cures" that will ultimately end in tragedy or disappointment.

A related question is whether therapists, as they mature and become increasingly self-actualized, inevitably relinquish the desire to transform others or to be transformed themselves. One of my brighter patients asked me a short time ago how long I would continue to be a therapist. I asked her what prompted the question. She said that she could see a person doing this for a time in life, but that after ten years or so, what was there left to accomplish? What was really in it for me at a personal level? Hadn't I worked out most of the things it was possible for me to work out by engaging in these intense long-term relationships with my patients? And didn't I want to go on to do other things? Not surprisingly, these comments coincided with her approaching termination following a lengthy treatment. Yet her comments seemed born out of a keen awareness of the mutual nature of the therapeutic relationship and a genuine desire to see me have a happy life. She was planning to ease her way out of the successful business she had run for the past twenty years and embark on a new life that involved work in the arts and the pursuit of pleasure. She obviously felt some guilt about "leaving me behind" to continue the blood and guts struggle of transformation. She wanted me to be free, as she now was, to pursue a less difficult and stressful life. Needless to say, her comments gave me pause and reminded me of the insight that I had had in my analysis: as I gave up my guilt, I became somewhat less committed to a career as a full-time therapist.

Like many other therapists, as I get older I am less willing to take on very disturbed patients. I had always heard that more experienced therapists were less likely to treat difficult patients because they had lost the grandiosity of the neophyte, had less energy as they aged, and were more likely to have the luxury of picking and choosing who they treat. Until my patient said it, I had never heard anyone say that this preference could be related to the therapist "healing" herself through her occupation and no longer needing, on an emotional level, to take on the more damaged patients of the world—that to the extent that we had been transformed ourselves, we would no longer need to transform others, particularly at the deepest and most primitive levels.

Until or unless we reach such a state of satisfaction, we continue to work with our patients and to facilitate their transformation. We also know that one difficult aspect of life that we must help our patients face is that any transformations that do occur will be small and hard won— that it is not possible for us to "recreate" ourselves in analytic treatment, even though it is common for people to believe this is possible. Coming to terms with the limitations of life is something we can help our patients do only insofar as we have done the same for ourselves.

We also need to be more realistic in our assessment of the limitations of psychoanalysis itself. Earlier in this century, particularly during the heyday of psychoanalysis in the late 1940s and 1950s, the literature revealed the idealistic hope that psychoanalysis offered the possibility of complete cure—that there was nothing that could not be psychoanalyzed away—provided that the treatment was conducted properly. The literature focused on how this could be done with a variety of patients. Just as the authoritarianism of the Victorian era pervaded Freud's approach to treatment, so did the ebullient idealism of post-War America contribute to the notion that with psychoanalysis all things were possible.

This idealism may actually have been the undoing of psychoanalysis; the enthusiasm in the 1950s inevitably led to the traumatic de-idealization of psychoanalysis in the 1960s. As more people came for psychoanalysis, and more people trained as analysts, it was only a matter of time before the unrealistic claims of analysis would be discovered. Patients and analysts alike became aware that total cure was not possible, and that in some ways psychoanalysis was not helpful to many people who were analyzed. Not only was psychoanalysis too rigid and authoritarian, but in the erroneous belief that it provided the magic cure, many people were analyzed who possibly could have benefited more from a different type of treatment. In reaction, existentialism, humanism and behaviorism came to the fore in the 1960s, along with the belief that psychoanalysis was *passé*.

This came as a rude awakening to many analysts, who went from having long waiting lists to having few analytic patients at all. And it forced the analytic community to take a second look at itself. Issues of analyzability, the appropriate use of psychoanalytic psychotherapy, the notion that perhaps the personality and the character of the analyst might be significant and, most importantly, the idea that total cure was impossible, were discussed more openly. In the past twenty-five years we have continued to make progress, albeit slowly, in these areas. Instead of believing that we have been "cured" and are now infinitely capable of "curing" our patients, we try instead to meet the challenge of being "good enough," something achieved only through listening to our patients and knowing how fallible we are.

If the prevalence of a view in the literature is any indication of its popularity or acceptability, we still have a way to go before we fully address the implications for the compensatory aspects of our vocational choice. That is, we have hardly begun to explore the issues of "why" we become therapists, how our own personality organization fits or does not fit with the analytic approach, what is unique (if anything) about people who wish to conduct long-term intensive treatments, and how our own needs are met by being therapists.

But there have been a few notable exceptions. For example, in 1953 Racker (1968) raised this rhetorical question: "What motive (in terms of the unconscious) would the analyst have for wanting to cure if it were not he who made the patient ill?" Racker, and Little (1951), both emphasized *the inherent danger of the countertransference in that the analyst might need to keep the patient sick* long after the patient actually is sick, in order to re-experience the relief that comes from making him well. Little (1951) assured us that this continuous cycle of making ill and restoring can be and is used productively as a normal part of the analytic process. But it can also be used destructively:

> Unconsciously we may exploit a patient's illness for our own purposes, both libidinal and aggressive, and he will quickly respond to this.
>
> A patient who has been in analysis for some considerable time has usually become his analyst's love object; he is the person to whom the analyst wishes to make reparation, and the reparative impulses, even when conscious, may through a partial repression come under the sway of the repetition compulsion, so that it becomes necessary to make that same patient well over and over again, which in effect means making him ill over and over again in order to have him to make well. (p. 34)

The timelessness of these observations is clear in Brenner's writings twenty-five years later. In response to the question, "What drive derivatives are gratified by being an analyst?" he stated, "Different ones for different analysts, of course, but one which often plays a part is the wish to see another suffer" (1985, p. 158). The patient enters treatment suffering and, in making him well, the analyst relieves herself of guilt at the same time. In general, the truth is probably that we sometimes seek and find relief in our patients' suffering. Every aspect of their struggle is potentially relieving to us, because our position as transformational facilitators provides endless possibilities for vicarious experiences. Although the notion of our need to make our patients "ill" and then make them "well" may be abhorrent to some, it is in fact how we go about helping them to achieve a reasonable transformation. The problem does not lie with our need to do this, but rather it has to do with the fact that our own needs may prevent us from allowing the patient to move on. The process of making the patient better may be too gratifying to give up, our own competitive strivings and envy may get in the way of allowing the patient to get better, our fears of abandonment can result in our not letting the patient leave, and our own need to be healed through the specific mechanism of making the patient ill may not have been dealt with adequately. In other words, we may still be symptomatic or conflicted, for example, even though the patient, relatively speaking, is not. As long as this is so, and to the extent that we wish to be healed in relation to a particular patient, we will need to keep making him symptomatic or in conflict as a way of restoring ourselves.

For example, let us say that Patient A, a 19-year-old boy, comes to therapy for the purpose of mourning his father's death. His therapist also lost *his* father at about the same age as Patient A and never adequately mourned his own father's death because of his fears of being out of control or insufficiently masculine. Patient A, however, has no such problems dealing with grief. The reason he has not grieved adequately is because people keep trying to comfort him by telling him he will get over his loss in time, and that he is now the man of the family and has to be strong for his mother. Given the opportunity to express his feelings in his therapy sessions, Patient A is perfectly ready and willing to do so and grieves deeply. His therapist finds these sessions very gratifying, not only because his patient is feeling much better, but because he has found relief for himself in vicariously experiencing Patient A's deep sadness. Because the therapist cannot actually break down sobbing in the sessions as his patient has done, he does not get the full therapeutic benefit that comes from expressing deep emotion and cannot make the same progress on this issue as his patient has done. As a direct result of the therapist's continuing need to participate in his patient's grieving, he has recently begun to cut off the patient's affective experience soon after it begins, causing the patient to feel rejected and to inhibit his sadness. This stifles the patient's progress and insures that he will remain in treatment longer, thus satisfying the therapist's need to continue his own grieving process. The treatment continues to proceed well only after the therapist becomes aware of what he is doing, adequately mourns his own father's death, or both. It is my opinion that therapists are rarely consciously aware of affecting a treatment in this way, in part because of the guilt and shame that might accompany the awareness of keeping a patient "down" in therapy.

Though this example involves a specific issue, the therapist's inability to move forward with the patient could also exist in relation to broader developmental issues and overall level of interpersonal functioning. What I am basically saying is that I doubt that any therapist can take a patient much beyond where she has gone herself. When the patient reaches the therapist's limit in a particular aspect of functioning, yet needs to go further, he will either have to bring the therapist along, or give up trying to make progress in that area with that particular therapist. Since all of us have our limitations, I think that our patients, particularly the higher functioning ones, inevitably run into these limitations all the time. Even though I basically advocate accepting our personal limitations and being realistic about them, I think we also need to be committed to the value of stretching and growing as much as we can in the interests of maximizing each therapy we conduct.

Brenner also points out that the "making well" part of the cycle can be the product of a reaction formation in the analyst:

> They [analysts] repress their wish to watch others suffer, they disown any such wish, they attribute it to others whenever possible, they emphasize the opposite wish—to help, to cure—they identify with great healers, like Freud, and with lesser ones, like their own analysts and teachers. In short, they defend against the wishes that cause them anxiety and depressive affect in every possible way. (p. 159)

But he fails to address the undesirability of maintaining a defensive stance like this during the symbiotic phase of an analytic treatment, be it psychoanalysis or psychoanalytic psychotherapy. At this time in particular, I think it essential that the analytic therapist be free to participate in periods of psychological merging with the patient, as well as prepared to face the primitive fears and aggression that are inevitably stimulated during such a period of mutual regression. Just as the patient cannot be healed without giving up his defenses, the therapist cannot facilitate healing unless she is capable of doing the same.

Let me cite a brief example of an instance when I had trouble letting a patient feel what she was feeling, for a reason that I believe to be quite common. Sarah, a psychology graduate student in her late twenties, was prone to great depressions that often culminated in intense feelings of hopelessness and suicidal depression. When she reached this nadir and told me she was thinking seriously of ending it all, I always had difficulties handling the situation. She was very sophisticated, intelligent, and mournfully philosophical, insisting that she could not work with me if I did not respect her right to take her own life. On one hand, I believed she had such a right and I truly did respect it; on the other hand, I did not want her to commit suicide—for both our sakes.

She became irritated whenever I would inquire regarding her actual intent, brushing this off as mundane and distracting her from her intense affect. Most of the time when I was uncomfortable with Sarah's suicidal depression it was because I feared that she would actually commit the act. It was clear to me that I didn't want her to die, and that I didn't want the emotional and professional consequences that would result for me if she did. But she was right when she said that these concerns of mine took both of us away from what she was experiencing. My own fears kept me from just staying with her in the midst of her despair.

Also, if I am to be honest, I have to admit that there were times when I identified with Sarah, recalling my own past existential crises that included wondering if life was really worth living. And, depending on my own state of mind at the time, I was sometimes too threatened by simply sitting with Sarah and feeling the full extent of her pain and hopelessness. On a bad day I think I unconsciously feared that if I did not defend against what she was feeling there would be two severely depressed people in the room instead of one. But as I listened to her complaints about my defensiveness and worked on giving up those defenses and allowing myself to feel what she was feeling, I found that I was less fearful, gaining trust that both of us could tolerate our worst experiences of depression, even if we felt them simultaneously. Though I had discovered this truth previously in my personal analysis, I had only become comfortable with it as a patient. What Sarah taught me was that it was in her best interest to allow myself to submit to this deep despair in my role as her therapist as well. And, not surprisingly, to do so resulted in both of us ultimately feeling better and having a better therapeutic relationship.

The Mutuality of the Healing Process

In my experience, many analytic therapists are typically ambivalent at best regarding the possibility of being healed by a patient, though I do not find this attitude in most patients. They are typically much quicker to see both the desirability and necessity of some degree of mutual healing. Not that they are interested in healing their therapists at their own expense—they are not. But our patients are interested in healing us, their therapists, *as they are healed.* Most patients do not consider the process to be split in such a manner that either the therapist or the patient is healed, but not both. I have found that my most insightful and sophisticated patients intuitively understand and accept the notion of mutuality, not only in the therapeutic relationship, but in all relationships. For many of them, part of their need for therapy stems from having this healthy desire for mutuality thwarted in their earliest relationships. It is their hope that the therapist will be better able to deal with this, as well as other aspects of life, than their caretakers were.

Searles (1975) has long noted his patients' need to be therapeutic to him, to heal him *as a part of healing themselves, rather than as a defense or inappropriate role reversal.* He stresses the patient's ability to unconsciously perceive the therapist's "ill components" and introject them during the symbiotic phase of treatment. Searles believes that most patients have "failed" for one reason or another in their therapeutic effort toward the mother, and he discusses how this can leave the patient guilt-ridden and subsequently unable to grow and be happy. Searles seems to be the only person writing about analytic treatment who understands the importance of mutuality in relationships, and the guilt, shame and feelings of inadequacy that result when a person is thwarted in this healthy pursuit. Many parents, as well as therapists, do not understand this, believing instead that the optimal parental stance involves only giving to their children rather than also receiving from them.

Though Searles' contributions have chiefly been the result of working with more disturbed patients, I believe that his observations are equally applicable to healthier ones. In discussing the importance of allowing the patient to be therapeutic toward his analyst, as he was not able to be toward his mother, Searles (1975) states:

> In my experience of recent years, it is only insofar as he can succeed in his comparable striving in the treatment, this time toward the therapist, that the patient can become sufficiently free from such guilt . . . so that he can now become more deeply a full human individual. (p. 99)

The concept of "mutual healing" is naturally a controversial one because it stimulates fears of needy therapists abusing their patients under the guise of providing something healthy for them. Allowing patients to be therapeutic toward their therapists does not mean taking turns discussing childhood pains. Rather it means permitting the patient, in his own time and at his own behest, to respond emotionally to the therapist and to have this communication acknowledged.

Searles seems somewhat reluctant to discuss the specifics of technique regarding the patient's therapeutic striving, stating that it is simply too complex an issue and too dependent on intuition and timing. He says he does not in any formal way acknowledge that he is receiving help from a patient. However, I think that small-scale acknowledgements are appropriate, such as when a patient notes that you look tired, and then says something like, "Well, don't worry, I won't give you a hard time today, I can tell you've had a difficult day." I think that at those times it is beneficial to say "I appreciate your concern, but I hope that you are not so interested in protecting me that you will not go ahead and say what is on your mind." Depending on how difficult a day I've actually had, I may also need to say something like, "Yes, it has been a tough day, but I really want you to talk freely to me anyway." In this way I receive and acknowledge the patient's empathy, which can often enable him to go on with the session more successfully than he would have otherwise. And the patient feels both respected and relieved. Though I will deal with examples of this kind more thoroughly in the chapter on techniques (see Chapter 5), the point I want to make here is that the therapist can achieve the effect of acknowledging the patient's therapeutic strivings through the accumulation of exchanges like the one just mentioned. To say, "Yes, I'm tired" or "Thanks for asking, but I'm okay," provides recognition of the patient's need to nurture the therapist without making too much of it. I agree with Searles that the patient would not need the therapist to make some grand interpretation about his overall therapeutic strivings toward him. As with most aspects of the analytic process, progress is made through the build-up of small but significant therapeutic moments.

What is most important, of course, is that the therapist should not make the mistake of sabotaging the patient's efforts to be therapeutic. Frequently this is what occurs when a therapist refuses to admit to a feeling that the patient has accurately identified. Patients who are denied access to their therapists' emotions feel rejected and demeaned. And to the extent that they intuitively perceive their therapists to be needy or disabled, they will feel guilty about doing well. Well-meaning therapists who remain silent in the interest of not "burdening" their patients, or those who insist on analyzing why the patient inquired about their health rather than first answering the question, may paradoxically do them harm. They operate under the illusion that controlling their overt verbal responses serves to control what they are communicating to their patients.

Countertransference Dominance

Since we repeatedly tell our patients that control of the type just mentioned is not possible, it is a mystery that we continue to perpetuate this idea as it applies to ourselves. Belief in this type of omniscient self-control ultimately leads to periods of *countertransference dominance*; by this, I mean that the treatment is dominated not by the patient's attempts to repeat the past, but by the analyst's. This notion is so abhorrent to us that it is virtually never mentioned. We always talk about the patient's repetition compulsion, but never about the therapist's, even though the therapist has the authority to control the direction of the sessions and the relationship. Can we afford to be so naive as to assume that the therapist's power is not used inadvertently at times for the purpose of attempting to heal herself? And can we deny that the therapist who cannot admit to her need to be healed will be more likely to respond *unconsciously* out of this need—or out of the frustration of this need? Let us take the worse-case scenario of a therapist who is out of control—one who sexually abuses a patient. Searles (1975) discusses this event as an expression of the therapist's neediness:

It has long been my impression that a major reason for therapists' becoming actually sexually involved with patients is that the therapist's therapeutic striving has desublimated to the level at which it operated in childhood. He has succumbed to the illusion that a magically curative copulation will resolve the patient's illness which tenaciously had resisted all the more sophisticated psychotherapeutic techniques learned in his adult-life training and practice. (p. 129)

Destructive action by the therapist, be it keeping the patient frustrated or depressed for unduly long periods of time, subtly encouraging the patient's repression of anger and dependence, or social or sexual acting-out with a patient, are the result of the therapist's inability to admit to herself that she needs the patient in some very significant way. As long as the therapist is in the dark about her own motivations for working with the patient, and the needs that are stimulated by that patient, she will be incapable of acting on this phenomenon in a productive, helpful way. The following example will serve to illustrate my points.

I consulted on an out-of-state malpractice case some years ago in which a well-known psychoanalytic psychologist, Dr K, was accused by his patient of having had sex with her during one of her sessions. Having agreed to review the case, I was inundated by the patient's attorney with a mountain of depositions, case material, numerous letters from the patient to her therapist, and statements by several other therapists in the community, some of whom had also treated the patient.

As I pored over this material I was struck by its novelistic nature. Here was a very disturbed young woman, with a diagnosis of borderline personality, who had agreed to a twice-weekly psychoanalytic treatment, clearly in great need of help. She was attractive, seductive, committed to treatment, yet impossible. After the first year she began to fall into periods of hopeless depression, alternating with periods of rage at her therapist for not helping her. She criticized him constantly, yet was also so truly pained and vulnerable that she stimulated not only feelings of rage, guilt, hopelessness, and inadequacy in him, but also great pathos. As if this were not enough, when all else failed, she begged, pleaded and cajoled him to love her as she loved him, and to make love to her.

In response to her pleas, he interpreted. And the more he interpreted, the more agitated she became. In response to this, he became *aggressively interpretive*. He accused her of trying to make him feel as lousy as she did, and of trying to defeat him and ruin the treatment by seducing him. In his deposition he described how she routinely adopted seductive poses, particularly when sitting up on the couch, rather than lying down. Dr K said that the patient repeatedly sat with her legs just far enough apart to show her underwear. To my amazement when reading his deposition, he *never once informed her that he could see up her skirt.* Rather he continued to look, yet resented all the ways in which she stimulated him. He reported in his deposition that he had told her a number of times that she was seductive toward him, but this seemed to occur only when he was angry with her. It was a weapon he used to counter her blaming of him.

In the depositions of both the patient and Dr K it was evident that the frustration on both their parts reached unbearable proportions. Attracted to each other and desperate to validate themselves and the treatment, they persisted until the tension in Dr K's office became intolerable. Gridlocked into mutual seduction, frustration and rage, the patient alleged that they finally had sex on the couch.

This case was ultimately settled out of court, with the therapist denying the patient's allegations. Clearly, the sexual act was not the culmination of a love relationship, nor was it a simple matter of an irresponsible therapist grabbing some gratification where he could find it. It was the desperate act of a therapist who was out of control, primarily with frustration and rage. His patient had continuously accosted him and rendered him impotent as a therapist. He, in turn, blamed her for his inability to take control of the situation, and no doubt fantasized having sexual power where legitimate power as a therapist no longer existed.

If Dr K did in fact have sex with his patient, he probably did so to relieve his feelings of powerlessness, to relieve his sexual tension, and to take the ultimate revenge on her for exposing his weakness. Searles would probably conclude that Dr K hoped that in granting his patient's constant overt wish for sex he would truly heal her, and I think this was no doubt one aspect of his motivation. But I also believe that Dr K committed an act of violence against his patient. Just as borderline patients must live with their ambivalence, so must their therapists. And Dr K's ambivalence toward his difficult patient culminated in his act of taking advantage of her sexually.

Dr K's deposition revealed that he not only failed to let his patient know when she was being inappropriately seductive (legs spread apart), but that he never directly informed her of any of his negative feelings toward her. He made pejorative interpretations, became rigid and distant, but never directly expressed to her that he was becoming terribly frustrated. He also never let her know that he was pained at not being able to do more to ease her constant distress. I do not believe that he would ever have reached the point where he felt compelled to act out sexually had he been willing to admit to his own sexual attraction to his patient, and to the intense ambivalent feelings that she stimulated in him. Apparently unaware of his deep need to heal her, and equally unaware of his deep need to see her suffer for having thwarted him in his task, he took the greatest revenge on her that was available to him.

Though I would agree with those who might say that much of this self-awareness should have gone on in Dr K's own mind, I believe that this particular patient is characteristic of the kind of patient who so desperately needs an affective response from a therapist that no amount of self-analysis, personal analysis, or consultation could ever serve to break the tension that built up between her and Dr K. Rather, he would have needed consultation in order to gain a perspective on his feelings and gain enough control over them in order to express his countertransference reactions to his patient constructively. I believe that the only type of intervention that logically could have broken through their continuous stalemate was a personal, affective confrontation between them. Had Dr K been aware that this was what his patient really needed, I believe he would have attempted to provide it. It took years for him to succumb to their mutual frustration, and during that period he obviously made numerous misguided and ineffective attempts to break their therapeutic stalemate, including approaching her about seeing another therapist. (She responded to this idea with the threat of suicide, which is the patient's way of saying, "Sorry, you're not getting off that easy.")

This case illustrates many of the points I am making in this chapter, but none more clearly than the inadequacy of personal analysis, clinical experience, and consultation in breaking intractable therapeutic stalemates. Dr K was a very experienced, well respected analytic clinician who had been analyzed and who pursued several consultations in his efforts to be successful with his borderline patient. Referral out would have been traumatic to the patient and could have resulted in a suicide attempt. There was simply nowhere to go except to work things out with her or destroy the relationship. In my opinion, he was doomed to destroying the relationship because he had *no idea* how to work things out with her. Everything he had been taught told him to simply persevere and keep on interpreting. This obviously did not work with this patient, but it was all Dr K knew how to do. I cannot state too strongly how unworkable I think it is to try to break a therapeutic stalemate without consulting the patient and enlisting his help. We presumably expect that our patients will at some point be able to work out their difficulties in their relationships, not only with us, but ultimately with the people who they live with in the world. We do not tell them that when they run into roadblocks they should seek a consultation. We try to help them to be able to sustain relationships on their own, through good times and bad, and to tell others when they feel that something is wrong. Why do we not apply these values to their relationships with us? Why do we think it better to discuss the problems we are having with them *with someone else?* And how can we imagine that someone outside the relationship will know better than we and our patients about where the heart of the difficulty lies? None of these things makes sense to me.

It is paradoxical that while we insist that everyone needs treatment *before* becoming one who treats, we persist in disavowing the therapist's *continuing* need to be healed. We have finally arrived at the point at which we can concede that we cannot entirely "cure" patients, but we have yet to make the leap to acknowledging, first, that we aren't cured by our own treatments, and second, that our patients can help to cure us through their interactions with us. And we deny the impact that this knowledge has on the treatment. Even in training, we deny that part of the original and ongoing motivation of the therapist's vocational choice is the need to both heal and be healed. Refusing to acknowledge this, as well as other significant aspects of transference–countertransference interplay, can result in an unnecessarily limited, stalemated, or destructive treatment. If a strong countertransference cannot be recognized and dealt with directly in the treatment, it will inevitably be acted out in some way. The acting out can take the form of keeping a non-therapeutic distance from the patient or refusing to merge with the patient out of fear of being out of control. Or it can take the form of obtaining some direct gratification from the patient, either during the treatment or following termination. In any event, the patient pays the price by being denied the therapeutic regression and subsequent independence that he needs and that the therapist is responsible for facilitating.

Mutual Regression

Bollas (1987) emphasizes the importance of mutual regression in a therapeutic relationship, noting that this shared experience additionally provides the deepest level of empathy possible:

> Only by making a good object (the analyst) go somewhat mad can such a patient believe in his analysis and *know that the analyst has been where he has been and has survived and emerged intact* with his own sense of self, an evolution in the countertransference that will match the emergence of the analysand within the transference from his family madness. In this sense, the transference–countertransference lifetime is necessarily a going mad together, followed by a mutual curing and a mutual establishment of a core self. (p. 254)

The example of Dr K and his borderline patient represents any therapist's worst nightmare. They *did* go mad together but, because of their lack of ability and awareness, they could not cooperate in mutual healing. They went mad, and stayed mad, until they could destroy the relationship as a way of escaping. Analytic therapists often avoid, resist, or attempt to abort the experience of shared madness in the belief that it will be destructive. But it is not the experience of madness that is destructive, but rather the inability to deal effectively with it. Let us look at another case example that illustrates the concept of mutual healing.

Sam, who had been in treatment for three years, was ready to confront how his constant anger interfered with his relationships. He had often expressed sadness that he would never be able to have a relationship with me, noting that he could live with this reality if only he could believe that he was good enough for me. He often said that he could only go on with his life if he believed that we could have been together had we met under different circumstances. During a difficult period in the treatment when he was struggling over giving me up, he was very angry with me, but couldn't admit it. Instead he remained depressed and was highly critical of me. Each session seemed pointless, as Sam's depression and rage only deepened, in spite of my best efforts. I was beginning to dread seeing him since all I experienced with him was being punished for not being able to help him. After a couple of weeks of this, he desolately stated that he knew I would never want to be with him, even if I wasn't his therapist, because I could not stand to be with someone who is always so angry. Then he looked hard at me, as if he expected an answer.

I was feeling very beaten down by weeks of criticism, pouting, and expressions of disgust from Sam. He would also leave messages on my answering machine telling me what a lousy therapist I was. I was feeling desolate, too, but not nearly to the degree that Sam was. Nonetheless, I did feel overwhelmed and felt that I had "gone mad" with Sam in that I was now sharing his feelings of hopelessness and that nothing he ever did was right. I felt like bursting out with my frustration, telling him he was right—that he was making me crazy and that I could hardly stand to see him at all. But that obviously would have been destructive, both because I would have been out of control and because talking to him that way would have been terribly hurtful.

But I knew he was looking for something from me, so when he looked hard at me and stopped talking, I asked him what he wanted, noting that he seemed to be asking me to answer. He said he *did* want an answer. I asked him how he would feel if I told him that his anger was, or was not, too much for me to bear. He said it didn't matter. He just wanted an answer.

In a controlled, but not emotionless way, I told him that he was right, that I found his constant anger to be draining and trying, and that I would not have been able to sustain a social relationship with him had we met outside of treatment. He said he was crushed to hear me say that. I asked him what his response would have been if I'd said the opposite. He said he would not have believed me—that it would have been a lie. We then discussed how he *knew* that his chronic anger drained the life out of any relationship he was in, even though he constantly fled from this reality and liked to think that it was the other person's fault. The other reason he knew it was hard for me to bear his anger was because it was hard for him to bear, too. I felt sad for him, which he clearly saw. He then said that he also knew the truth about how defeated I was feeling and wondered if I was giving up on him. I told him it was hard not to feel defeated when nothing I did seemed to help him very much right now, but that I was by no means giving up on him. I said I was still committed to working with him, that he had made progress with his anger, and that we would keep working on it. When this session ended he was obviously relieved and we both felt much better.

In my opinion, these periods of being "stuck" in mutual hopelessness, depression, anger, or defeat are both inevitable *and constructive.* Sam and I had had difficult times before, and did again. But they were always resolved through some shared distress that was acknowledged and worked through together. If Sam was in distress, and I wasn't, he would stay worked up until I finally joined him.

I have found this need for shared madness, shared pain, shared vulnerability, or whatever you may call it, to be particularly prevalent in many patients with narcissistic and borderline personality disorders. The need for merger and as much shared experience as possible is not sought for the purpose of tormenting the therapist, but rather to provide the symbiosis and almost primitive type of empathy that is essential to the healing process. We, as analytic therapists, may not feel that so much emotional involvement is desirable, but don't try to tell that to our personality-disordered patients (not to mention the schizophrenics that Searles discusses.) They do not want to hear it and they do not believe it. They want us to join them, at least for a while, in their world. They want us to feel their pain while reliving our own, and temporarily not know the difference. Admittedly, this is asking a great deal from us. But if we are not prepared to travel on this journey with them, following their map and their itinerary, then I am afraid we cannot treat them.

Any attempts to avert these periods of mutual madness only result in the patient attempting to attenuate his experience or in the therapist defending himself by remaining aloof. I wonder if part of the need for mutuality is not based on the avoidance of humiliation as well as the pursuit of empathy. There is something about human nature that says that if I am in the stew then I want you to be in the stew, too. We should be equal. Our patients can accept the asymmetry in dependence, regression, and love. They can accept the asymmetry in power because they know these things must be true for the therapy to work. Someone must be in control, or no change will occur. All that they ask is that we occasionally lose ourselves in the experience with them, that we not always be on the outside, looking in. If we do this, then we cannot possibly look down on them. Because if we were to reject them for their vulnerability and pain, then we would have to reject ourselves as well. And the power they have to help heal us additionally serves to lessen the inequality in the relationship. From the patient's point of view, we are in the stew together. Even though we may or may not be as disturbed as our patients, and certainly will not regress in the relationship to the extent that they must, they want to have some sense that we are in it with them. They also want and need to believe that they have something more to offer us than just money. And the more we share this view, the more helpful we will be.

The idea of getting lost for periods of time during any treatment has not enjoyed a great deal of popularity in the analytic world. The ideal of the analytic practitioner is someone who understands everything and is always in control—of herself, of her patient, and of the treatment situation. She anticipates many of her patients' moves or quickly grasps the meaning of any unforeseen event. For some, the ideal is to be lost without experiencing anxiety (see especially Bion (1967), who discusses this ideal and its relationship to creativity in the therapeutic process). In reality, of course, we are lost quite frequently. In a monument to understatement, Tower (1956) said:

> Every analyst of experience knows that as he gets deeper and deeper into an analysis, he somehow or other loses a certain perspective on the total situation. (p. 166)

The idea, of course, is to be lost in the interest of being found at some later time. I believe that more errors result from the expectation of always understanding and being in control than result from acceptance of not knowing and feeling lost or confused. A therapist who knows she is lost keeps seeking the truth. A therapist who must believe she is always in control reaches premature conclusions and cuts off the affective experience of herself and her patients. Repressed conflicts then go underground, usually to surface later in some form of acting out.

The following example sheds light on what can be the worst of outcomes when a therapist resists the experience of the patient's anguish. In the case of the following patient, the therapist's resistance led to countertransference dominance. Both the following case and the preceding one with Dr K involve sexual abuse of a patient. I have chosen both these examples because sexual abuse is generally considered to be the worst possible outcome in a treatment, and an outcome which emphasizes loss of control and responsibility on the part of the therapist. The examples also illustrate that the merger involved in having sexual relations is *not* the type of merging with the patient that I am advocating here. I see sexual acting out as a flight from experiencing deep pain with the patient.

Joanne, an attractive lesbian in her late twenties, consulted me regarding her two failed treatments—both of her female therapists had gone to bed with her, even though they had both had psychoanalytic training. Joanne told me that she had abruptly fled her first treatment after she and her first therapist, Dr S, had ended up in bed fondling and kissing each other. Shortly after this incident, Joanne, suffering from an extreme anxiety reaction as a result of what had happened with Dr S, was admitted to a hospital emergency room and treated by a young female psychiatrist, Dr T.

This second treatment seemed to go well for about eighteen months, with both Dr T and Joanne forming an intense attachment to each other. However, at the end of this time, Dr T announced that she was moving to another city with her husband, who had a career opportunity he wanted to pursue. Dr T may have felt as helpless and abandoned as Joanne did in response to this forced separation.

Following Dr T's move, letters were exchanged between Dr T and Joanne for over a year. Shortly after this first year had passed, Joanne received a letter from Dr T, who professed her love for Joanne. She asked to begin a long-distance love affair with Joanne, perhaps as a solution to the painful distance separating the two of them, and Joanne agreed. Dr T, who was well-to-do, paid for all of Joanne's expenses related to the affair. They were in the midst of a passionate relationship, and Joanne flew anywhere at a moment's notice to see Dr T. They saw each other quite often. But, as time passed, Joanne wrote less, called fewer times, and generally seemed less interested. Dr T, aware of Joanne's withdrawal, seemed frustrated, hurt, and confused, and she offered to leave her husband and to "run away" with Joanne. But the affair ultimately ended in a heated argument, which centered around Joanne's neglect of Dr T.

Even though Joanne knew that her therapists had behaved in an unethical and irresponsible manner, she blamed herself for these traumatic affairs. They were both married women who claimed that they had no homosexual history, and Joanne felt that she had seduced them. She was worried that this might happen again.

Joanne asked me what I thought had happened. Of course, Joanne's ambivalence about the relationships was related to their incestuous and inappropriate nature. And her ambivalence also illustrated how Joanne, who had difficulty with intimacy, behaved in most close relationships.

It was inevitable that Joanne would ultimately try to keep Dr T at arm's length, which was what she had done in all of her relationships. Dr T did not seem to realize this about Joanne. Joanne could not tolerate true intimacy, which was why she had come to therapy in the first place. Rather than succumbing to Joanne's expectations, it was Dr T's responsibility to delineate what was going on in the relationship and to help Joanne understand how her behavior precluded any serious involvement with anyone.

I, of course, had asked Joanne some questions about her early relationships, particularly inquiring as to whether she had been sexually molested. She said that though relations in her family had been sexually tinged, there had been no incest or molestation of any kind. Then she said, "But both of my therapists told me that *they* had been molested as children. Is that important?"

I believe that in this particular instance both treatments became dominated by the therapists' early pathology and unfortunate experiences as victims of sexual abuse. Caught up in the pathos of Joanne's life and reliving their own painful childhood experiences became more than they could bear. Though it is impossible to determine exactly what took place in the minds of these two therapists, they clearly became over-involved with their highly intelligent, ambitious and talented patient, and denied their own vulnerability and neediness through sexual acting out. Joanne probably frustrated and hurt both of them with her distancing and rejection (she sounded merciless when she described her two therapists to me, and it was clear that she could be quite cruel by very coldly rejecting other people).

Joanne's homosexuality laid the groundwork for potential sexual abuse, which I believe took place because neither of these therapists could acknowledge to their patient, and probably to themselves, that they had lost themselves in identification with her and in a frustrated need to restore the emotional merger that Joanne had abruptly severed. Joanne had successfully stimulated, in both of these women, the experience of her intense longing, frustration and feelings of aloneness and abandonment. Unable to tolerate these feelings, the therapists sought sexual gratification to re-establish the merger that Joanne had broken.

In interviewing Joanne I found her to be quite likable. She was charming, witty, very perceptive, psychologically-minded and fearless in her readiness to confront others. I did not, however, find her to be particularly nurturing and noted from her history that she was intensely ambivalent about intimacy. My fantasy about what happened with her therapists is that she successfully "seduced" them, then backed away, leaving them frustrated and lost. Overstimulated and abandoned, they found the only way they knew to re-establish intimacy with their elusive patient. Had they been able to acknowledge to her and to themselves what had happened, I think there could have been a much more positive outcome. Joanne could have been confronted with her ambivalent, perhaps even sadistic, behavior and seen the results of it. And the therapists could have acknowledged the genuine hurt they felt as Joanne became cold and indifferent to them. If the therapist over-involvement was so great as to make this type of intervention impossible, acknowledgement of the therapists' inability to continue the treatment would certainly have been preferable to the sexual acting out that took place, leaving the patient as victim. As things turned out, the only sense of responsibility Joanne felt she had for the disastrous outcomes of her treatments revolved around grandiose visions of herself as evil, irresistible, and untreatable.

Resolving Countertransference Dominance Problems

Even though most clinicians reading this book will shake their heads with dismay in reaction to the behavior of Joanne's therapists, more benign forms of countertransference dominance are not easily avoided. Every time we dilute a patient's anger or unnecessarily provoke it, or fail to accept the patient's love or revel in it too long, or remain stuck in an intractable period of silence or depression or anger, the therapy is being dominated by the countertransference. Most instances of counter-transference dominance are stimulated or provoked by a need to preserve the therapist's narcissism and block negative transferences. Finell (1985) makes this point well:

> . . . the analytic situation offers much gratification for analysts with intense needs to be loved, idealized, and to feel a sense of power and control over others. Analysts with such dynamics will tend to promote idealization, power, and control by taking a dominant position in relation to the analysand who is essentially submissive and masochistic in these dynamics. In these circumstances, analyst and patient collude and form a misalliance in the sense described by Langs (1975). The narcissistic character structure of both is protected, and both receive a great deal of gratification that leaves the basic pathology untouched. (p. 436)

Finell describes how the analyst can easily be blinded to her own narcissistic defenses, and points out that it is the very nature of the defenses of splitting, projection, and denial that make them totally unconscious processes. By definition, the analyst who uses them cannot possibly know through self-analysis that she is doing so. Finell argues that the only possible solution to this problem is an extensive personal analysis, presumably with the hope that narcissistic analysts would be sufficiently cured to be able to conduct a treatment adequately. Otherwise, the analytic clinician is doomed to preserve her narcissistic equilibrium at the expense of her patients. Finell believes that in these cases the patient stays in treatment, unable to leave the disabled analyst, yet stuck with his desire to heal her.

Finell is obviously correct when she says that self-analysis cannot possibly address the problem of narcissistic defenses. But I do not share her optimism regarding personal analysis as the solution to the problem. Kohut (1977) and Miller (1981) refer to the prevalence of narcissistic disturbances in therapists, and since these disturbances cannot be eliminated even in the best of personal treatments, there must be some mechanism for identifying problems that arise as a result of these weaknesses in the character of the therapist.

Since self-analysis and personal analysis are not enough, how is this dilemma resolved? I think that in many cases it is not. Patients who leave treatment early may be unmotivated or untreatable, but they may also be aware that their therapists are incapable of treating them. In other cases the therapist forces termination in a flight from the patient. (Though this method of dealing with therapist disablement is benignly called "referring out," when it is totally against the patient's wishes I believe referral of this sort is always harmful and traumatic. If referring out is absolutely necessary, I think the therapist must take responsibility for discussing the problem frankly with the patient and finding a timetable and method for achieving a referral to another clinician that is not traumatic, even if this means bringing in a consultant.) Then there are the patients who merely dig in for the duration, as Finell notes. Perhaps this is one reason why so many analytic treatments seem to go on forever.

The question is, "How do we effectively limit the potential for therapist gratification and the overall consequence of countertransference dominance?" It is the responsibility of the therapist to deter any unnecessary gratification of the patient. Yet it is also the therapist's responsibility to monitor herself in the therapeutic relationship. But if we are realistic about our own residual conflicts and narcissistic vulnerabilities, and if we also realize the limitations of personal- and self-analysis as well as consultation, how can we expect to effectively self-monitor? Because of the power and control we have in the therapeutic setting, aren't there times for all of us when this resembles having the hawk stand guard over the chicken house?

I do not mean to imply that there are no successful treatments or that all therapists secretly lie in wait to take advantage of their patients. But because we are human, even the most successful treatments have their periods of stalemate or rupture of the therapeutic alliance. And, thankfully, we have evolved to the point where we can no longer blame the patient for any and all problems in the treatment. Yes, there are difficult patients. There are even *very difficult* patients, who would try the patience and soul of any person attempting to help them. But this does not excuse us from the enormous responsibility we have to work with even the most trying people.

To work well with patients I think we need to face our need to be healed and transformed, in spite of the narcissistic defenses that can leave us oblivious to these motivations as they manifest themselves in treatment. How do we take responsibility for something that we may not even be aware of? Again, it is the concept of mutuality that makes a large contribution to maintaining a truly therapeutic relationship. Just as the patient needs us to facilitate his self-awareness, we need him for the same reason.

Langs (1978) says that the best way to know what the patient needs and how he is experiencing the therapeutic relationship is to listen carefully and empathically to both the manifest and latent content of the sessions. Langs' method depends upon the ability of the therapist to "hear" the latent content, which means being very open and self-aware. Though I thoroughly agree with Langs' approach to understanding what the patient is telling us, he stops short of addressing one of the most difficult problems in treatment—how to handle the therapist's unconscious motivations or blind spots.

How do we go about letting the patient tell us when we are acting in a non-therapeutic manner? The most obvious answer is that we listen to him, as Langs suggests, and not merely write off criticisms or expressions of hurt as resistance. The less obvious answer is that we accept *all* heartfelt emotional reactions of the patient as valid, whether we understand them or not. But we do not stop here. To stop here would be to endorse empathy, much in the way that self-psychologists write about it, but this does not go far enough. Empathy alone fails to address the issue of responsibility; it implicitly states that the patient's disturbance with us is solely a function of his own psychopathology. The next step is to understand what happened, to sort it out with the patient, and to take responsibility for our contribution to the conflict.

As an example, let us take the case of Susan. One of the ongoing issues for her in treatment was that she had to grow up too fast and took too much responsibility for raising herself. This left her feeling chronically emotionally deprived and cheated. This was further aggravated by her family's standing as the "poorest" people in a very affluent neighborhood. Most of her schoolmates and neighbors had much more money than she did, contributing to her feeling that she received much less in life than others did. To some extent this was realistic, in that her parents gave her little attention and nurturing. Yet she was physically well cared for and had educational and social opportunities far beyond what the average child receives.

Early in Susan's treatment, I was aware that I had difficulty when her sense of deprivation led to an attitude of entitlement. I could say that this was simply because entitlement is not a very appealing stance. But it was more than that. I began to realize that, even though I came from a much more loving family than Susan did and had been much better off emotionally, I, too, took on too much at an early age and had felt burdened in this way. Also, I came from a family with a modest income and never had the opportunities for good schools and travel that Susan did, let alone the private tennis lessons and country club membership. Lastly, I had sacrificed considerably to pay for my own psychoanalysis and Susan had an excellent insurance policy that continuously paid 90% of the fee for her four sessions per week. So when she demanded something from me, or complained about having less in life than *anyone*, I could feel this little switch inside me shutting off any real emotional connection with her.

I usually dealt with this by having an internal conversation with myself about how this was defensive on my part and not very therapeutic, and would try to figure out what I needed to do to extract myself from this non-therapeutic position. For the most part, this would work. But one day she came to her session asking for something I thought was totally unreasonable. A student at the time, she came with her schedule for the summer, and was upset because courses she needed in order to graduate conflicted with two of her session times. I told her I would try to make a switch for her, since I had a couple of people who were flexible. The next session I told her I was confident about being able to facilitate this, but wanted to wait until it was closer to when she needed the switch, because one of the persons who would probably switch with her was also a student, but would not know her schedule for a few weeks.

At this point Susan looked distressed and informed me that she had hoped that she could make the switch a full month earlier than she had told me. I asked why. She said that she had felt really *deprived* of her singing lessons, which she hadn't had time to take since she was in high school, and wanted the earlier switch so she could take voice lessons with a very talented teacher during the month before her academic classes began. I said I was sorry, but I did not consider that to be a good enough reason to disrupt other people's schedules. She became very upset with me and said that I was taking this far too lightly and did not appreciate at all how much her singing meant to her. Why wasn't I willing to at least ask and see if the switch could be made without difficulty? She said if this was not possible she could accept it, but she couldn't accept my refusal to even attempt to arrange it.

I found myself responding internally with outrage. I couldn't believe that she was seriously asking me to change her session times for *voice lessons*, and was irate about her apparent disregard for the inconvenience to me as well as the potential inconvenience to the other patients whose appointments would be changed. I again told her I thought she was being completely unreasonable, and that I *would not* consider doing what she asked. She cried and protested further, but to no avail. Even though I knew I was overreacting internally, I felt confident that I had taken the right action in refusing to indulge Susan's sense of entitlement. Once she had calmed down, I also tried to discuss it with her in terms of her wanting me to make up for what she didn't get from her mother—something she had acknowledged easily in the past.

However, this time nothing worked. Though she calmed down and no longer emotionally demanded anything from me, she persisted in the sessions that followed in saying that I was being unreasonable, since I didn't even know for sure whether this change would really make any difference to anyone. The more she talked, of course, the less I wanted to do it. She then said that she really didn't understand my attitude, and that I seemed uncharacteristically rigid and withholding—almost as though *I didn't want her to have the chance to sing.* Her persistence, along with this comment, made me realize that she was refusing to accept my decision because of her *accurate perception* that I was not interested in seeing her have this experience. In fact, things had been going quite well for her of late, in part because of all the hard work I had done with her, including many phone calls during a period of extreme distress earlier in the year. And I think I unconsciously had decided that she had enough. In many ways she had more than I had at her age, especially since her treatment was going quite well and considering that she entered therapy a full ten years younger than I was when I managed to afford the time and money for my analysis. Once I realized this was true, I wrestled with myself for a while, still troubled by the fact that I felt her request was basically unreasonable. But finally I decided to inquire of my other students whether they could make the aforementioned change. As it turned out, it actually was *better* for both of them to change to new times, and they quickly agreed to it. I then went back to Susan and told her that I was granting her request.

Naturally, she was stunned and wanted to know why I had changed my mind. I told her that I realized that I had overreacted to her request and had been too withholding. Also I understood that she had *not understood* my position at all and that I knew it was bad for the therapeutic relationship for her to perceive me as begrudging her something that was important to her, something that in many ways symbolized her lost childhood and opportunity for creative play.

That night she had a dream about having a mother who really loved her, which she reported at her next session. She said that she awoke from this dream with an incredible feeling of relaxation and comfort, unlike anything she had ever experienced before. The next few months proved to be one of the most productive periods in the treatment, wherein she became more aware of her own unproductive envy of others that led to her hostile withholding and rejection. Subsequently, she was able to establish close friendships, something she had never succeeded in doing previously.

This case example illustrates how the countertransference, particularly blind spots due to narcissistic defenses, can be illuminated through interaction with the patient. It would have been easy to maintain my original position with Susan, categorizing her protests as resistance. I had consulted with two colleagues regarding this problem with Susan, both of whom supported the idea that she was wrong and that I should hold my ground. Yet I knew somehow that it was *me* who was really wrong in the situation. My own vague feeling of discomfort led me to initiate the consultations, yet this effort was not successful. It was the break in the therapeutic alliance that told me I was wrong, no matter how much reassurance I had received from my colleagues.

Susan did not just disagree with me, or get angry with me. She became profoundly disappointed, dismayed, and defeated. And she questioned my motivations and how they contributed to the current state of affairs. I think that this kind of heartfelt protest, one which is obviously not just a protest over not getting what the patient wants, but one that conveys to the therapist a deep sadness and indicates a rupture in the relationship, should always be taken as the patient's attempt to enlighten the therapist regarding some error or empathic lapse. Even if the circumstances seem to endorse overwhelmingly the therapist's actions, the patient would not respond as I have described unless something had gone wrong somewhere. In this way, the patient is capable of monitoring the therapist's blind spots, provided that the therapist is open to the patient in this way.

Granted, even when the therapist is being open and receptive to the underlying reasons for ruptures in the therapeutic alliance, difficult judgement calls must still be made—ones that rely on a certain amount of intuition, good sense, maturity, and insight on the part of the therapist. In the case of Susan, I had to discriminate between indulging her because she was angry and disapproving of me versus responding to an anguish that was born out of being thwarted and rejected by me. And since there is no foolproof way to conduct any therapy, sometimes I am wrong. But even when I am wrong, at least the issues are out in the open and have the potential for being worked out and understood. A therapist who lays low all the time virtually pre-empts this type of struggling with the patient, and forecloses the possibility of ending unnecessary anguish through successfully concluding the struggle.

After all, it is in the patient's best interest to make accurate calls on us, and even the most difficult and recalcitrant patients will rise to the occasion when they feel the relationship is being threatened. When the relationship breaks down, everyone loses. And patients realize this at some level every bit as much as we do—sometimes more. So why not accept their help in staying on track, and accept that no one is in a better position to give us feedback on our motivations and behaviors than our patients are?

If we are committed to facilitating deep, long-term analytic treatments that draw their strength from the curative aspects of regression, then it seems apparent that we would do well to pay more attention to the reality that this experience will always be somewhat mutual. Once we accept the idea of mutual regression, then the impact of the therapist's current needs, as well as psychological history, become far more important than what has been acknowledged to date. And the role of the patient as guide and mutual healer, rather than passive recipient of the therapist's wisdom, becomes crucial to the conduct of a successful treatment. As analytic clinicians, our level of expertise can only be as great as our level of self-awareness and our capacity to bear being seen realistically by others.

CHAPTER 3

The Unfolding of the Transference and Countertransference: The Drama Re-Enacted

Having discussed my philosophy on the effectiveness of and necessity for a mutual and interpersonal approach to analytic treatments, I shall now take a closer look at transference and countertransference issues. For this discussion, transference is defined as the conscious and unconscious responses—both affective and cognitive—of the patient to the therapist. In parallel fashion, the countertransference is defined as the conscious and unconscious responses of the therapist to the patient. The unfolding of the relationship between patient and therapist, including the transferences and countertransferences, the interplay between responses and the manner in which they are (or are not) addressed—by either or both parties—leads to an intricate psychological dance between patient and therapist. As therapists, we need to understand the nature of and tremendous variety of nuances in this dance, and we especially must know how to manage the countertransference.

Countertransference is once again in vogue, having faded into relative unimportance after its original development in the 1950s by Gitelson (1952), Heimann (1950), Little (1951), Racker (1968), Tower (1956) and others. In the interests of brevity and of keeping to my basic thesis, the reader is referred to McLaughlin (1981), Slakter (1987), Tyson (1986), and Tansey and Burke (1989) for comprehensive literature reviews, including historical perspectives and debates regarding both the definition and disclosure of the countertransference. The literature will be quoted here only as it pertains to particular points I am making.

In this chapter, I am especially interested in explaining how the countertransference develops in relation to the transference and what functions it can serve in the therapeutic endeavor. I believe that the therapist's fear of his own pathology and primitive affects has led to an unfortunate neglect of the use of the countertransference that persists to the present day. Much of this chapter will be devoted to examining the potential of the countertransference as the sleeping giant in psychoanalytic treatment.

First, let us look at what happens when a patient comes for analytic therapy. Essentially, the first year is devoted to developing the relationship and setting the stage for the expression of the transference. Basic trust and empathy are the primary concerns—the patient wants to know that his therapist understands, is reliable and trustworthy, and is genuine in his desire to help him. In this initial stage, the self-psychological approach to treatment is very effective. Sustained empathic inquiry is ideal because the patient is telling his story and is seeking some symptom relief for the pain or crisis that brought him to treatment in the first place. He is usually not looking for a confrontation and is rarely interested in knowing very much about his therapist. The therapist's life and feelings are for the most part unimportant. As long as his therapist appears to be well and able to function, the patient is happy and needs no further information. More than anything else, what he wants and needs is for someone to listen to him and be there for him. After all, the therapist is a relative stranger to whom he may be paying a considerable sum for exactly this purpose. The asymmetry of the relationship at this point is seen as desirable by the patient. The prospect of not having to be concerned about the other person is a wonderful luxury and source of relief and pleasure. It is exactly what the patient wants. Though the transference material may surface from the first day of treatment and continue to expand as the relationship builds, in a long-term treatment a transference neurosis or state of dynamic conflict does not usually arise in the early phase of therapy. (In time-limited treatments, however, this general guideline does not apply.)

As the end of the first year of therapy approaches, however, the therapist begins to emerge as a distinctly separate person. Even though the patient may not mention it, he becomes aware of changes in his therapist's mood, style of dress, voice tone, facial expression, body tension, signs of fatigue or illness, use of silence, and use of talking, and he begins to consider how these things might relate to the therapist's values and opinions, surges of energy following vacations, and all other manner of verbal and non-verbal phenomena that contribute to the definition of the therapist as a person. As the patient takes in this information over time, he reacts to it, consciously and unconsciously weaving his responses into an emotional fabric that will someday, if all goes well, be expressed in what is known as a full-blown transference reaction or transference neurosis. Regardless of your preference for terms, *the objective of an analytic treatment is to go beyond the establishment of a good working relationship or positive transference to a stage of dynamic conflict.* A successful treatment is predicated on the notion of the relationship developing to a point at which the patient's conflicts and deficits are expressed within the context of the therapeutic relationship, thus offering the possibility for resolution and integration. Facilitating the patient's move from phase one (empathic understanding and establishing basic trust) to phase two (emergence of dynamic conflict) demands that the therapist be keenly aware of his limitations. As the first phase of treatment proceeds, part of the establishment of basic trust will center on the therapist's willingness to acknowledge errors or weaknesses. The patient may note that the therapist failed to understand something said in the previous session. Or the patient may note some lack of patience on the therapist's part, or a tendency to intellectualize when the patient emotes strongly. At these times, it is crucial that the therapist be able to quietly acknowledge the correctness of the patient's observations in order to establish an environment that is free and safe enough to facilitate the second phase of treatment, dynamic conflict and regression. I believe that the therapist's ability to acknowledge his limitations and his potential for stimulating idiosyncratic transference responses in his patient often determines the extent to which the patient is able to regress for therapeutic gain.

(As a note regarding shorter-term treatments, obviously the timetable I have outlined above would not apply. As I have stated previously, I believe that the same basic stages of treatment will occur in an analytic therapy of shorter duration, but without the depth and complexity characteristic of psychoanalysis and intensive psychoanalytic psychotherapy. The telescoping down effect of the transference in time-limited treatments means that the therapist has less of a margin of error and cannot afford to be overly cautious. The objective in shorter treatments is to work fast, while working *well*, and therapists in this setting must be not only astute but decisive in order to deal effectively with both the transference and countertransference.)

Regarding our limitations, it may be that we do not respond as warmly, genuinely or spontaneously as someone else in the patient's past or present life, or that we are somehow *less* than the patient in some notable way. Whether we can treat someone, for example, who is nicer, smarter, healthier, more talented, more intelligent, wealthier, or more sensitive than we are depends on whether we can accept the truth about ourselves and work with it within the relationship. Determining whether the match between patient and therapist is "good enough" can be troublesome and is an issue that must be resolved between patient and therapist to the satisfaction of each. Inevitably this means admitting that we are less, both as human beings and as therapists, than we hoped we would be. Abend (1986) says:

> Every analyst, in the course of his psychoanalytic education and subsequent professional maturation, has to come to terms with those limitations on our

wishes that both analysis and analysts could be more powerful and more ideal than is actually possible. (p. 574)

Acknowledging our limitations leaves us free to observe how the transference and countertransference act on each other from the first moment that patient and therapist meet and to perceive how the resulting relationship is unique, for better or worse. As Racker (1968) stated when speaking of the countertransference:

> I would have liked to refer to it together with the transference, for transference and countertransference represent two components of a unity, mutually giving life to each other and creating the interpersonal relation of the analytic situation. (p. 59)

Kasin (1986) cites Sullivan's pioneering contribution to the definition of the therapeutic relationship in interpersonal terms, and he notes that once having accepted the notion of the analyst as participant observer, he then had to concentrate on how to optimize his participation for the patient's good. Sullivan's awareness of mutuality and the limitations of both people in the relationship was an inherent part of his effectiveness. Kasin states:

> I remember Sullivan defining the therapeutic relationship as follows: Two people, both with problems in living, who agree to work together to study those problems, with the hope that the therapist has fewer problems than the patient. (p. 455)

It might seem that I am advocating a rather humbling perspective regarding the mental health of the therapist, and I am. I do this not to denigrate the profession or to imply that we are less healthy than anyone else; I do not think we are. *But we are not necessarily healthier*, either. We need to acknowledge the reality of our personal limitations so that we can develop a mutual and respectful relationship with our patients, as well as rid ourselves of unrealistic expectations which merely create blind spots and make us defensive in the treatment situation. Racker (1968) called for such a realistic approach almost forty years ago:

> We must begin by revision of our feelings about our own counter-transference and try to overcome our own infantile ideals more thoroughly, accepting more fully the fact that we are still children and neurotics even when we are adults and analysts. (p. 130)

Accepting the ideas that the transference unfolds in conjunction with the countertransference, that each helps determine the other, and that the therapist's awareness of his own weakness and pathology allows him to view this process clearly, naturally leads to a view of analytic treatment that varies greatly from classical analysis. From an interpersonal perspective, the countertransference can be as important as the transference, and the person of the therapist can be almost as important as the person of the patient. Benedek (1953) made this same point when she defined the analytic procedure as

> . . . the unfolding of an interpersonal relationship in which transference and countertransference are utilized to achieve the therapeutic aim. This definition indicates that the therapist's personality is the most important agent of the therapeutic process. (p. 208)

Conceptualizing the treatment relationship and integrating the therapist's role in this relationship in such a way so as to maximize his effectiveness is the challenge that lies before us. It begins with an awareness of how the transference and countertransference unfold together, is further highlighted by examining how to optimize the great array and depth of transferences, and culminates in the active use of the countertransference for the purpose of resolution and facilitating termination.

The second phase of treatment, the emergence of the dynamic conflict (transference neurosis), calls for the therapist to expand his repertoire, both in terms of how he conceptualizes the relationship and of how he responds to the patient. It is now that the therapist is tested. He is tested for his stability, endurance, flexibility, tolerance, generosity, strength, loyalty, honesty and trustworthiness, as well as his ability to protect and preserve himself and the treatment.

All of the above occurs within the context of the patient setting the stage to replay the past, while challenging the therapist to recast his role so that the outcome is different. According to Wachtel (1986), the patient needs "accomplices" to maintain his neurosis and he attempts to cast the therapist in just such a role. Objecting to the traditional view that the therapist must refuse this role, Wachtel believes that ". . . it is in the very act of participating that the analyst learns what is most important to know about the patient" (p. 63). On the same topic, Gedo (1989) says:

> In order to reenact these old transactions, the analysand needs the compliance of the analyst—if not as an actor in restaging the old script, at least as a willing puppet to whom the necessary roles might be attributed. The ever-shifting consequences of these complex cybernetic mechanisms have generally been mistaken for static internal conditions characteristic of the analysand. Systematic correction of the resultant misconceptions is an enormous task awaiting the next generation of analysts. (p. 13)

I agree with Gedo's point that much of what was formerly attributed solely to the intrapsychic process of the patient was actually the result of a series of ongoing conscious and unconscious exchanges between therapist and patient. When a patient acquires insight and relinquishes his defenses, we attribute his progress to his capacity to use some interpretation fruitfully. But do we arrive at this conclusion because we *know* that interpretation always leads to these results, or because this is *what we have been taught* about how analysis works and what we were taught must be true? It seems to me that we actually do a great many different things with our patients, yet we feel compelled to call everything that we do "interpretation" because we have been taught it provides the only path to true success in treatment. Everything else is only "transference cure." Yet can this really be true? If it were, no-one in a non-analytic treatment would ever get any better. And we know they do—some people receive tremendous benefit from a variety of alternative psychotherapies that involve little or no interpretation. We do know that the transference-countertransference mechanisms are steadily at work in the treatment relationship, but whether we can always articulate the exact nature of those mechanisms is uncertain. McLaughlin (1981), for example, says:

> Gill (1979), Dahl *et al.* (1978), and Langs (1976), from quite different operational positions, have provided rich data to demonstrate that both parties are caught up in a communicative field of incredible sensitivity and subtlety, with transferential–countertransferential shadings constantly at play in enormous affective intensities—a field in which the possibility of a neutral or catalytic comment, given or received, is remote indeed. (p. 658)

These subtle communications are particularly important as patient and therapist mutually regress and become immersed in the symbiotic phase of treatment. As the regression proceeds, an increasing amount of the interaction between patient and therapist centers on pre-oedipal issues, and the patient demands more from the therapist. The regression itself, as well as patient demands for greater self-disclosure on the part of the therapist, are directly proportional to the extent of pre-oedipal or narcissistic problems of the patient. Consider, for example, the symbiotic phase of treatment and the diversity of therapist behaviors that are required when treating psychotics or severe personality disorders. These patients tend to be very vocal about what they want and need and there is absolutely no way of escaping the symbiotic phase of treatment when treating them. Other patients, like those with anxiety disorders or mild personality disorders, are much more likely to try to follow the therapist's lead and behave in a way that will please the therapist and fit the expectations that both persons have regarding the nature of an analytic treatment. Less severely disturbed patients are more concerned with approval and have also received reinforcement in life for their ability to contain themselves, something that more primitive personalities have never had the luxury of experiencing. (There are also a number of patients who defend at the oedipal level and are quite compliant, but they might not be as docile if they regressed to a pre-oedipal stage.)

In some ways the capacity for certain personalities to contain themselves works to their disadvantage because they will not scream for what they need. Instead, they are likely to blame themselves and become depressed, believing that they did not get much better in analysis because they just weren't good enough or did not know how to properly make use of the treatment. Worse still, their therapists may agree with them and settle for symptom relief when much more would have been possible.

In my experience I find that people who are generally very contained have difficulty with the regressive phase of treatment and may not be able to participate in it without the active encouragement of their therapists. But, by definition, a treatment that does not include a regressive phase cannot be called analytic. I do not believe that four or five or even eight or ten years on the couch, with no loss of control by the patient, no blurring of boundaries, no infantile expressions, and no unreasonable demands on the therapist and, most importantly, no deep grieving of past losses (Miller, 1981), can be called a truly analytic experience.

Giovacchini (1972) compares the regressive phase of treatment to early childhood experiences and notes that even healthy patients will regress to symbiosis if given the opportunity:

> . . . among patients with relatively well-integrated egos, one finds evidence of fusion during the transference regression. This should not be surprising because if one accepts the existence of a symbiotic fusion as a beginning developmental phase, one should expect its persistence in the context of more integrated superstructures. During regression it can become activated again. (p. 301)

To one extent or another, we are all capable of regression and we must all regress in order to heal ourselves. Without a regressive phase in treatment, no matter how many sessions a week or how many analytic credentials the therapist holds, all that results is a supportive treatment. Not that years of such a treatment cannot produce some significant outcomes. I think they can. Many people stabilize and grow in a long-term holding environment. And it must be acknowledged that some people are so afraid of regression that they will not regress no matter what the therapist does. Though there may be good reasons why a treatment remains at a pre-regression level throughout its entire course, I believe it will produce less complete results than if the patient had engaged in a regressive experience. I have always thought that anyone who seeks a second, or third, or even fourth analysis is someone who, for whatever reasons, has failed to achieve, maintain and emerge naturally from a regressive phase of treatment. And he is still looking for this— perhaps hoping that the next therapist down the road will hold the key to making it happen.

As I previously implied, during the regressive phase of treatment, the patient exerts a great deal of pressure on the therapist to assume a predetermined role or roles. The traditional analytic response to the patient's efforts involves trying to remain as cool and calm as possible, while interpreting to the patient how he is attempting to re-enact the past. The problem with doing this while the patient is in the throes of some primitive affect is that it does not work. Even worse, with many, if not with all patients, interpretive activity during regression is experienced not only as unhelpful but also as intrusive or assaultive—hardly a desirable effect. (In many treatments this effect is ameliorated by the therapist's genuine concern and facial or vocal expressions of emotion, but this does not negate the fact that interpretation is not the most effective intervention when the patient is regressed.)

Many treatments begin at the oedipal level but eventually, if they are to be succesful, move along to the pre-oedipal level, then back again to the oedipal. (This generalization does not do justice to the many oedipal and pre-oedipal fluctuations that occur, even within a given session.) Thus it is vital that the therapist knows when particular interventions will facilitate the therapeutic process and when they will not. Since even patients with oedipal problems in the forefront are likely to go through a pre-oedipal phase of treatment (therapeutic regression), the therapist must be ready and willing to participate at both levels with all patients. Balint (1968) discusses the difference between interventions that respond to repressed conflicts (oedipal) and those that respond to significant early developmental failure (pre-oedipal), which is referred to by him as the "basic fault":

> At the oedipal—and even at some of the so-called pre-oedipal—levels, a proper interpretation, which makes a repressed conflict conscious and thereby resolves a resistance or undoes a split, gets the patient's free associations going again; at the level of the basic fault this does not necessarily happen. The interpretation is either experienced as interference, cruelty, unwarranted demand or unfair impingement, as a hostile act, or a sign of affection, or is felt so lifeless, in fact dead, that it has no effect at all. (p. 175)

Regarding the emergence of pre-oedipal or oedipal material, Gedo (1989) discusses how the behavior and expectations of the therapist control the tone, flavor and depth of any treatment. He notes that the therapist's verbal behavior influences how the transference is manifested, with particular emphasis on the differences between affective expressions and interpretations:

> . . . one of the most important of these concerns the degree to which we infuse our communications with the affect appropriate to our words. . . .

the more direct and affect-laden our communications are, the more likely they are to tilt the analytic relationship in the direction of transferences of relatively archaic origin. Interpretations . . . call upon our patients to exercise secondary-process capacities . . . only available in mid-latency or later. (p. 8)

Gedo notes that this is why both classical and self-psychological analysts are able to claim that their observations of the treatment process are accurate. The classical analyst, responding to the analysand in a certain manner, provides a treatment that remains primarily at the oedipal level. The self-psychologist (or interpersonalist), responding to the analysand with more "affect-laden" communications, facilitates a more archaic treatment experience. In essence, then, the definition of what treatment is and how it should work sets the stage for a self-fulfilling prophecy. That is, every person has a mixture of pre-oedipal and oedipal concerns and we, as therapists, often decide what will be explored and experienced, rather than leaving these decisions to the patient. And it seems to me that Gedo is correct: no matter what approach we take, we run the risk of distorting the transference so that it will blend with our psychodynamics and intellectual views of treatment.

Bollas (1986) articulately argues for the analyst to admit that deep regression is desirable and that "work," interpretation, or any conscious attempt at organization during the regressive phase of treatment is unfruitful. He notes that therapists who deny this reality will only fail:

If the analyst cannot acknowledge that in fact he is offering a regressive space to the patient (that is, a space that encourages the patient to relive his infantile life in the transference), if he insists that in the face of the "invitation" *work* must be carried out, it is not surprising that in such analyses patient and analyst may either carry on in a kind of mutual dissociation that leads nowhere (obsessional collusion), or in a sudden blow-up on the part of the patient, often termed "acting-out." (p. 96)

Self-psychologists recognized the limits of "working" during the regressed stage of treatment and turned to "sustained empathic inquiry" as a way out of the intellectual quagmire created by classical analysts. For self-psychologists, empathy is a compassionate way of responding to the regressed patient. It does not interfere with the patient's regressive experience either by challenging his subjective emotional experience or by rejecting his emotionality and demanding that he *think* instead of *feel*. However, using "sustained empathic inquiry" on a prolonged basis with a regressed patient often leads to a passive position that does not directly respond to the patient and, as such, may also be regarded as rejection.

A patient who is looking for his therapist to participate in his personal drama by acting out a certain role can become extremely frustrated by the ever-empathic self-psychologist. The patient who needs help in containing his rage, for example, will not appreciate his therapist's *understanding*.

This is why the patient must be allowed to direct the scenes of his own play. If we intercede with what *we* think is best we will essentially be writing our own play, not the patient's. The fact that we might produce a better play with a happier ending is irrelevant because it has little or nothing to do with the patient's reality.

Exactly how far the patient will need to go with his need to recreate the past depends on the patient, of course, but the usual rule of thumb applies: the more disturbed the patient, the more difficult and traumatic the re-enactment will be for him (and perhaps for us as well). He obviously did not get disturbed on his own. Cataclysmic and unbearable things happened to him. And as burdensome as they might be to the therapist, they must be repeated.

An example of what I mean can be seen in the case of Ethel, a highly intelligent, middle-aged woman who had achieved considerable wealth through her own efforts. She had been in treatment almost continuously since the age of fifteen and, by the time she arrived at my office, she had seen about six therapists plus a half dozen other assorted "gurus." She was described by a psychoanalyst I consulted with during the first few years of her treatment as "the sickest functioning borderline" he had ever seen. What he meant by "functioning" was that she was able to sustain a work and personal life as opposed to being institutionalized. But she did have a history of one- or two-month hospitalizations every few years. Ethel abused every medication she was ever given and I finally refused to participate in her acquisition of medication in any way. This did not disturb her since she was accustomed to medicating herself with marijuana, cocaine, quaaludes, Valium or anything that she or any of her friends happened to have handy.

Treating this woman—who was extremely outrageous in her behavior yet able to get away with it because most people she acted out with were either family members or employees—was the challenge of my therapeutic career. Over the course of ten years of treatment I went through a great deal with her, not the least of which was the loss of a lover she was devoted to and for whom she had divorced her husband. This event occurred in the sixth year of her therapy with me. At that time she had significantly reduced her polymorphous perverse sexual behavior, being close to monogamous with her lover. She also had restricted her drug use to marijuana, had stopped her periodic bouts of shoplifting, and was making significant progress in terms of greatly reduced denial and splitting as ways of dealing with the world. Unfortunately, even as she began to actively join the real world, she still maintained a pattern of verbally abusing her lover, calling him at all hours of the day and night for him to soothe and comfort her, and letting him know that she occasionally cheated on him with a "one-night stand." He grew weary of trying to reason with her or be close to her when she was so often under the influence of marijuana. (She had been in drug treatment centers numerous times, to no avail.)

Her lover had tolerated Ethel's bad behavior and abuse for so many years that Ethel erroneously assumed that he would tolerate it forever. But he did, in fact, leave her. His departure was an event that Ethel had never imagined possible, since she knew he loved her very much. I cannot find the words adequately to describe the extent of her grief and despair as she responded to this loss. To say that she was beside herself and remained beside herself for years is an understatement. She was like a raging, stampeding elephant. Grief-stricken, enraged and terrified, she ran in every direction with no destination.

Most of her efforts in the first few months after he left her were devoted to an attempted reconciliation. But the harder she tried and pushed for this, the colder and more distant he grew. The reality began to penetrate her that this was not just another of their many lovers' quarrels: it was the end. As this reality became apparent, she looked for ways to ease her pain. She ate too much, talked too much, and drank too much as she tried to soothe herself. Treating her had always been difficult and I took some pride, perverse as it might have been, in having lasted longer than any of her previous therapists. I was determined not to suffer the fate of those other therapists, which included giving up in despair, placating her so that she would become disillusioned and quit, angering her by maintaining a considerable distance, and being "bought off" by accepting expensive gifts. In spite of her offerings of similar temptations to me, I remained pristine and idealistically determined to do right by her, if not cure her.

She had always been a very difficult and demanding patient, making many phone calls to me. At one time, I had had to restrict her to using my answering machine because she had decided that her morning depressions were "emergencies" and she began calling my home at 6:00 a.m. Following the break up with her lover she was especially demanding and called my answering machine compulsively and incessantly, sometimes leaving 20 minutes of messages at a time— barraging me with her presence and her pain. At this time, she also began to abuse marijuana heavily. I suggested that she consider hospitalization, but she absolutely refused, saying that she hated hospitals and was never going to one again. I told her that her constant phone calls were unacceptable to me; she decreased them, but she increased her drug abuse.

She did this even though I told her that I could not and would not treat her while she was engaging in heavy substance abuse. One evening when she was particularly pained she desperately searched her medicine cabinet for something to anesthetize herself and found an old bottle of stelazine. She took it throughout the night and arrived for her morning session with acute dyskinesia, a result of an overdose of stelazine. One of her children, appalled and frightened by her condition, brought her to my office. I arranged to have her hospitalized immediately. Owing to her physical symptoms, she did not resist and spent the next three weeks in the hospital.

Coincidentally, at the same time that my patient was so distressed, I was going through a very difficult period in my own life. Ethel's hospitalization required me to travel across town every other day, after I had finished with all my private patients, to see her at the hospital and conduct staffings on her, which only added to my own distress. When I visited her at the hospital, I realized that I could no longer work with her. After years of constant effort she was not that much better, and she continued to be unable to contain herself so that she could make use of the psychotherapy that I offered her. At times in the past I had hated her. But I began to feel something worse than hatred: I felt only pity and disgust, and I wanted out. I told this to the consulting psychiatrist who had hospitalized her, and he was very understanding. He assuaged my guilt by telling me that I had more than done my duty and that it was perfectly acceptable to refer out a demanding patient with such a poor prognosis. He said she would no doubt be in some kind of treatment for the rest of her life, and it was certainly all right to pass the baton.

I continued to see her during her hospitalization, and she eventually stabilized and got a pass to come to my office for her sessions. At this time I informed her that I would no longer be working with her. I told her I would give her time to talk to other therapists and find someone suitable, and I would generally do anything within reason to facilitate a referral. I told her I was sorry, but that I simply could not help her anymore. She cried and told me that she didn't want another therapist and would not accept the referral. I told her that I would set a date to end with her anyway. She implored me to reconsider and I said my mind was made up.

At her next session Ethel cried and begged me not to terminate her treatment. She said she knew I was "burned out" on her case, that she was difficult, uncooperative, demanding and persistent in her bouts of drug abuse, but would change if only I would stay with her. She said I was giving up on her just like her lover did. She also said she knew that her violent reaction to the break-up with her lover meant that she must have felt abandoned in this way by her mother, too. How could I add to this traumatic experience? I acknowledged that her point was well made—but it didn't change the fact that I no longer *wanted* to treat her, nor did it change the fact that she responded to all crises by abusing drugs and that she defeated the point of the treatment in doing so. I held my ground and maintained that we would set a termination date for a time within the next month, even though she said she would change if I would only continue with her.

However, that weekend I found that I could not relax. I kept thinking about Ethel sitting in my office crying and begging me not to leave her. But when I thought about keeping her I felt overwhelmed by the burden and strain of working with her, and felt martyred by the prospect. After a few wrenching days with much soul-searching, I finally decided that I couldn't end her treatment against her will. *As much as I wanted to, I just couldn't.* So I made peace with myself, and made up a new set of rules that had to be followed if I were to continue with her. I limited her to two phone messages on my machine per day, with no message to exceed a few minutes. I also limited her to two phone contacts with me per week. And I told her that if she ever started a downward spiral of being upset, taking drugs, deteriorating further, taking more drugs, and ultimately ending in decompensation and hospitalization, I would terminate the treatment on the spot.

I continued to treat Ethel for another four years, during which time she kept to all of the above-stated conditions. More importantly, with the option of ''going crazy'' having been removed, she became more and more sane. She never did stop all of her self-indulgent behavior. She still spent too much money, ate too much and used marijuana recreationally. But she was never crazy again and showed an impressive degree of insight and integration during the period after our ''showdown.'' She terminated with me of her own accord and said she would be back periodically for supportive care.

During her termination phase we reviewed our ten years together, exchanging observations about each other and the process. She told me that in the early years I was too young and uptight to do the right thing with her—that I was too concerned about following the rules—and could not let myself openly go mad with her as I finally did when I told her I couldn't take it anymore and wanted to end her treatment. She said that even in the later years I did not show enough emotion, that I was too much of a ''tight-ass.'' Perhaps she was right: I don't know. In response I told her that I could only be who I was. And, of course, there was no question that age and experience helped me to work better with her as the treatment progressed.

I also told her that I had the feeling that our moment of truth after her hospitalization was somehow a re-creation of the past that she was determined to play out—that I *had* to end up like her mother, her lover, and many others, who finally could take no more and had to leave her. This was the repetition of the past. And throughout those years when I played the long-suffering therapist who would stand by her and continue to work hard with her, I was only prolonging the inevitable. My persistence meant that she had to "keep upping the ante" until I finally relented and gave up. She was amused by this and said she was sure that was true, because *once she succeeded in repeating the past, and then changing it*, she was free to get better. Had I actually gone through with my threatened termination, she simply would have continued the old pattern, been hurt again, and forced to look further for someone who would participate in her drama to the point of crisis but who would ultimately remain with her.

Though Ethel was a severe borderline personality with limited growth potential, I think her re-enactment of the conditions for abandonment is not unique. Many borderline personalities re-create intense dramas with the precipitous loss of the therapist as the focal point. And these dramas must be played out. The therapist cannot simply interpret to the patient that he is trying to drive the therapist away or to alienate him. This does not register at more than an intellectual level. Even if the patient accepts the interpretation and acknowledges its truth, this insight will not change the patient's need to re-enact the past. As I stated earlier, exactly how much has to be replayed, and with how much trauma and pain, depends on how disturbed the patient is. But I believe that every patient, regardless of diagnosis, has a drama that must be re-enacted in terms of emotional equivalency to the original problem relationship, and that the patient will re-enact it if sufficiently regressed.

The patient needs to repeat the past trauma, not for the sake of masochistic suffering, not for the sake of making the therapist suffer, but for the sake of his own transformation. The crux of the problem lies in the level of difficulty that this repetition of the traumatic situation presents for us as therapists. Obviously, there is a limit to how much any therapist could participate in regression. But since not all patients will regress when given the opportunity, and others will regress only partially or for a very short time, it is not necessary that we be able to participate in this continuously with all the people we treat. Even though I believe a controlled regression offers the greatest opportunity for healing, it also presents the greatest stress and difficulties for the therapist. After all, if I am advocating a more mutual relationship that involves openness and non-defensiveness on the therapist's part—one that eventually leads to some period of symbiosis and mutual regression, with the therapist at times experiencing his own or the patient's madness—with how many patients is this possible? Obviously, no therapist could possibly participate in this type of relationship with too many patients at the same time. Awareness of the strains inherent in working with people who can and do regress easily is evident when you hear clinicians say that they cannot treat psychotics or that they can only treat two or three borderline personalities at a time. In fact, my treatment approach relies on the observations that, first, many patients do not regress significantly in treatment and, second, a therapist can balance his case load so that he is not overwhelmed by too many patients who are very regressed.

What is equally evident is that every therapist will have his own tolerance for regression, and this tolerance must be respected. We need to know and accept our limitations; they should be considered seriously without holding any particular set of expectations, other than that every therapist must have a tolerance for *some* deep regression or he will not be able to do analytic work. Those therapists who cannot tolerate the regressive experience and the subsequent chaos that it brings will need to regularly stop it by intellectualizing or by remaining outside of it. Regressed patients want and need us to be "with" them, not safely ensconced behind the line of fire. They also need to know how much and in what way they are affecting us emotionally.

When Ethel and I reached what seemed like the point of no return, I *had* to tell her the full truth about how she was affecting me. She would not accept anything less. And it had an impact on her when I told her that she was wearing me down; I felt defeated, helpless, frustrated, and angry, and I did not want to continue to work with her. When I said these words and showed the feelings that went with them, I saw her pay attention to me and allow me into her world in a way she previously never had. Not that I had never shown any emotion to her. Most of the progress she had made was related to me showing anger toward her. But she had never tapped—nor had she ever seen—such deep and pervasive negative feelings in me. Like many others in her life, I sat before her as a person who cared very much about her, had given her years of energy and personal involvement, had been reliable, consistent and trustworthy (her ex-husband was especially like this), yet somehow had reached a point of personal defeat and despair, and wanted out. Ethel had always disavowed the deterioration of any relationship; she would only realize that she was losing the person when it was too late to do anything about it. Then she was left alone and in despair. Our relationship provided her with the emotional stay of execution that she had always longed for. And there is no question that she used it profitably.

Ethel's case illustrates the basic concept of allowing the patient to play out his or her drama, with the therapist following the patient's lead and, ultimately, disclosing the countertransference for the patient's benefit. And, perhaps most important of all, I think it serves as a vivid example of how some patients are compelled to literally repeat the past with their therapists and will not rest until they succeed—the only caveat being that the therapist must know how to play out his role so that the final scene is a hopeful, restorative one, rather than tragic and painful.

If we believe that all patients need to return to the scene of the crime, and that some of them need to do this completely and in a way that recapitulates the original depth of feeling, then the unwillingness or inability of the therapist to participate lends new meaning to the concept of *resistance*. With the understanding that the patient—not the therapist—is in treatment, I should like to pose these questions: How much do we use intellectualization to protect our patients and ourselves from primitive affective states that can so easily be stirred in the therapeutic situation? Isn't intellectualization our only legitimate defense? How often do we squelch, under the guise of offering understanding through interpretation, the emotional release that our patients are seeking?

As I stated in Chapter 1, interpretation is overvalued to such an extent that, for all intents and purposes, it excludes other equally valuable interventions that could be used in analytic treatments. And, it seems to me that interpretation is so highly valued because the interpretive stance offers a high degree of emotional or psychological protection to the therapist. When the patient's feelings or the therapist's own response to the patient's feelings become too much to handle, the therapist merely interjects an interpretation—which has the immediate effect of squelching the affect. Of course, there are other ways for the therapist to abort a difficult emotional experience. But intellectualization seems to be the defense of choice for many of us who have chosen analytic treatment as a specialty. This choice is difficult to justify, because interpretation (or any other intellectual intervention) is seriously detrimental when working with a regressed patient. Interpretation is an entrenched and accepted analytic technique for two basic reasons: (1) the short-term goal of a single interpretation has become confused with the long-term analytic goal of patient understanding, and (2) intellectualization and authoritarianism allow the therapist to disengage from the patient's experience.

Regarding the first reason, I sometimes feel that we have become myopic in discussing analytic technique, focusing excessively on defining and redefining interpretation and other technical terms, and excluding fresh perspectives on the overriding analytic principle of illumination and understanding. Schafer (1976) has already made the point, and made it well, that our language becomes increasingly esoteric and obfuscating rather than serving as effective communication. If our language no longer addresses the heart of the analytic experience, then what about our philosophy and our technique? (Also, if we are no longer speaking plainly and clearly to each other, can we be so different with our patients?) Have we become like scholars in another field who spend endless hours counting the semicolons in a Shakespearean play for the purpose of attributing some meaning to it? Have we lost sight of the fact that the only technique that is truly "analytic" is the technique that succeeds with a particular patient in discovering the truth and working with it? Have we become so ritualized that we emphasize form over content? And does it really matter whether we offer an interpretation, or a confrontation, or a laugh, or a tear, provided that whatever we offer is genuine and truly helps the patient to understand and accept himself and others?

I realize that as I write these things I am inviting accusations of encouraging all manner of crazy behavior from therapists. It may be true that when some therapists believe there are no rules they are likely to behave in an irresponsible and destructive way. But I refuse to believe that most therapists are so inherently unstable or self-indulgent that, *if they are encouraged to use their intuition and emotions in addition to their intellect in a responsible manner*, the only result will be wild and destructive acts. I believe that most therapists, like most patients, want more than anything else for the therapy to succeed and to see both their patients and themselves do well. Yes, our patients and our own limitations can make things difficult. But neither negates our basic desire to facilitate a positive transformation.

Regarding the second reason why we use intellectualization so much— i.e. the need to disengage from the patient's intense affects—I believe that it is reasonable and human of us to need to make this break from time to time. If we get lost in our patients' sea of emotion and drown with them, what good are we? We must be able to move in and out of their emotional experience at will so that we can maintain a perspective, as well as a structure to guide the therapy. Also, there will be times when we need a respite purely because of our own vulnerability, and there is no need to apologize for this. We have an obligation to maintain our equilibrium because if we lose it for very long we will no longer be functioning as therapists. My argument is not with the need to step back from the patient, particularly during or after a challenging emotional experience. My argument is with failing to admit to the patient that this is what we are doing. Pretending that the time is ripe for an intellectualization is dishonest. Admitting that we need a moment to think or to gather ourselves together emotionally is direct, honest and respectful of the patient's experience. It also ameliorates the fear of being rejected that patients often feel when faced with their therapist's intellectual responses to their emotions.

It is hard to find anyone who argues, at least in principle, with the goal of uncovering the truth in an analytic therapy. The problem lies in determining the best method for achieving this goal, as well as in deciding whether it is an intrapsychic or interpersonal process. Beginning with Sullivan (1953), a segment of American analytic practitioners always believed that the analytic process was essentially interpersonal. In Britain the prominence of the object relations school has virtually made the notion of autonomous experience extinct. Yet few innovations in analytic techniques that fit an interpersonal model have developed. This appears to be a result of a desire to maintain the integrity of the analytic experience, as well as a fear that, while therapist self-disclosure might serve the relationship, it will also deprive the patient of the fullest possible intrapsychic experience. The thought of significantly altering psychoanalytic technique rouses fears of sacrificing that which is considered uniquely analytic, as well as fears of being accused of the same. Understandably, most analysts tread gingerly regarding technique, not wanting to risk being innovative at the price of ostracism. Therapists who are analytic are usually deeply committed to analytic principles and are naturally sensitive to any criticism of being "non-analytic." We would all like to believe that the pressure to conform would not affect us, would not stop us from using something that we thought would work, or would not stop us from talking about it if we did. But, after all, we are only human. And I think we do succumb to the pressure.

Perhaps this is why there is so little discussion regarding analysis and disclosure of the countertransference. A counterargument might be that it simply is not an idea worthy of consideration, which many probably believe to be true. But if this *is* true, why do discussions of theory and technique generate such heated arguments? Why is it that we cannot discuss countertransference in a calm, even-handed manner? If there is nothing there of significance, then why is the subject so consistently belittled or angrily dismissed? Benedek (1953) noted that "as the history of psycho-analysis shows, the discussion of countertransference usually ended in a retreat to defensive positions" (p. 202). She further elaborated on *why* therapists become skittish when the topic of countertransference comes up, noting that they regularly defend against being known in the analytic setting:

> The point which I want to make is that the complication in therapy arises usually when the therapist has a blind spot against being recognized and reacted to by the patient as a *real person*. I have seen often that an analysis came to an impasse because the therapist either did not realize that the patient was talking about *him*, or if he realized it, he tended to avoid the issue, or he misunderstood the intention of the patient, because it put the therapist on the defensive. (p. 204)

Tauber (1954) commented on what happens to the patient whose therapist adopts a somewhat secretive attitude about himself in the treatment setting:

> The very nature of the analytic setting is such that the analyst plays a
> relatively passive role and maintains an incognito. Many patients seem to
> respond to this setting by presenting an incognito of their own. (pp. 331-332)

This notion of the "incognito," of the analyst hiding from the patient
and therefore subtly encouraging the patient to hide from him, is at the
heart of the countertransference debate. People like Tauber and Little
believe that hiding does not further the uncovering of truth in the
relationship, and therefore cannot further the analytic endeavor. On the
other hand, those who think that the analyst should remain "incognito"
believe that it is vital to focusing on the patient's—and not on the
analyst's—truth. Therefore the key factor in taking a position on the
appropriateness of disclosure of the countertransference seems to be
whether you believe that it is possible to get to the heart of the patient's
truth without also revealing some of the therapist's. On a more personal
level, therapists must decide whether they are willing and able to reveal
more of themselves to their patients, even when it *is* for the better.

While many—Langs (1974), Greenson (1967), Gill (1982), Kohut (1971,
1977), Stolorow, Brandchaft and Atwood (1987)—favor acknowledging
the patient's perceptions, most are quite conservative when it comes to
actually expressing the countertransference; at best, they will only admit
to gross errors when confronted by the patient. To my mind their stance,
while emphasizing empathy with the patient's feelings and representing
a compassionate and enlightened view, still attempts to maintain the
therapist's "incognito." In reviewing some of these positions, Langs has
served as an eloquent spokesman for acknowledging the real perceptions
that the patient reveals in the manifest and latent content of his sessions.
Yet even Langs regards countertransference disclosure by the therapist
as taboo, which severely limits the possibilities for admitting or finding
the truth. Particularly as the interpersonal aspects of the therapeutic
relationship are more widely recognized and acknowledged, therapeutic
anonymity seems even more absurd.

Relatively few individuals advocate regular disclosure of the countertransference, but the literature is punctuated with warnings of its dangers.
Tansey and Burke (1989) have categorized disclosure perspectives as
conservative, moderate and radical. Conservatives, like Reich (1960),
Heimann (1950) and Langs (1978), state that while countertransference
is useful to the analyst, direct communication of it is burdensome to the
patient and unnecessarily self-indulgent for the therapist. Moderates, like
Giovacchini (1972), Greenson (1974) and Winnicott (1949), advocate
occasional disclosure, but only with more seriously disturbed patients.
Radicals, such as Little (1951, 1957), Tauber (1954), Searles (1979) and
Bollas (1983), favor disclosure and active use of the countertransference,

treating it as an integral part of an interpersonal analytic process. (But, I disagree with Tansey and Burke's inclusion of Bollas as a radical, because he is less enthusiastic about disclosure of the countertransference than the others in this category.)

Though I advocate what has been referred to as the "radical" position on countertransference, I do respect the sincere concerns of the conservatives for the patient. Most of their warnings pertaining to disclosure are based on the fear that the therapist will use the session to serve his own ends rather than those of his patient. For example, Langs (1975), who puts so much trust in the patient, unfortunately seems to have an equally significant *distrust* of therapists. Even when acknowledging an error, he says:

> . . . the therapist should not go beyond a simple recognition of it to the patient and, at times, a comment to the effect that the patient can be assured that he is endeavoring to understand its basis within himself. It is inappropriate for the therapist to discuss the inner sources of his mistake. (p. 249)

Heimann (1950) argues *against* the detachment of the analyst and *for* constructive awareness of the countertransference; but when it comes to actual disclosure, she said:

> This [the awareness of the countertransference], however, is his private affair, and I do not consider it right for the analyst to communicate his feelings to his patient. In my view such honesty is more in the nature of a confession and a burden to the patient. In any case it leads away from the analysis. (p. 84)

In reviewing the literature I was amazed by the number of people who have written on countertransference but who have made no direct statement at all regarding its disclosure (Tower, 1956; Kernberg, 1965) or who have hedged, saying that the topic needed to be researched further (Racker, 1968). Slakter (1987) says that self-revelation may be useful at times, but cautions the therapist to take time to reflect before doing so. Even Bollas (1987) is cautious in advocating disclosure:

> . . . on rare but significant occasions the analyst may analyse his experience as the object of the patient's transference in the presence of the patient. (p. 201)

Tansey and Burke themselves might be categorized as moderates, since they do not advocate systematic disclosure of the countertransference:

> In the overwhelming majority of instances the therapist is better advised not to disclose direct countertransference material, but rather to make silent

use of his responses to the patient in an effort to guide interpretations pertaining primarily to the patient's subjective experience. (p. 102)

Again, the primary reason for caution regarding the disclosure of the countertransference relates to the possibility that the therapist might simply dump all of his own problems into the patient's lap, thus doing him harm. Tauber (1954), who advocates disclosure, answers this criticism:

> If one wishes to appraise the possible injurious effects of exploring countertransference reactions in the therapeutic situation, the only injury which I believe requires serious consideration is that which could be imposed on the patient by the therapist's own attitudes. If the therapist is serious, responsible, competent, and resourceful, it seems highly improbable that the patient will react with panic or a depression, or that he will suddenly leave treatment. It is, moreover, significant that in my own experience the examination of countertransference reactions has not led to further bogging down and resistance. The more usual result has been the re-establishment of varying degrees of contact, further activity, and greater hopefulness. (p. 336)

Little (1951) was the first champion of countertransference disclosure. She understood acutely how the interplay of transference and countertransference naturally led to a mutual regression that inevitably threatened the equilibrium of the analyst. It was clear to Little that the only way to avoid being overwhelmed by this experience was to admit one's countertransference to the patient. She went further, stating that failure to admit it could result in what Kernberg (1965) was to later call a "fixed countertransference," which is often distinguished by a "microparanoid" reaction to the patient. Little felt that the only viable way out of this destructive, passive position was to become emotionally active in the relationship:

> To my mind it is this question of a paranoid or phobic attitude towards the analyst's own feelings which constitutes the greatest danger and difficulty in countertransference. The very real fear of being flooded with feeling of any kind, rage, anxiety, love, etc., in relation to one's patient and of being passive to it and at its mercy, leads to an unconscious avoidance or denial. (p. 149)

Gitelson (1952) felt strongly that part of the therapeutic process was the analyst's acceptance of his "unconscious community with the patient." Also seeing the analytic process as the unfolding of a past drama, he says:

> Countertransferences thus constitute an accidental casting of the analyst in an intrusive part in the psychoanalytic drama. Through the analysis of the countertransference the analyst can reintegrate his position as an analyst

and regain a position from which he can utilize the interfering factor for the purpose of analysing the patient's exploitation of it. In some instances this may mean a degree of self-revelation (by which I do not mean confession). But in a going analysis it may be found possible. *In such a situation one can reveal as much of oneself as is needed to foster and support the patient's discovery of the reality of the actual interpersonal situation as contrasted with the transference–countertransference situation.* (p. 7) [Emphasis mine.]

In Gorkin's opinion (1987) the reason for disclosing the countertransference is sometimes overtly stated, but often it is only implied. He provides an excellent review of the literature on why the countertransference is disclosed, and cites reasons (pp. 85–86) for doing so:

1. to confirm the patient's sense of reality;
2. to establish the therapist's honesty or genuineness;
3. to establish the therapist's humanness;
4. to clarify both the fact and the nature of the patient's impact on the therapist, and on people in general; and
5. to end a treatment impasse or break through a deeply entrenched impasse.

The reasons stated above are all valid as justifications for revelation of the countertransference. Yet they are all very specific and as such do not provide an underlying or generalizable principle that can be applied to questions of countertransference disclosure. As Compton (1988) says:

Change, while it occurs in the mind of the patient, is brought about by the interaction of the patient and the analyst, and, accordingly, must be conceptualized in some way that recognizes that interaction. (p. 227)

In my view, the underlying principle that should guide disclosure of the countertransference is as follows: *The therapist must disclose whatever is necessary to facilitate the patient's awareness and acceptance of the truth.* And the guiding principle for how and when this is done is simple: *The timing, nature and extent of the countertransference disclosure can only be determined by the therapist in consultation with the patient.* This second principle addresses the longstanding problem of how to determine what will be helpful to the patient and what will be "burdensome." The answer to the question, "How will you know what to say and when to say it?" is, "Ask the patient." Particularly if done within the context of the mutual, non-authoritarian relationship outlined in previous chapters, it is easier than you might imagine to have the patient tell you what he needs, whether this is done by direct communication, through projective identification, or some combination of the two.

To illustrate this concept, I would like to examine a case study presented by Silverman (1985). This case was part of an article on counter-transference in which he attempted to demonstrate how a countertransference dilemma was averted. He presents the case history of a man who came from a wealthy family, but who was attempting to separate from them and wanted to pay for his treatment. Since the patient had very little money at the beginning of the treatment, Silverman took him as a patient at a considerably reduced fee. As the treatment progressed, however, his patient's financial status greatly improved; he became quite wealthy and acquired a mountaintop estate with stables and tennis courts. Even as his client accumulated wealth, Silverman did not raise the fee. Instead, he waited for the patient to struggle with the unfairness of the situation and with his complementary desires to both nurture and defeat Silverman, believing that the patient would ultimately decide to raise the fee himself. During this period, both Silverman and his patient became quite upset. For example, Silverman began to keep his patient waiting for sessions, which he explains as follows:

> It did not take a great deal of self-scrutiny for me to realize that I resented my patient's teasing me by dangling offers to reward me for my labors, which indeed had been of enormous assistance to him, but then pulling back short of fulfilling them. He had been teasing me by accelerating his progress toward a good analytic result and by hinting at using some of the greatly expanded income I had helped him obtain, via an analysis that had proceeded for a long time at a low fee, to pay me more money, only to put the brakes on each time I became interested. (p. 190)

This quote illustrates that Silverman was well aware of his resentment toward his patient and that he was struggling with his self-awareness in the interests of facilitating the treatment. But, I disagree with his decision to keep his feelings to himself, ostensibly because he felt that the patient was trying to lure him into expressing his anger and raising the fee. Silverman seemed to feel that he would be falling into a trap of being sadistic, envious, and punishing his patient for his success, much as the patient's own father had done.

As the treatment progressed, the patient became increasingly agitated, attempting to humiliate and goad Silverman into raising the fee through verbal assaults and even smearing mud on his new couch. Silverman says, "He continued to subtly encourage me to lose my patience and demand more money from him." After failing to get an emotional response from Silverman, the patient fell into a long period of silent withdrawal, which was accompanied by the patient's contempt: at one point Silverman's patient asked, "Where would I be if I had your balls?", which I interpreted as his growing disgust over Silverman's reluctance to act. Eventually, Silverman reports, they agreed on a fee increase, but only after a very anguished period.

In reading this case, along with Silverman's commentary to the effect that he was refusing to take the part of the punitive, sadistic, and castrating father, the unfettered anguish of this patient can be felt. And the question arises as to why Silverman refused to take the legitimate power of the analyst in raising the fee: since when do patients set fees? Silverman says that he was avoiding the countertransference trap of expressing envy and resentment at his patient's success—feelings that he, in his article, admits to having. And yet, while I believe that Silverman was sincere in his wish not to punish his patient for his success, it appears to me that he unconsciously got his revenge on the patient after all, judging by the patient's considerable distress and therapeutic block.

It seems to me that if Silverman had been comfortable with his feelings of competition, envy and resentment toward his patient, he could have *used* his countertransference to help his patient and to avoid the long stalemate that occurred in this otherwise successful treatment. Had Silverman realized that his patient was trying to tell him what he needed him to do, rather than believing that his patient was leading him astray, I believe the outcome could have been quite different.

I think that whenever a patient is blatantly provocative, he is telling us that he desperately needs a response—and probably an emotional one. Viewing the patient's provocations, as Silverman does, as an attempt to bait the therapist into doing something wrong, is a statement of distrust and indicates an inability to ally with the patient. At the beginning of his report, Silverman warns of

> . . . falling prey to the implantation of misleading views by an analysand who is playing upon the analyst's biases and personal inclinations to lead him astray. The ability of certain patients to subtly but skillfully produce desired feelings in and reactive responses by their analysts can be impressive. (p. 180)

It seems to me that Silverman succumbed to the countertransference state labeled "microparanoia" by Kernberg, as mentioned earlier. This is what got Silverman into trouble with his patient in the first place; over time, it intensified, and, as Silverman's patient continued with his provocations, an impasse was reached which continued for some time. Silverman's patient was not trying to lead him astray, but rather to invite, persuade, cajole, or do whatever was necessary to get him to play out his role in his own personal drama. Silverman, aware of the pressure from his patient and his own countertransference, believed that the only way to avert disaster was to refuse to accept his assigned role and to keep the countertransference hidden. But I believe he would have been more effective if he had accepted the role and played it out honestly and directly, using the countertransference to facilitate a different and more therapeutic outcome.

It seems likely that part of Silverman's reluctance to play his role was because he would have been forced to admit to feelings of envy and resentment. Hirsch (1980-81) discusses the inevitability of such feelings and how they complement the patient's fear and sense of loss regarding leaving the therapist behind. He refers to the

> . . . analyst's anxiety about being surpassed by his or her patient in important ways. The degree of resolution of issues of competitiveness, jealousy and envy are important here. Nonetheless, it is rare not to experience those feelings in the context of an intense relationship. Our patients are often younger, smarter, in better health, better looking, have more potential, have more excitement in their lives, have better relationships with their loved ones, have more money, and on and on. *Analysts who are unable to acknowledge both the fact of such differences and the ensuing jealousy or competitiveness run the risk of acting unconsciously to stifle the patient.* (p. 127)

This brings me to the issue of recognizing and admitting to "negative" feelings on the therapist's part. In order to use the countertransference effectively we must be reasonably comfortable with any feelings we might have, including envy, hatred or sexual attraction. But just as sex and aggression cause the most difficulties for our patients, so do they for us as therapists. It is seldom that one hears any reference to hating a patient or being sexually attracted to a patient that is accepted as natural. Usually such feelings signal not only the presence of a significant countertransference reaction, but also alarm on the therapist's part. Much guilt is associated with having these feelings, the emphasis often being on how to get rid of them as soon as possible.

Kernberg (1975) has discussed the inevitable feelings of anger, frustration and hopelessness that are stimulated in therapists who work with borderline personalities. And Searles (1975) has noted that, particularly with very regressed patients, the therapist will naturally regress to primitive sexual and aggressive strivings. But no-one has so eloquently argued for the naturalness and potential benefit from recognizing negative feelings toward patients as has Winnicott (1949). Rather than viewing hatred as something that demonstrates a sickness in the therapist, Winnicott stresses the vitally important role that hatred plays in the development of the capacity to love:

> . . . it seems to me doubtful whether a human child as he develops is capable of tolerating the full extent of his own hate in a sentimental environment. He needs hate to hate.
>
> If this is true, a psychotic patient in analysis cannot be expected to tolerate his hate of the analyst unless the analyst can hate him. . . . Until the interpretation [of mutual hate] is made the patient is kept to some extent in the position of the infant, one who cannot understand what he owes to his mother. (p. 74)

Even though Winnicott's comments are directed to the treatment of psychotic patients, he draws his conclusions from observations of normal development. Taking his point one step further, could we not say the same about all patients? And could we not accept the normalcy and necessity of feeling envy, jealousy, intolerance, and all other human emotions, including hatred, with the understanding that what we refer to as "negative emotions" are essential counterparts of the "positive emotions" of love, respect, generosity, and empathy?

And if Winnicott is right when he says that hate cannot be tolerated in a sentimental environment then I am afraid that many self-psychologists are adopting a posture that forces the inhibition and denial of hatred and other negative feelings. In our well-intentioned efforts to understand our patients, have we not denied vital aspects of our own experience—and therefore theirs? Unlike the analysts who practiced in the 1940s and 1950s who seemed freer with a broad range of feeling (and perhaps in reaction to the more distant and removed style of the 1960s, 1970s and early 1980s), are we leaning toward accepting a sugar-coated version of humanity that ultimately depersonalizes both therapist and patient, and unknowingly stifles the most positive human expressions in the process? How successful can we be in helping our patients to accept themselves when they are hateful, or petty and mean, or selfish and niggardly, if we cannot accept these feelings in ourselves?

Tansey and Burke (1989) admit that the therapist is bound to have negative feelings, and caution therapists against attempting to compensate for these feelings with expressions of "unconditional positive regard." Yet they do not say exactly what the therapist should do when having negative feelings. Emphasizing the counterproductive aspects of hiding these feelings does not go far enough. Though they encourage self-analysis and understanding of the transference–countertransference interplay, they never say what a therapist should do when the negative feelings either will not go away or are periodically rekindled in the therapeutic relationship.

Similarly, Stolorow, Brandchaft and Atwood (1987) base their intersubjective approach on the proposition that "transference and countertransference together form an intersubjective system of mutual reciprocal influence" (p. 42), which is philosophically very compatible with the basic approach to the treatment relationship outlined here. However, when it comes to technique, they relegate acknowledgement of the transference–countertransference interplay to a predominantly intellectual exercise performed by the therapist. Defined in terms of therapist awareness, the interplay is something for the therapist to acknowledge internally and factor into his understanding of the patient. It is something to be used internally for the purposes of achieving a higher degree of empathy. But it is not to be recognized verbally with the patient. As with classical analysis, the most important information about the patient and the relationship remains the exclusive and silent domain of the therapist. Even though the purpose is to understand the patient better, what results is the ultimate in what Winnicott called the "sentimental environment" and the therapist subsumes his independent identity in the interests of validating the patient's subjective experience. McLaughlin (1981) speaks of the need for a vital interaction between therapist and patient, emphasizing the aspect of mutual validation:

> What becomes mutually accepted as experientially "real" in the two-party system of privacy and isolation can only be a shared consensus wrung from prolonged testing and verification by both. The "therapeutic alliance" is not then a pregiven for analytic work but rather a gradually shaped trust which patient and analyst build up about the reliability of their shared views of what goes on between them, a consensus and comfort that allow the deep explorations of psychoanalysis to transpire. In this sense the outcome of successful analysis reflects an evolving, mutual authentication of the psychic realities of the two parties in the analytic search. (p. 658)

McLaughlin's conceptualization emphasizes authentication of the realities of the *relationship*, rather than the reality of the *patient*. If the analytic relationship is viewed in this way, then virtually anything and everything that transpires between therapist and patient is potentially important to recognize and verbally acknowledge. Viewing the relationship in this light has a great leveling effect, in that all that is important is the truth— whatever that might be. Love is not more important than hate, integrity is not more important than an obvious lack of character. What is real about each person and what is happening between them is the highest priority. The therapist's constant empathy or positive regard for the patient actually becomes irrelevant. The most essential attribute for the therapist is an unyielding commitment—a commitment to the truth, to maintaining the integrity of the relationship and the process, and to being aware of how the transference molds the countertransference and vice-versa, for better or worse.

When I first started my practice I did not believe any of what I have just written. I believed that a good therapist cared deeply about his or her patients, and that the most successful outcomes would occur with patients whom I truly loved and respected. But this has simply not been the case. In reality, my worst failures have always been with patients I cared about deeply. And one of my greatest successes was with a patient I often hated and who badgered and criticized me constantly. It is thanks to her that I learned the value of acknowledging hatred in the therapeutic relationship.

Nancy, a 30-year-old borderline personality whom I had been seeing for about 2½ years, repeatedly implored me to love her the way she "loved" me. When she would cry and become agitated, and insist that I love her, I either empathically noted her desperation and need to receive the mother-love that had always eluded her or, when this failed, said nothing, both of which did nothing but enrage her. At these times she would criticize me for being cold, withholding, and unhelpful. Over time I became increasingly frustrated and angry at the repetition of this scene and noted to myself that I did not feel loved by her at all. After endless repetitions of this scene I thought we would both go crazy if we could not find a way out of this dilemma. When empathy did not work, I tried taking her criticisms seriously as an indication that she wanted me to admit that I was not handling her case well and should refer her to another therapist. When I asked her if she wanted me to do this she became hysterical and said that if I abandoned her she would be lost forever. She said she did not want to see someone else. She wanted me to find a way to help her.

I began to feel as though I was lost in some mythological journey, the path to the holy grail being totally unknown to me. I sought consultations, which helped me to deal better with my feelings of frustration, rage and helplessness, but did not change the basic situation with Nancy. One day, when she was again imploring me to love her, and I was feeling desperate to escape from the drama that entrapped us both, I said to her, "What you say is not true. You do *not* love me. I believe you would like to, but you don't. And you know that I cannot say what you want me to say because I don't love you either. How could I when I always feel as though you've got me by the throat and are pushing me against the wall? That's not love. It's anger or hatred."

Somewhat to my amazement, this intervention proved to be the catalyst for a dramatic turning point in Nancy's treatment, counterpointed humorously by her retort, "We've been through this so many times, why didn't you tell me this before?" She then went on to relate emotionally how much she had *wanted* to love her mother and be loved by her in return, but had actually hated her more and more as she grew older. She re-enacted with me her angry attempts to extract love from her mother, with the same futile outcome. The more she pressed me, the more I felt angry and distant from her. When I finally accepted my role, but behaved differently from her mother by confronting her with the reality of the situation, she was released. She also told me how important it was that she could be free to hate me. She said that throughout her life she had denied her hatred for her mother because she felt so ashamed of it. And she was sure that if she ever let her mother know how she felt, all would be lost. This applied equally to me, of course, so I had to be the one to acknowledge her hatred. If we had waited for her to do it, it is unlikely that it would ever have happened. It was my role and my function to accept her hatred and express it. My feelings of frustration and anger were clear in my voice when I confronted her and I believe that this was critical to the success of this encounter.

Nancy had made steady progress up until the stalemate that led to our intense exchange, but there was quite a dramatic change in her behavior from that point on. She never again made a hostile demand for my love, or for anyone else's, as she reported to me. And she became much more relaxed and at ease than I had ever seen her before. My attitude toward her naturally changed, too. I began to enjoy working with her rather than dreading the sessions, as I had prior to our confrontation. While there was still much work to be done, particularly as we proceeded to the termination phase of the treatment, it was accomplished without the strain of the previous years and to the satisfaction of both of us. The treatment ended well, with both of us proud of the excellent work we had done together, and happy for the considerably altered and more satisfying life that she could now enjoy with her husband and daughter. What I have always marveled at, however, is that I disliked working with Nancy through at least two-thirds of her treatment and often wished I could be rid of her. What I realize now, but did not then, is that Nancy did not need my understanding or empathy. (In fact, she constantly received empathy and sincere comfort from her husband, which only relieved her momentarily and left her feeling guilty and ashamed that his love and acceptance didn't really change anything.) She needed me to demonstrate that I could tolerate seeing and feeling her rage and my own; and that I would not leave her if I knew she hated me.

Sexual Feelings

A very controversial area, which must be addressed when confronting the countertransference and attempting to modify technique in a way that incorporates it, is the area of sexual feelings toward patients. If hatred and envy have been viewed in the past as difficult and unsavory, it is safe to say that sexual feelings have been viewed as taboo and unacceptable. Gorkin (1985, 1987) notes that the therapist's sexual feelings are not as acceptable as those that are aggressive:

> It is worth noting that, in spite of the burgeoning interest in counter-transference issues, scant attention has been paid in the literature to the analyst's sexual feelings and fantasies toward his patients. One can only speculate as to the reasons for this. I do not think it is primarily a matter of analysts' repression of their sexual fantasies, though one does sometimes have the impression that it is more comfortable nowadays for an analyst to fantasize throwing a patient out of his office, than it is to imagine joining him or her on the couch. Still, in today's more liberal milieu, with the

growing acceptance of the clinical importance of countertransference, it is impossible to believe that analysts are unaware of their sexual fantasies and feelings about their patients. (p. 424)

Gorkin is generally not in favor of disclosing the sexualized countertransference, admitting to poor results when having done so. I agree with his position, primarily because sexual feelings toward patients are viewed so negatively by almost everyone, not only because of the symbolic incest taboo that may be violated by disclosing sexual feelings, but also because of the increasing number of therapists being prosecuted for sexual misconduct. Thus any disclosure of sexual feelings has great potential for scaring the patient to death. Since the purpose of any countertransference disclosure is to affirm the integrity of the patient and of the relationship, any disclosure that results in high anxiety and a break in the alliance is at cross-purposes with these goals and thus unacceptable. Though disclosure of the sexualized countertransference will be discussed further in the techniques chapter, suffice it to say that this area of disclosure is too prone to stimulating anxiety to be useful very often. And the risk of damaging the therapeutic alliance is simply too great to take.

It is also worth noting that sexual responses fall into a different category for patient and therapist than do other human emotions. This has to do with the re-creation of the parent–child relation and the incest taboo, so that most patients are very uneasy about the prospect of stimulating their therapists sexually. If a parent's sexual feelings toward his child are intense and long-lasting this usually means that something has gone awry in the parent or in the relationship. I think the same might be said for therapist–patient relationships. In Chapter 1, I mentioned that patients who are unduly frustrated in the therapeutic relationship and who do not feel free to hate their therapists may respond with the reaction formation of being intensely in love with them. Similarly, at times therapists may respond with intense sexual feelings toward a patient whom they secretly hate. This is especially likely, of course, if the patient is very attractive or seductive.

When sexual feelings are not defensive, but rather a reflection of the therapist's true feelings, it is likely that they will be transient and manageable. This does not mean that they will not be intense at times; but if the therapist is not in conflict regarding these feelings, they should be as manageable as any other feeling and not pose a threat to the treatment. For example, they should not produce seductiveness or sexual acting-out on the part of the therapist. If, however, the therapist falls in love with the patient, and remains in love, the treatment must be aborted.

Contrary to traditional practice, I think that the patient has a right to know *why* he is being referred out, and that this should be discussed frankly. When a therapist has fallen in love with a patient there exists a very strong and mutual attachment. To simply inform the patient that the relationship is ending because the therapist is not capable of continuing it is cruel. The patient cannot help but feel abandoned and assume that he has done something wrong. He has a right to know that he is being referred out because his therapist feels so strongly about him that the therapist has lost all potential for maintaining a professional relationship and therefore cannot continue. The patient should be able to talk about this with the therapist, have his questions and fears addressed directly and, if need be, meet with a consultant to facilitate the least traumatic ending possible to the unfortunate circumstances that exist.

Though I generally feel that greater caution must be used when considering disclosure of the sexualized countertransference, and that it will not typically be productive, I am not saying that sexual feelings should be exempt from possible disclosure. What I am saying is that I do not believe that many patients actually want and need to know if their therapists are sexually attracted to them. They may muse about it from time to time, and admit to wishing that the therapist would be attracted or in love. But this is not to be confused with a serious confrontation and demand to know. And to make the mistake of disclosing when the patient does not want it can have serious consequences.

In Summary

The delicate and constant interplay of transference–countertransference builds during the first phase of treatment, with the patient primarily seeking the therapist's understanding. This phase gradually gives way to a phase that is ideally characterized by a symbiotic phase in which the patient regresses significantly and the therapist regresses to a lesser but complementary degree. As this period of mutual regression progresses the relationship becomes more dynamic and conflicted, with the patient heading toward replaying the most damaging dramas from the past. Selective and timely disclosure of the countertransference is recommended for the purpose of altering previous outcomes in the patient's drama, and facilitating a different and more productive final scene.

CHAPTER 4

The "Real" Relationship Versus the Transference and the Countertransference: The Impossible Distinction

Initially, the term "transference' described all of the patient's reactions and behaviors aimed at the therapist in the analytic situation. No matter what the patient perceived about the therapist, it was transference. This definition was simple, neat, orderly, parsimonious and efficient. But over the years many therapists came to realize that their patients were in fact quite capable of independent observation, perceiving their therapists' changing moods and behavior, as well as discerning their basic character—no matter how hard the therapists may have tried to keep this information hidden. Therapists also discerned that many of their patients could experience mature love and empathy in the therapeutic relationship. Similarly, therapists began to understand that some of their strong feelings toward their patients were "neurotic," in that some patients behaved in a way that stimulated hatred and some behaved in a way, or revealed a certain character, that unmistakably inspired love. Once it was fully realized that patient and therapist could *accurately perceive* the other, attempts were made to distinguish between the "real" relationship and the transference and countertransference (Greenson, 1971; Searles, 1973, 1975). Attempting to delineate the differences between transference and reality was not only in the interests of validating the patient's feelings and perceptions. If there was such a thing as "reality" then strong emotional reactions on the part of the therapist could be labeled reality-based, rather than countertransference (implied here is the earlier definition of countertransference which was said to reflect the therapist's pathology). Making the distinction between either the therapist's or the patient's transference and reality thus served to free both to have reactions that would not be dismissed as distortions.

There is no question that attempts to distinguish between the real and the imaginary or the healthy and the neurotic are constructive in theory.

The need to make such distinctions stems from an honest wish to help the patient and to "cure" him of his "illness." If we could isolate and identify all that is healthy and all that is unhealthy, as in comparing normal cells to malignant ones, it would be much easier to diagnose and treat our patients. Likewise, it is an integral part of psychoanalytic therapy that some reasonable attempt be made to understand how the past is replayed in the present and to aid the patient in acquiring insight into this process.

The Problem with Distinctions

However, in practice, there are enormous difficulties in making distinctions between the "real" and the imagined, projected, displaced, or distorted. Traditionally, making such distinctions has been a major part of the therapist's role. It is the therapist who decides what is transference and what is not. It is the therapist who decides what is countertransference and what is not. The therapist assumes this power based on the belief that the patient is in no position to make these distinctions himself. The therapist is seen as a more objective person with no personal ax to grind and it is she who is seen not only as being in the favored position for making such judgments, but as the one who has the responsibility to do so. But is it not presumptuous on the part of the therapist to think that she can define and know *everything*? Has the analytic therapist exceeded her authority in taking responsibility for deciding what is transference and what is not? Acknowledging the seminal nature of transference, Szasz (1963) says:

> Transference is the pivot upon which the entire structure of psycho-analytic treatment rests. It is an inspired and indispensable concept; yet it also harbours the seeds, not only of its own destruction, but of the destruction of psycho-analysis itself. Why? Because it tends to place the person of the analyst beyond the reality testing of patients, colleagues, and self. (p. 443)

Reich (1950) and many other traditionalists argue that the analyst's integrity and her use of self-analysis and consultation result in an even-handed judgment regarding reality that is fair to the patient and not threatening to the analytic process, let alone prone to the apocalyptic consequences envisioned by Szasz. Others believe that even though the therapist is in no position to determine what is real and what is not, her job, nonetheless, is to interpret the transference (Arlow, 1985), which strikes me as a notion that turns in on itself and is contradictory. How do you interpret the transference without first making the judgment about what is transference and what is not?

Another factor to consider in distinguishing between the real and the transference or countertransference is that the relative objectivity of the therapist, which is somewhat pronounced at the onset of treatment, will give way as the relationship continues, particularly during the middle phase that ideally is characterized by some mutual (but not equal) regression. Searles (1973) discusses how difficult it can be to sort out feelings and their point of origin, since so much non-verbal and unconscious-to-unconscious communication takes place as the therapy progresses.

> The symbiotic instability of ego boundaries makes it impossible to know whether the anger or depression, for instance, which one suddenly experiences, is one's "own," or whether one is empathically sensing a feeling of the patient's "own" against which he is successfully defended unconsciously (as by projection). (p. 254)

The difficulty in determining what is transference, particularly during periods of mutual regression, applies equally to the countertransference. Because of the impossibility of making these distinctions, I suggest that therapists not attempt to do so. This may sound like abandonment of one of the most basic and essential analytic concepts, but it is not. The notion of transference is indispensable to the analytic endeavor. There is no question that it is invaluable to understand that people re-create the past in the present. But I think it is *not* essential that we presume to be able to make moment-to-moment judgments about when that is happening—particularly when those judgments are about *someone else's experience.* I agree with Szasz when he says:

> In psychoanalytic *theory*, the concept of transference serves as an explanatory hypothesis; whereas in the psychoanalytic *situation*, it serves as a defence for the analyst. (p. 435)

Who Decides What Is Real?

In my opinion, the person who is in the best position to say what is transference and what is not transference is the patient. The history that he gives us, along with our experience of him in the present, helps us to explore the nature of his reactions in a joint inquiry. There is certainly nothing wrong in asking the patient if the situation with you seems familiar. Nor do I think there is anything wrong with the therapist saying that she is reminded of the patient's past by some current circumstance, so long as the validation is left to the patient. Most clinicians would agree that efforts by the therapist aimed at connecting the past and the present must take the form of sincere inquiry, rather than an assumption or *fait accompli.* Yet, in practice, this is often not the case.

In the instances when sincere inquiry becomes difficult or impossible, such as when the therapist feels sure the patient is forcing her into a mold which does not fit and she has strong feelings about this, then I think this situation can often be remedied by disclosure of the counter-transference—as opposed to insistent repetition of an interpretation that the patient has already rejected (even though it may be accurate). Because an affective response is more likely to permeate the patient's defenses, this approach offers the potential for breaking the stalemate and aiding the patient in achieving insight rather than becoming more entrenched in self-protection. In fact, one of the rules of thumb that I discuss in the next chapter pertains to using interpretation, or any other intervention, to keep the patient in line. Whenever the spirit of joint inquiry breaks down and is replaced by an adversarial struggle, a countertransference disclosure may be the intervention of choice. The initial purpose of interpretation was to facilitate the process of making the unconscious conscious. And this cannot possibly happen when a power struggle is in progress.

Granted, it would be neater if we could just *know* what is transference and what is not—and what is countertransference and what is not. In the early years of psychoanalysis the unrealistic assumption held that we were, in fact, capable of making such distinctions. In the past twenty years, as we have become more realistic, we have recanted this view to a great extent. But, as is often the case, we overlay new concepts and terms on top of the existing ones, apparently because we cannot bear to alter the essential nature of our ideas or to throw any of them away. Rather than eliminating the notion of transference as resistance and as something easily distinguished from reality, we have incorporated new ideas and terms to fill the void left by these old ideas. As we have come to understand that the patient truly wants to get better and expends considerable effort in that direction, and that he is capable of real feeling and genuine concern for us as his therapist and a human being, we have created new terms to describe this. These terms include "working alliance" (Greenson, 1965), "therapeutic alliance" (Zetzel, 1956), and "real relationship." However, as Gill (1985) notes, these well-intentioned attempts to acknowledge the patient's humanity are misguided in that they result in splitting. For example, writing on the issue of "real" versus "transference" in the therapeutic relationship, Gill says:

> In a general sense, one of the difficulties with that kind of concept is that it implies that the nature of the patient's experience of the relationship can be cut up into various kinds of things: there is a real relationship, and there's the neurotic relationship; there's a distortion of the real relationship; there's this kind of alliance and that kind of alliance. There may be some conceptual advantage to be gained in that sort of cutting things up, but I think when

it comes to the actual work with the patient, this effort only interferes with one's ability to empathize with what the patient is experiencing. (p. 131)

Because we have created new and separate terms rather than changing the basic notion of transference–countertransference and the nature of the analytic relationship, we have failed to integrate our new ideas and clinical observations with the old. This only hampers our ability to help ourselves and our patients to integrate our own experiences.

Greenson (1971) was so sensitive to the accuracy of his patients' observations about him, and their ability to "know" him whether he self-disclosed or not, that he was moved to write about it. And there is no question that he made an enormous contribution when he recognized his patients' strengths and the futility of the therapist's attempts to be a blank screen. However, his observations were never integrated into the existing notion of transference, nor was a new term that more completely described the patient's attitude toward the analyst coined. Perhaps because of his classical training, Greenson was intent on discriminating between transference and reality. In fact, it was Greenson who defined what are now the oft-quoted characteristics of a transference reaction—it is an undiscriminating, non-selective repetition of the past, which is inappropriate and ignores or distorts reality. Yet even using this definition, he admitted that there were many times when it was very difficult to distinguish between transference and reality. But he persisted in trying to ferret out the difference between the two for the purpose of taking the patient seriously when he had a valid point to make about the therapist and his behavior.

A simpler solution to this problem, of course, is to take the patient seriously as a matter of course, knowing that no matter how extreme or "inappropriate" his reaction may be, it is always reality-based in the sense that it is a response to something the therapist has done or said. Thus, when the clinician acknowledges his role in eliciting a patient's response, it is unnecessary to mention to the patient that his intense reaction is born out of some past experience. And the reason is that the patient naturally goes to it himself once the need to defend himself against the therapist's threat to his reality-testing has been removed. Generally speaking, the patient is infinitely more willing and able to accept responsibility for his reactions and to assess whether they are "reasonable" if the therapist is able to do the same. And, patients make the best "transference interpretations" themselves. While interpretations and general understanding of the patient's experiences are invaluable to clinicians, they are rarely as useful when verbalized to the patient.

Grotstein (1987) discusses the concept of the patient's reactions being based in reality as it pertains to projective identification:

Projective identification never occurs in a vacuum. There must always be an external realization which justifies the projection so that the projection can take place. Mother must frustrate, err, disappoint, etc.—seemingly purposely so as to justify the projective identifications into reality—and mother must acknowledge these "goofs," as must analysts, so that the Memory of Justice can be restored. (p. 70)

When I acknowledge to a patient that there is indeed a stimulus for his reaction, and that I myself am often that stimulus, I also make a point of discussing with him how he reacts to that stimulus and how his reaction relates to his self-image and past experience.

For example, Ellen, a narcissistic patient who is hypersensitive to any mood changes in me or variations in my emotional availability, regularly reacts strongly when I am less than optimally available. One day when I had a mild case of the flu, being somewhat tired and lethargic yet not visibly ill, I was less responsive during her session. On an emotional level, I was less involved when she was telling me what was upsetting her that day and, on a behavioral level, I was less talkative.

The next day she came to her session distraught and enraged. She railed at me for not wanting to hear about her pain and difficulties in life, saying I was just like everyone else—if she was too needy then I did not want to have anything to do with her. Since I had felt quite sympathetic to her during the previous session, I was at first quite stunned by what she was saying. I asked her what made her think that I had rejected her. She said that it was quite obvious that she failed to engage me during the previous session and that I seemed quite separate and apart from her, as well as having very little to say.

After giving her sufficient opportunity to express all of her feelings of hurt, disappointment and rage, I told her that she was absolutely accurate in what she had perceived, but not in the conclusions that she drew. I let her know that I had had the flu and was unusually subdued the previous day only for that reason. She was surprised and it took her a few minutes to process this information and to decide whether she should believe it. Her initial reaction was to wonder if I was only coming up with an excuse for my rejection of her. She had to hold on to this reaction for a while since part of her longstanding self-image is that she is unacceptable and unlovable when she is in pain. But after a bit she began to accept that I was telling the truth, because of my sincerity and surety in speaking to her, and because of her past experience of me.

It might seem quite evident to many readers that it is essential to realize that patients' behaviors, no matter how extreme, are related to something in the analytic situation. Yet I find this recognition in actual practice to be more difficult than I had imagined. I find that I struggle internally when criticized or verbally assaulted by a patient, wanting somehow to justify my attitudes or behavior. Particularly if what the patient is saying makes no sense to me, I want to dismiss his argument as irrational. This is especially true if the "something" that the patient is responding to in the treatment situation seems trivial. (I once had a patient spend one whole hour questioning my capacity for nurturing when she observed that one of the plants in my office was wilting and had lost some leaves.)

The other point I consider to be essential is that the patient often takes what is a correct observation and then, based on fear, comes to an incorrect conclusion. I have found that most people who are in therapy owing to difficulties in relationships (this includes most patients) arrive at their conclusions by using inference rather than by talking to the other person in the conflict; and patients who are quite bright and perceptive are often the "worst" ones, since they are confident in their ability to perceive others' behavior accurately. Armed with this confidence, they are equally sure that their inferences are accurate, and part of my job is to bring them compassionately to an emotional understanding of what amounts to a total breach of logic. (Consider, for example, my patient Ellen, who jumped from the accurate perception that I was less involved to the erroneous conclusion that I had rejected her sadness, when in fact I had the flu.)

The work with patients on their reality testing usually begins with me and gradually becomes part of my patients' repertoire outside of treatment. Along with their experience with me, I encourage them to examine their responses to others and to think seriously about whether their conclusions are supported behaviorally or if they are purely speculative or intuitive. If speculative, I encourage them to find a way to discuss the problem with the other person in such a way that would test their hypotheses. If they discover that the problem primarily lies with them, in that they are reacting based on fear and past history, then I encourage them to mediate their responses to others based on this and to develop insight and perspective on how these internal events affect their relations with others. I also point out that there is no absolute line of demarcation, that the determination of "what's me and what's you and what's the result of our interaction" is relative, that it's hard to define reality, and that the assumption of responsibility is a very delicate and difficult process. The ultimate objective of the dialog is to arrive at some reasonably fair appraisal of a situation that can be agreed upon by both parties. An appreciation of the inseparability of internal and external events is crucial to a realistic resolution.

If we look at the patient's reactions in this light—i.e. everything the patient says is both intrapsychic (a product of early experience and internal conflict) and interpersonal (a product of the relationship with the therapist), then *everything* is transference and *everything* is real.

(Of course, the same can be said for the countertransference.) This blending of transference and reality is evident when you consider that most conflicts involve repeated exchanges between the two persons involved. One person speaks and the other responds, taking in the reality of the other person and mingling that with past history. Then the *other* person responds to this combination of transference and reality with yet another combined response. This cycle continues as the dialog does, with the weaving of intrapsychic and interpersonal becoming increasingly complex and, to a great extent, inextricable.

If we cannot distinguish between what is real and what is transference (or countertransference), then we cannot decide how much each of us is contributing to the conflict. We are faced with trying to make distinctions that are impossible to make in the absolute sense and the only way to resolve this is to hammer it out between the two of us as the transference–countertransference interplay is enacted and analyzed.

In terms of hammering out "reality," I am mindful of Szasz's admonition that what is useful to the therapist in theory may not be so useful when it comes to technique. Ideally, of course, the therapist has some reasonable notion about what is going on with the patient and how it is a repetition of the past, which is imminently useful in terms of organizing and guiding the therapeutic experience, but may be anything but useful if verbalized to the patient—particularly at a time when he is struggling to retrieve repressed feeling. And once the patient has been able to experience this affect he more often than not is able to make the necessary interpretations himself. Additionally, any intellectual discussions about the genetic origin of a patient's feelings is much more useful if instigated by him rather than by me.

Thus, the process whereby the transference–countertransference interplay is sorted out, discussed, felt and understood is best initiated by the patient. The patient cues the therapist regarding what response is needed. As stated in previous chapters, the patient will tell the therapist what he needs and what he is capable of handling at the moment. If he needs to know what the therapist is feeling he will either ask directly or prompt this response through repeated projective identifications or other provocative behavior.

The Mental Health of the Therapist

One of the most difficult and controversial aspects of hammering out some reasonable assessment of reality between patient and therapist concerns the relative mental health of the therapist. How can a therapist who does not know the truth about herself facilitate the patient's awareness of what is true about himself and the relationship? The only answer can be, with great difficulty. After all, the extent to which the therapist cannot accurately perceive herself and the patient is evident in any treatment and has an impact, whether it becomes obvious through self-disclosure or some other avenue. The therapist influences and shapes the patient's experience through interpretation, with pertinent interpretations being determined by the therapist's view of herself, the patient, and their interactions. However, without self-disclosure the full extent of the therapist's limitations, including any severe or characterological pathology, will be less evident to the patient on a conscious level.

While the masking of the therapist's pathology may be in the therapist's best interest from a professional standpoint, the same cannot be said for the patient. For he will be influenced and limited in his treatment by his therapist's pathology, yet will not have the opportunity to oberve and understand this. What can happen when the therapist cannot distinguish between reality and her own distortion is that the patient becomes increasingly confused, anxious and, if the situation is not resolved, hopeless and depressed. Even if this occurs only transiently in the duration of the treatment, which is probably inevitable, the patient can quickly exhibit the symptoms described above. One of the most important tasks of analytic treatment is to accept limitations, loss, and human frailty, but this does not mean that the patient should accept responsibility for the therapist's limitations as well as his own. Should this occur, it will significantly and unnecessarily undermine the patient's confidence and optimism, both during the treatment and after.

The therapist's ability to transcend her own pathology also determines the extent to which the treatment will be fueled and directed by the countertransference. Without the benefit of disclosure, I believe there is little hope of resolving anything but the most transient countertransference responses to the patient, paving the way for a countertransference-dominated outcome. When people ask me how I can advocate the therapist dumping her pathology on the patient by disclosing it, I answer that if she discloses it responsibly she at least has a *chance* of working it through successfully with the patient. If she does not disclose her countertransference she may well do more damage to the patient by influencing him covertly, never taking responsibility for this influence, and never giving herself and the patient the opportunity to ameliorate the negative consequences.

I have stated in earlier chapters that there is no one right way to do treatment, no technique that cannot be used ineffectively, and this includes disclosure of the countertransference. I do not dispute that some therapists may use this technique abusively, simply because some therapists *are* abusive. But I believe that the majority of therapists are *not* abusive and would have the opportunity to work through much more with their patients if they were emotionally freer in the treatment and had countertransference techniques in their repertoires. I also believe that disclosure of the countertransference, as defined in the following chapter, offers the therapist the potential for greater awareness of how her pathology becomes operative in a given treatment, thus increasing the possibility for insight that would further the patient's progress.

Even though Benedek (1953) engages in the splitting of transference and reality that I have taken issue with in this chapter, I think her point regarding the emotional freedom of the therapist is worth noting:

> As long as the therapist is emotionally free in handling the patient's reactions toward him, whether they be transference reactions, or actually valid responses to his personality, the countertransference is kept in check. (p. 206)

Little (1951) speaks of the "subjective states" of the analyst, a reference to the analyst's pathology. Little, perhaps because of her own emotional breaks and subsequent treatment by Winnicott, seems unusually at ease with her own imperfections, accepting that none of us will ever reach the ideal of mental health to which we aspire. An advocate of countertransference disclosure, she is skeptical about personal analysis as the cure for countertransference difficulties:

> The ever-quoted remedy for counter-transference difficulties—deeper and more thorough analysis of the analyst—can at best be an incomplete one, for some tendency to develop unconscious infantile countertransferences is bound to remain. Analysis cannot reach the whole of the unconscious id, and we have only to remember that even the most thoroughly analysed person still dreams to be reminded of this. (p. 38)

Because few authors since Little have delved into the problems of the analytic therapist's psychopathology, this aspect of the treatment relationship has been largely ignored with regard to technique. Most articles on countertransference assume that ongoing pathological tendencies in the therapist can be "cured" through personal analysis, and that transient difficulties due to life crises or idiosyncratic responses to particular patients can be dealt with adequately through self-analysis and consultation. If this formula is accepted then the issue of the therapist's pathology virtually disappears. There is no need to develop an analytic technique for addressing something that either does not exist or is always short-lived.

What has happened as a result of this denial of the therapist's neediness and conflicts is that the patient is often blamed when a treatment fails. Therapists are expectably uneasy when a treatment ends badly and some feel compelled to cover their guilt over their contribution to the breakdown of the treatment relationship, chiefly because they have been taught *that there is no valid reason for them to be responsible*. Following conventional analytic wisdom, if the therapist *is* responsible then she did not have a successful analysis and should return to treatment. Some allowances are made for life crises, but on the whole anything more than a transient difficulty is viewed as an unacceptable weakness in the therapist. You rarely hear analytic therapists discussing their character flaws or ongoing conflicts and how they struggle with these issues when doing treatment. The assumption is that they have been cured of these problems, if not in life, at least in the sense that the "work ego" takes over in therapy and permits them to transcend themselves and to behave in a healthy way. To admit that this is often not the case is tantamount to admitting to being unfit as an analytic therapist. So therapists often feel compelled to minimize their own pathology to their patients, their colleagues, and themselves in order to save face and maintain some semblance of respect for themselves as clinicians. Many people believe that for the analytic therapist to admit to her pathology is dangerous. I believe that it is the need to preserve the mask of sanity that is dangerous. It distorts the true reality and assigns the burden of responsibility for anything unhealthy in the relationship to the patient.

I realize that not everyone does this. Some therapists are quite flexible and reasonable and willing to admit to their patients that they have been unreasonable, aggressive, inattentive, angry, envious, bored, unresponsive or whatever. And I am confident that most therapists do this at least occasionally. The problem is that this behavior is not sanctioned in the analytic world, which forces clinicians to hide what they really do and how they really feel, and dampens any efforts that are made to develop techniques for addressing the therapist's weaknesses and mistakes. Without such advances in technique the therapist has little choice but to interpret the patient's response defensively to her "subjective reaction" and hope that the patient will be willing to focus exclusively on the intrapsychic rather than the interpersonal. Too often, when a patient refuses to do this and demands that the interpersonal situation be analyzed and discussed, he is labeled as difficult and resistant. Granted, some patients do like to find fault with their therapists to deflect away from themselves, but the solution to this problem is certainly not for the therapist to engage in the same behavior. As I stated earlier, if the therapist can non-defensively acknowledge and take responsibility for her attitudes and behavior, then the patient is likely to respond in kind.

Perhaps the therapist's psychopathology is so neglected because of fears that the therapist, or some aspect of the situation, will get out of control. Revelation of the countertransference may seem like declaring open season on the therapist, stripping away what may be perceived as requisite anonymity. If Freud had people use the couch initially because he could not tolerate being stared at all day, how can we expect to endure the much closer scrutiny involved in disclosing the countertransference? Do we not run the risk of driving ourselves mad by demanding an unreasonable degree of openness, particularly from a full-time clinician?

Also, do not many therapists fear that disclosing their own distortions, illusions, weaknesses and wishes will potentially result in them losing control? Like other aspects of analytic technique, disclosure of the countertransference requires rigorous self-discipline. However, applying such discipline when one's own feelings are exposed can be difficult and is understandably a questionable or threatening proposition to many. Most of us like to think that we are fairly healthy and that our personal treatments were relatively successful. But proper disclosure of the countertransference puts this notion on the table for validation, and may force some therapists to admit to character flaws and residues of infantile neuroses that provoke narcissistic injuries or profound disappointment. Facing our own pathology, even after a relatively successful personal treatment, can be a grim task. After spending all that time and money it is not uplifting to ponder the inescapable traces of our infantile neuroses. And the fear may be that once we start admitting to the ways in which our own pathology affects our conduct as therapists, the situation will become damning and out of control. After all, what *would* happen if one of the therapists on the negative end of the normal curve of psychopathology started unleashing her craziness on her unsuspecting patients?

My solution to this problem is a bit simplistic, but not unrealistic: very troubled therapists absolutely need to keep a lid on their emotional responses to their patients. But they are also unlikely to be interested in using any countertransference techniques. And, what is likely to happen to those who *do* is that their patients will leave them. I do not take lightly the fact that emotionally disturbed therapists who reveal their counter-transference will be destructive to their patients. Yet at the same time, I do not believe that their inhibition of their poor responses actually facilitates a good treatment. What happens instead is that the patient does not have enough *evidence* to justify leaving an unhealthy and unhelpful therapist who hides his true feelings, and he probably ends up continuing with a treatment that is actually deleterious to his mental health. A more obvious and early revelation of the therapist's inability to be therapeutic, though it may be upsetting to the patient, could ultimately put an end to a relationship that is not in the patient's best interest.

What concerns me more is that too many therapists have exaggerated fears pertaining to their own pathology. I have found that discussions with colleagues regarding disclosure of the countertransference often results in expressions of anxiety concerning the therapist's ability to handle the situation well. Since their own analysts rarely, if ever, acknowledged their own struggles and weaknesses they have no model for what constitutes an "acceptable" level of pathology—let alone how to express their personal feelings constructively.

Naturally the first step in managing the countertransference requires the therapist to be keenly aware of her own strengths and weaknesses— to know where she is most effective and where she usually has difficulties. And she must be willing to admit that all the analysis in the world will not make her perfectly sane—that she will always say and do things that are not necessarily healthy and may even be quite irrational or destructive. If we admit to neurotic reactions to our patients with equanimity I think most of them will not flee from us or damn us. Even among those who expect perfection lies the wish to know that perfection is not necessary or even desirable.

In Summary

Transference and countertransference are defined as the total reactions of patient and therapist to each other. Distinctions between what is real and what is transference/countertransference are held to be impossible to make and insistence on doing so is considered unproductive and detracting to the analytic process. Reality is seen as a relative concept that only has meaning in the therapeutic setting if mutually agreed upon by both patient and therapist. The struggle for this truth in the therapeutic dyad is central to the therapeutic process and relies on the capacity of the therapist for acknowledging the countertransference, even if this involves disclosing unhealthy aspects of the therapist's personality. Therapists are encouraged to be aware of the ways in which they are likely to manifest their own pathological tendencies in the treatment relationship—and to do so without shame or self-deprecation.

CHAPTER 5

Countertransference Techniques: Constructing the Interpersonal Analysis

There are three basic reasons for revealing the countertransference. The first is that the patient is aware of his therapist's feelings and he suffers from the distortions and confusion that arise when his therapist denies or circumvents his reactions to the patient. The second reason is that the patient's opportunities for delineating, understanding, and taking responsibility for his own motivations and behavior are limited by the therapist's refusal to do the same. And third, to the extent that the countertransference is not resolved within the treatment relationship it can lead to an outcome characterized by *countertransference dominance*, in which the past of the therapist is repeated and determines the course of treatment.

I believe that incorporating revelation and analysis of the countertransference into analytic technique increases the opportunity for dynamic conflict and its resolution within the therapeutic relationship. Bird (1972) has suggested that many analytic practitioners, ignoring the goal of facilitating a transference neurosis because it is too personally demanding, contentedly settle for long and unresolvable positive transferences. While it *is* far more challenging and stressful to have patients who are regularly in conflict with us, an ongoing dynamic conflict is the essence of the analytic process and, therefore, I see countertransference techniques as offering the potential for greatly enhancing the analytic process.

Incorporating revelation of the countertransference into psychoanalytic technique enhances the here-and-now relationship and reduces the protective distance and personal anonymity to which many analytic practitioners are accustomed. Coming out from behind our shield of neutrality which protects us from our patients' inquiries, their needs for an emotional response, and their sometimes virulent attacks, may be seen as undesirable by some therapists. (This is particularly true of those who embrace the analytic position not only for the ideological fit, but also for the personal distance it requires.) And, as Little (1951) said, using the countertransference in treatment has probably been neglected precisely because of the interpersonal demands that it places upon us.

In spite of these demands, I advocate expression of the counter-transference because, while it forces the therapist to deal actively with his own feelings, thoughts and even unconscious desires, it also offers a unique opportunity for significantly facilitating the analytic endeavor. Disclosing the countertransference can lead to earlier surfacing of conflicts, subsequent opportunities for deeper emotional experience and resolution, and fewer stalemates and empathic breaks in the therapeutic relationship.

If what happens in the analytic relationship is the result of the dynamics between patient and therapist, including libidinal urges that fuel and perpetuate any relationship, then the potential usefulness of expressing and analyzing the countertransference is evident. As Little (1951) says:

> What is the driving force in any analysis? What is it that urges the patient on to get well? The answer surely is that it is the combined id urges of both patient and analyst, urges which in the case of the analyst have been modified and integrated as a result of his own analysis so that they have become more directed and effective. Successful combination of these urges seems to me to depend on a special kind of identification of the analyst with the patient. (p. 34)

This chapter is about how the therapist can modify and integrate his internal experiences and ultimately master expression of the countertransference. But I would first like to define a few terms and delineate the general course of treatment before I discuss specific techniques.

Disclosure of the countertransference, analysis of the transference-countertransference and, less often, analysis of the countertransference alone comprise the technical use of the countertransference. Using the countertransference begins with thoughtful and timely disclosures, which should precede any attempt with a patient to analyze transference-countertransference psychodynamics or to analyze the countertransference alone.

In early stages of treatment, patient requests will be almost exclusively concerned with disclosure of the countertransference. It is a rare patient who is ready in the early phase of treatment to accept analysis of either the transference–countertransference interplay or of the counter-transference on its own. Most patient requests or provocations will be in the direction of stimulating countertransference affect and seeking the therapist's expression of that affect. But as analysis of the transference moves into full swing, many patients will seek a greater understanding of the psychodynamics at play in the interpersonal realm. They will want to know more about why the therapist feels and behaves the way he does, and what role the patient's behavior and history have in determining what surfaces in the relationship.

With psychologically sophisticated patients, the desire to have the interpersonal psychodynamics revealed will increase as the treatment relationship matures. Eventually this will lead to questions pertaining to the countertransference, with less emphasis on the transference. Attempts at understanding and analyzing the countertransference occur primarily during the termination phase (see Chapter 6) and occur *not* as a result of the patient wanting to defend by "analyzing the analyst" but as a result of the patient's increasing maturity and capacity for recognizing and understanding the therapist as a separate person.

Disclosure of the countertransference, analysis of the transference–countertransference, and analysis of the countertransference alone can thus be seen as a developmental continuum in the therapeutic relationship. The patient moves from one level to the next as he becomes capable of handling greater degrees of insight and intense feelings, and as he achieves a greater capacity for object relations. Since some patients will never reach higher levels of functioning, or will have some areas where lower levels of functioning are sustained, all patients will not go through all of the above three stages of countertransference work. Admittedly, others will not fit this pattern at all, seeking revelation and understanding of the countertransference as each new issue arises, or in response to stalemates within the relationship, regardless of when they occur.

But how do we know when a patient is ready for analysis of the transference–countertransference or countertransference alone? The patient will tell you. He will dig further, asking and needing to know more. If he does not, then he is probably not ready and you should not volunteer it out of your desire to have the patient know and understand you. When the patient needs this knowledge, he will seek it.

Before addressing specific aspects of technique, I would like to provide the framework for effective use of the countertransference. First of all, the techniques outlined in this chapter have been developed in long-term psychoanalytic treatments, with patients coming at least twice a week and no more than five times per week. Countertransference techniques are predicated on the existence of a stable, ongoing relationship between therapist and patient that is analytic in nature, be it psychoanalytic psychotherapy or psychoanalysis.

I am aware that many analytic practitioners do not have the luxury of seeing patients for years and must address transference and counter-transference issues in time-limited treatments. I feel sure that this can be done effectively, particularly in light of Schlessinger and Robbins' (1983) findings that it was possible for comprehensive mini-transferences to surface and be worked through in a matter of days. It seems likely that the patient will present the transference as best he can in whatever time he is allowed to do so. Considering this reality, I encourage therapists doing short-term or time-limited psychodynamic therapy to use the general guidelines provided here to address the countertransference. Since I do very little short-term treatment myself, I will leave the development of appropriate technical considerations in this setting to those who do. However, it seems evident that any therapist working against the clock is forced to take more risks. I encourage therapists using the counter-transference techniques in short-term treatment to be more aggressive not necessarily in initially revealing the countertransference but in confronting the patient to see if this is what he is truly looking for and needs. A therapist in this situation cannot afford to be in doubt and needs all the more to educate the patient about his role as an active and responsible partner in the therapeutic endeavor. It is also assumed that any therapist intending to implement countertransference techniques will have completed a personal analysis or psychoanalytic psychotherapy before attempting to do so.

The focus in this chapter is specifically on *expressive* uses of the countertransference. The interested reader should refer to Tansey and Burke (1989) for an excellent step-by-step guide to receiving communications from the patient and processing them internally, as well as integrating the transference and countertransference in a manner that promotes understanding of the dynamic interplay between the two. They discuss important issues pertaining to the therapist's initial receptivity to a patient's messages, processing what is received from the patient (including how this resonates with the therapist's feelings or personality), and responding to the patient's communication, both verbally and non-verbally. But Tansey and Burke do *not* advocate systematic disclosure of the countertransference; I am essentially augmenting their system to include it.

Ideally, the therapist's understanding of the patient and the subsequent self-reflection that Tansey and Burke advocate should precede any decision to disclose the countertransference. Also, the patient should be directly asking for or attempting to provoke a countertransference disclosure. The therapist's disclosures should be responsive to and focused on the patient's experience, with the therapist weeding out unnecessary personal information and gaining reasonable control of intense affects prior to disclosure.

Even among those who advocate disclosure of the countertransference, the issue of technique is thorny. Searles (1979) begged off the issue completely, calling it "too complex," while Wachtel (1986) expressed a wish for clear (but clearly non-existent) rules pertaining to when disclosure would be helpful. Pierloot (1987) says, ''If psychoanalysis is an art, the structuring of the countertransference without any doubt constitutes an important part of it'' (p. 226). Gitelson (1952) posed some good questions pertinent to technique, but answered them only in the most general way:

> What and how does the patient need to know in order to correct an illusion or to validate a real insight? How much will be useful to the patient and how much will be the burden imposed on him? One does not ask the patient to share one's own problems. But one does make use of what has palpably intruded into the analytic situation without begging the issue. (p. 8)

It seems to me that the difficulty in knowing when and how to express the countertransference has historically led to avoiding the subject altogether. Since everyone seems to agree that the potential dangers are great, and because no-one, including myself, is anxious to suggest any techniques that might be misinterpreted and misapplied, there simply are no guidelines for expressing the countertransference. The feeling has been that countertransference technique is just too intricate and complex to teach, and should be left to the discretion of experienced analytic therapists who have managed to find their own way through the maze and who know what they are doing. Better this than to unleash an army of semi-trained therapists, particularly neophytes who do not possess the necessary confidence vital to doing good therapy, on an unsuspecting public. Visions of out-of-control beginners ''spilling their guts'' to their patients certainly makes everyone's blood run cold.

But writing off disclosure of the countertransference as too risky is equally unacceptable. For those who accept the basic premises outlined in this book, the countertransference cannot be adequately addressed without timely disclosure. Even therapists who are uncomfortable with disclosure remain faced with the challenge of how to respond to patients who raise the issue of the therapist's countertransference and seek to have their perceptions validated. Many of them regularly demand that the countertransference be acknowledged and will accept nothing less. And many of us know in our hearts that patients have left us, often in depression or rage, because we could not or would not give them what they were asking for in terms of access to us. We sometimes comfort ourselves by saying that they were hopeless (''untreatable''), but we know that such a damning proclamation is not always called for. Sometimes there is the feeling, if not the knowledge, that a particular patient *was* reachable—we just did not know how to do it. Granted, disclosing the countertransference will not put an end to all treatment failures, but it is a valuable and unique tool for improving the quality of treatment, particularly when working with patients who have a stated need to know their therapist's thoughts and feelings.

When to Disclose the Countertransference

Let us start by reviewing the underlying principle of *when* to disclose and analyze the countertransference. The general rule of thumb could not be easier to remember: in the vast majority of cases, *the patient will simply tell you*. Usually, he will not seek intense encounters with his therapist nor will he ask much of anything in the first year or so. He may well test the water for future requests, however, by inquiring as to whether his therapist is married, has children, believes in God, or by asking about some other aspect of his therapist's life that seems innocuous to him. He will take a cue from his analyst's responses to these seemingly harmless questions and record any discomfort that is revealed. The traditional analytic approach calls for a refusal to answer such questions; but, instead, the therapist should focus on their meaning and inquire as to why the patient is asking them at the present time. In theory, answering such questions will result in the patient inhibiting his fantasies and reasons for asking. However, my experience with patients has not confirmed this. In my early years of practice I followed the traditional approach and found that many patients refused to answer my questions at all if I did not answer theirs. Worse still, some were quite hurt and humiliated at asking for and being refused an answer—an outcome that always seemed to me to be quite *untherapeutic*. (I recall how naively surprised I was as a young therapist when patients responded with shame when I did the "right thing" by refusing to answer their questions.) So I began to talk to my patients about making an agreement that I would answer if they would. And I have never been disappointed with the results. I find that patients are much *more* willing to reveal their fantasies and motivations if I treat them respectfully and answer their questions. And this is true even if their fantasies are the complete opposite of the answer I give them. (Originally the agreement I had with my patients was that they had to answer my question first. But while some patients are more responsive if *they* answer first, others are more responsive if *I* answer first. So I work this out on an individual basis, talking it out with the patient. I let them tell me what the optimal conditions are for them.) Discussing with the patient why it is important for him to respond as fully as possible concerning his fantasies is an important aspect of a non-authoritarian treatment and the earlier in the relationship that this disclosure occurs, the better. It sets the tone for a therapeutic partnership that can continue to develop throughout the treatment.

As the treatment progresses, particularly once a dynamic conflict has begun between patient and therapist, the patient will make more requests, either directly or indirectly. The patient's need to know the extent and nature of his emotional impact on his therapist grows as the dynamic re-enactment progresses, and it will culminate and may even become dominant during the termination phase. Because of the heavy demands that patients can make on their therapists during this phase, and because of the complex psychodynamics that can affect the relationship at this time, Chapter 6 is devoted to this topic.

As stated previously, there are two main ways in which the patient makes his requests for disclosure of the countertransference. One is direct, the other is indirect:

1. *Directly.* The patient tells his therapist directly or asks for what he wants or needs. This most often takes the form of a question. For example, he might ask, "Are you angry with me?" or "What you said hurt my feelings. Were you trying to hurt me?" Or the patient may emotionally confront his therapist in a manner that demands a response. For example, he may, through constant verbal abuse, demand a limit-setting response by saying repeatedly, "Boy are you stupid. How am I supposed to get any better when I have such an idiot for a therapist?" (The implied countertransference disclosure would address the therapist's feelings and personal limits regarding continual verbal abuse.)

When the patient asks his therapist directly to make a personal statement regarding personal reactions to him, it is probably right to answer. If for any reason the therapist is not sure that the patient actually wants an answer to a question, or if an answer may be difficult for the patient to tolerate, the therapist should simply ask him if he is sure that he wants an answer. If he says "Yes" then he should be told. If he says anything other than "Yes"—which includes not only "No" but also "Maybe," "I'm not sure," "I guess so," or anything else that smacks of being tentative—then his question should not be answered. Further exploration of the issue is in order.

2. *Indirectly.* Alternatively, the patient will use projective identification, which is the likely option for the patient trying to communicate disavowed affect. Projective identification can be thought of as the unconscious mind of the patient attempting to communicate to the therapist that which is unavailable consciously. For example, the patient whines and criticizes his therapist endlessly for not being "loving" enough. The disavowed affect is hate, which is stimulated in the therapist. (This discussion of indirect provocation of affect in the therapist includes non-verbal methods, such as socially inappropriate seductive poses, and silence, noted by Arlow (1985) as a most potent countertransference stimulus.)

There is more room to make an error in deciding whether to disclose when the patient communicates indirectly through projective identification than when he does so directly. This is especially true when the emotion that the patient stimulates in his therapist coincides with what he was already feeling immediately before he saw the patient. For example, if the therapist is feeling sad because of something going on in his own life, and he finds himself becoming sadder yet in response to his patient, there is some question as to whether his sadness is a response to his patient or is primarily an internal event.

When a therapist's pre-existing affective state seems to overlap with his patient's affect or supersedes it, it is wise to consider the situation carefully before disclosing. A prudent course is to process the patient's provocation without disclosure and wait for another day. If the patient needed his therapist to feel sad for him and for his therapist to express this feeling for him, the patient will replay the scene again. Anyone who has treated a patient who needs an affective response will recognize the persistent pattern of provocation that usually establishes itself. As with almost everything the patient needs to have addressed, there will always be another opportunity. Anything that is truly important will keep resurfacing, affording another chance to respond in an optimally therapeutic fashion.

Once the essence of the patient's "request" is determined, there are still several issues to consider before deciding whether to disclose the counter-transference. First, has the patient's question or provocation been analyzed? That is, is the patient's question or provocation rhetorical in nature: is it intended to bring some underlying issue to the table, rather than a demand for a personal response? We certainly should not immediately respond to any question that the patient asks by simply answering it. This is naive, simplistic, and interferes with the analytic process. Many times patients ask questions as a way of initiating a topic, of deferring to the therapist, of changing the subject to avoid something threatening, or of testing the limits of the therapist or the relationship. I want to make it clear here that I am *not* advocating taking patient inquiries at face value and simply answering them as a matter of course. And any therapist who does so will quickly face a justifiably confused and discontented patient.

For example, I treated a man of my age with borderline personality disorder who coped with his fears of abandonment and of women by being unrelentingly seductive. When he started treatment he was hypersexual, having sex with as many as three different women in one day. Not surprisingly, when he was threatened in the treatment situation by some unwanted feeling, he would often change the subject to sex. At these times, he would turn to me and say, "So are you good in bed?"

or "So do *you* want to sleep with me?" He would then grin with a mixture of embarrassment and impishness, waiting to see if he had managed to distract or stimulate me, yet also fearing that I would punish him for his "naughty" behavior. It is quite obvious from this example that for me to answer these questions, no matter how often they were asked, would have been to miss the point entirely.

If the patient's persistence is a necessary yet not sufficient criterion for whether to answer, what else is essential to making a decision? The request from the patient should be one that is not deterred by exploration of the issue or interpretation. That is, if the patient is not truly seeking an answer to his question, he will usually move on to a discussion of the point at hand and will not persist in asking the therapist for a direct answer. If a direct answer is what the patient really needs he will not only tell his therapist that he wants an answer, but he will keep returning to the question. (The above patient would always quickly acknowledge that he was trying to change the subject and would express relief or even pleasure at my refusal to answer his questions.) And, though requiring a subjective judgment on the therapist's part, the patient's request should be not only repetitive, but serious and heartfelt. Granted, this is a hard call to make and one that is highly dependent on the therapist's capacity for empathy and on good intuition. One of the ways to judge this is whether the therapist feels compelled to answer out of respect for the patient and his feelings, and not simply because it might be relieving for him to do so. If a therapist feels himself cringing inside with embarrassment or shame for not answering, then he probably should. (This should not be confused with feeling intimidated by the patient's anger or disapproval, and feeling the desire to pacify him, which is quite different.)

But at other times, while it may be *right* to answer, in that it is the most therapeutic move and is in the patient's best interest, a therapist might not feel comfortable making the disclosure. In this case, the discomfort is probably related to fears regarding intimacy or to some other discomfort related to what may have to be revealed to the patient. Another possibility is that the therapist may feel that the topic at hand is a very sensitive one for the patient and he may fear that he is not confident enough to handle the situation well. If he is feeling any significant discomfort regarding disclosure of the countertransference, then he should generally not do it. As stated in previous chapters, any type of intervention is potentially harmful as well as useful. And ambivalence or insecurity do not bode well for a successful intervention.

However, a therapist might be in the midst of an "emergency" situation; for example, he feels sure that his patient is on the verge of leaving treatment and will do so if his therapist fails to rise to the occasion. In this situation, where there may be little left to lose, I would go ahead and make the disclosure. Otherwise, it is best to wait until the therapist can do whatever is necessary to make himself comfortable in dealing with the countertransference directly. (As an aside, I *do* believe that consultation, self-analysis, and returning to treatment can help facilitate this process of preparing to confront the countertransference with patients. What I do *not* believe is that they can act as a substitute for it.)

Other Signs that a Countertransference Intervention Is Needed

Ideally, once a therapist is committed to the notion of expression and analysis of the countertransference, he will do it in such a way that minimizes stalemates or other difficulties that might arise as a result of failing to use it. However, the ideal should not be confused with reality. In this vein, I would like to discuss some indications that a counter-transference disclosure may be past due.

Therapeutic stalemates represent some breakdown in the treatment relationship rather than arbitrary resistances on the part of the patient. When patients find a particular subject too difficult to confront they will usually quickly move to another that is more manageable so that the process is not halted. A stalemate is therefore indicative of something awry in the relationship. Stalemates include unproductive and prolonged affective states that are not responsive to standard interventions. For example, the patient is intractably anxious, depressed, compulsively stuck on one subject, silent, angry, or misses sessions. The therapist often begins to feel thwarted, frustrated, confused and inadequate as all interpretations and other interventions seem to fall on deaf ears. Stalemates may result from a power struggle between therapist and patient, which often leads the therapist to believe that the patient is merely being negative or resistant. My own clinical experience tells me that this is rarely, if ever, the case.

It can be too easy to focus on a patient's prolonged protest in the treatment situation and miss the real issue creating the stalemate. An example of this is the case of Kate, a 30-year-old professional with a diagnosis of depressive neurosis with significant narcissistic features. She had been in analysis with Dr W for about three years and had become intensely attached to her. Though prone to narcissistic injury and fears of abandonment, Kate did not fit the diagnosis of narcissistic personality disorder because she was very sensitive and responsive to others and was capable of great empathy. She naturally extended this warm regard to her analyst, noticing small changes in her mood and expressing concern if she seemed at all ill or depressed. Dr W, whose own mother had been quite cold to her, began to attach quite strongly to Kate, feeling deeply moved by Kate's uncanny ability to sense her mood and to respond to her so warmly. Kate saw Dr W five times a week and repeatedly told Dr W how much it meant to her to have so much time with her and how painful it had been for her to never have enough time with her own mother, who though very attached to Kate, was usually too busy to give her what she needed.

In the third year of treatment, Dr W began a session by informing Kate that she was altering her schedule to do some research and would have to cut one of Kate's sessions starting the following month. Kate responded to this news with disbelief, hurt and despair. It was clearly a narcissistic injury for her and she also felt betrayed by Dr W.

Dr W, on the other hand, felt that it was her prerogative to make such changes based on her own needs, and she simply could not allow Kate or any other patient to tell her whether she could do her research. Dr W was empathic to Kate and interpreted that Kate was feeling abandoned, just as she had been by her mother, who would sometimes threaten to pack her bags and leave when Kate misbehaved. Dr W also said she was sorry and that she had not meant to hurt her. These, and all other interventions by Dr W, accomplished nothing. Kate came to all of her sessions, but was remote and lifeless. She either said nothing or cried. And when Dr W tried to get her to talk she would only criticize Dr W for being so insensitive to her.

Dr W, believing that she was doing the right thing, sat patiently with Kate, trying to understand why she remained in such despair. Weeks passed and Kate showed little improvement. As before, when she did speak, Kate accused Dr W of wanting to leave her and of not being able to bear the intensity of her feeling for her. She refused to accept that Dr W's research interests were the real reason for the reduction in session time. Finally Dr W asked Kate what she needed to recover. Kate told her to reinstate her session—nothing else would do. Not surprisingly, Dr W refused. She believed that it was incumbent upon her to hold the line and not indulge any fantasies that Kate might have had about being important to her. She was kind but firm when she communicated this to Kate.

Still, Kate did not recover. Weeks passed and essentially nothing happened in the treatment. One day Kate informed Dr W that she wanted to seek a consultation with another analyst. Dr W reluctantly agreed, feeling defeated in her struggle with Kate. Each of them met with the other analyst separately, hoping to find the key to restoring the relationship and moving on with what had been an otherwise successful treatment. The consulting analyst agreed with Dr W that she, under no circumstances, should give in to Kate's demand to have her session reinstated. She felt that it was unfortunate that this alteration in Kate's treatment situation proved to be so painful to her, but that the only way to resolve the situation was to work harder at understanding the full meaning of the event. The consultant felt that Kate's belief that Dr W was fleeing her and rejecting closeness with her was somewhat grandiose and irrational, reflecting her narcissistic pathology.

Kate opted to continue with Dr W in spite of her dispirited attitude toward her treatment, believing that the problem was hers alone and wanting somehow to overcome it. Dr W, on the other hand, consulted with colleagues, her own analyst, and searched her own experience in an attempt to understand what was going on. She had a very strong attachment to Kate and feared that she would leave if this seemingly traumatic incident were not resolved. Everyone assured her that the consulting analyst was correct and that Dr W had done the right thing. She was advised to help Kate deal with her grandiosity. After about a year Kate terminated her treatment, with both her and Dr W feeling hurt, abandoned and defeated.

Some time later Dr W returned to analysis and, with the safety of considerable distance from her relationship with Kate, she realized that she *had* fled Kate. During this treatment, she remembered how wonderful she had felt when Kate had been so nurturing toward her and recalled wanting Kate to take care of *her*, the way her own mother never had. She had repressed these feelings during the incident with Kate, as well as her feelings of guilt and shame over wanting a patient to transform and heal her. She also recalled that shortly after having had these thoughts, she had been offered and had accepted the research assignment. Now she had new feelings of guilt to confront as she realized that Kate had been right, and that Kate had not been able to recover from what had happened between them because Dr W had not been able to admit the truth. Yet no-one had known Dr W's true feelings at the time of the incident. Not Dr W. Not the consulting analyst, who had spoken with both of them. Not colleagues. Not Dr W's former analyst. Because all of them had taken the situation at face value. Certainly, they could not have been aware of what Dr W had repressed. And they were no doubt distracted by the surface issue of a power struggle between therapist and patient. Even Kate gave up trying to get Dr W to admit to her true feelings and simply insisted that the status quo be restored. With everyone focused on the overt power struggle, the covert but real issue was buried, which proved to be fatal to an otherwise promising treatment.

The reader may say that these things happen. After all, Dr W did everything humanly possible. There was nothing more that could have been done. But this is where disclosure and analysis of the counter-transference could have been of genuine use. Dr W was aware of feeling defensive and guilty during the episode with Kate. However, she wrote this off as excessive guilt in response to Kate's distress, something Dr W knew was characteristic of her as an analyst and something she struggled with frequently. She was also *very* aware of being engaged in an intense power struggle with Kate that was not settled by a firm but compassionate reiteration of her limits. Had Dr W known that a defensive posture of this sort is *always* indicative of a countertransference problem (no matter what other problems the patient may be expressing), she could have tried something else. And that "something else" was disclosing her own emotional reactions to Kate. In this instance I believe that if a dialog had occurred between them, Dr W would have become aware of her disavowed fear of becoming dependent on Kate and would have known what was really happening. Even if she had not succeeded in mining this repressed material, her expression of her conscious feelings toward Kate would have helped the situation greatly. Just being willing to *consider* that Kate might be right, rather than arbitrarily deciding what the issue was and what needed to be done, would have had a positive impact. Had Dr W and Kate really worked together as partners to end the stalemate things could have been different. Dr W's rigid belief that she should hold her ground no matter what only encouraged Kate's attitude of helplessness and powerlessness in the treatment relationship and contributed to its premature demise.

I realize that if Dr W had admitted to Kate that she had tried to dilute their relationship because she was feeling overwhelmed, it would have presented a significant problem for them to address in the treatment. Such a declaration by a therapist would stimulate fear in a patient and could feed any grandiosity in a patient with narcissistic issues. But the problem *was* there and, like all interpersonal issues, it was going to find a way to surface in the relationship. It did not go away because Dr W denied it. It only went underground and sabotaged the treatment. (Initially, the problem may have been resolved simply by Dr W apologizing and restoring the session. But after a prolonged and painful struggle, I doubt that this would have been enough.)

Not everything can be worked out by disclosing the counter-transference, of course, but at least the opportunity is there if the problem can be identified and discussed. This gives both therapist and patient the chance to know and accept reality, no matter what it is, and to have some power over what happens. And even if the relationship has to end, it will end on a sad but certainly more sane and respectful note—leaving both parties with less guilt and remorse over the ending of the treatment.

In this example there was a therapeutic stalemate and power struggle— sure signs that the countertransference is significant if not dominant—

which I believe required disclosure to remediate the situation. The development of a therapeutic stalemate often follows a predictable pattern: first, the patient is frustrated and unhappy with the therapist. The patient continues to complain and asks or demands that the therapist respond differently. (The patient may or may not know what he wants.) By this time, the therapist is confused, possibly anxious, and either becomes critical of the patient or withdraws into intellectualization, continuing to offer interpretations that the patient rejects. The patient continues to be angry, and may become enraged. Some patients may threaten suicide or some other destructive act. Others may fall into depression. Ultimately, the therapist feels frustrated, thwarted and helpless to find a solution to the problem. The situation will not improve substantially until some transference–countertransference peace is made.

Signs of Therapist Defensiveness

Any defensive behavior on the therapist's part indicates a counter-transference problem, no matter how small or transient. Whenever the therapist removes himself from the patient *for any reason* the countertransference is dominating and obstructing the treatment. If this cannot quickly be resolved through self-analysis and analysis of the situation at hand, then the therapist should move as quickly as possible to disclose the countertransference. Examples of defensive postures on the part of the therapist include arguing with the patient, withdrawing from the patient and being overly intellectual or silent, becoming overtly or covertly judgmental or critical, aggressing against the patient passively by repeating interpretations that have already been rejected, responding intellectually—often through the use of genetic material—to the patient's intense affective expressions, consistently being late for sessions, "forgetting" a patient or double-scheduling patients, canceling or rescheduling of sessions at the last minute, failing to confront a patient regarding payment of fees, and refusing to answer reasonable questions posed by a patient. Obvious persistent anger or idealization regarding a patient reveals a countertransference problem, as do feelings of fear or uneasiness.

Countertransference dominance is also likely when a patient is continually seen as controlling or attempting to control the therapist in a way that personally upsets the therapist—creating the aforementioned state of "microparanoia" (Kernberg, 1965). Strong reactions or defensive language, such as feeling "hooked" or "sucked in" by a patient, indicate the presence of unresolved countertransference. Therapists who repeatedly refer to patients in this way, or who use other types of pejorative language, are afraid of being controlled in some way by their patients.

When fears of being out of control with a patient persist, the therapist may have nightmares about him and may dread seeing him or be atypically nervous prior to his sessions. Likewise, persistent feelings of being in love with a patient, accompanied by obsessive thoughts or erotic dreams, will usually result in some countertransference-based behavior of over-indulging the patient or defending against these emotions by distancing from him.

Like Kernberg (1987), I do not believe that merely having a patient on your mind outside of the hour, or even having him in your dreams, is necessarily a sign of a countertransference problem. Intense feelings, in and of themselves, toward a patient are not necessarily problematic. Particularly during the period of mutual regression (the symbiotic phase), these kinds of reactions should not be cause for concern, especially with severely regressed patients. Kernberg says:

> For the analyst to be excessively preoccupied with severely regressed patients outside the treatment hours may be healthy, not necessarily neurotic. In fact . . . a significant part of the analyst's working through of his countertransference reactions may have to occur in work outside the hours. (p. 815)

If a particular attitude toward a patient is extreme *and* consistent it may well result in countertransference dominance (the treatment course being determined primarily by a replay of the therapist's past rather than the patient's). As long as the therapist can experience his feelings while putting them into perspective and without feeling threatened or overstimulated by them, they need not be a problem. But often this is easier said than done. And the sooner the therapist recognizes when his attempts at managing the countertransference are failing and require an interaction with the patient, the sooner he will get the treatment back on track. This is why I stress that the therapist must be aware of his own weaknesses, infantile longings and dependency. This awareness paves the way for management of the countertransference or, when a problem arises, enables the therapist to move quickly to remedy the situation. Regarding dependency feelings, Hirsch (1980–81) says:

> I do not believe even the most extreme feelings of dependence toward a patient need be a problem. The effort to deny such feelings by assuming a position of apparent strength will most likely cause difficulties. (p. 126)

A therapist who believes that he should always be on top of things and in a superior, controlling position will deny any longings he experiences in response to his "sick" patients, and will define dependency feelings toward patients as unacceptable. If the therapist *does* find himself experiencing strong feelings toward a patient and is having difficulty managing those feelings, should he disclose them to the patient, even in the absence of an identifiable direct or indirect request from the patient? Generally, no. This is a concern of many people regarding disclosure of the countertransference: therapists will relieve themselves of their strong reactions to their patients at the patient's expense. Bollas (1987) warns therapists that:

> . . . however much it might relieve the analyst to describe his state of mind to a patient, such an action should never be undertaken solely for the purpose of the analyst's self cure. (p. 211)

Along the same lines, Gitelson (1952) says:

> Whenever the analyst feels impelled to do something "active," it would seem advisable for him to ask himself where he himself stands in the situation. (p. 10)

Disclosure of strong feelings toward a patient may indeed be relieving for the therapist in the very short term, but if such a disclosure does not occur in response to the patient's request it will only threaten and disturb the relationship. In accordance with my theory of mutuality presented earlier in this book, an uninvited disclosure by the therapist will ultimately not be in either parties' best interest since it will undermine the therapeutic relationship. Mutuality also dictates that it will not be long before the therapist's discomfort is evidenced in the treatment, at which time the patient will respond to it. The therapist should wait until this happens, even if it takes some time for the patient both to become aware of and prepare himself to address his therapist's problem.

Are there any times when a therapist should self-disclose in the absence of a request by the patient? Yes. But these are the exception. Sometimes, when a therapist is in distress, the patient will be adversely affected and may even become highly symptomatic. If he does not consciously know that his therapist is in distress, he may simply deteriorate and not know why. He might never say more than that he just does not understand why he is so upset. Under these circumstances the therapist might consider relieving the patient by telling him that he is responding to the former's distress. No elaboration on the form or content of the therapist's distress should be given unless specifically sought by the patient. I would also like to reiterate that the therapist should be comfortable with anything of a personal nature that he discloses and he should refuse to disclose anything that he does not want the patient to know.

Remember that the essential aspect of disclosing the countertransference is the nature of the *affective response* to the patient, *not the revelation of personal information*. Whenever a therapist considers disclosing information such as a death in the family, marital problems, an impending divorce, or illness, for example, he should remind himself that this is his personal business and that the patient does not necessarily have the right to know these things, *even if it would make him better*. Patients do have the right to know things that will surely have a direct impact on them at some point, such as a terminal illness of the therapist, a move to another city, or anything that significantly impedes the treatment. But other information regarding the therapist's personal life is usually not needed by the patient, and I think it is important to balance out the patient's need to know with the therapist's right to privacy. (If the patient's need to know frequently conflicts with the therapist's willingness to disclose, the issue of a "good enough" therapeutic match needs to be addressed by the two of them.) Each therapist has to assess the situation with a particular patient and make the best decision he can.

Before deciding to make a disclosure of information of a personal nature to a patient, the therapist might also seriously consider that confidentiality is a one-way street. The therapist has to weigh the probability of the patient repeating the information and consider how he would feel if this were to occur. Therapists who disclose highly personal information run the risk of inviting their patients to betray them.

The conventional belief that personal information burdens the patient unnecessarily is also pertinent here. Detailed information is not normally required to validate a patient's perceptions, and it has high potential for muddying the waters and inappropriately placing the emphasis on the therapist. Focusing on affect should be the therapist's main concern, not only for the patient's sake, but also for the therapist's. The main therapeutic benefit comes from the affective disclosure and this can often be accomplished without the therapist's disclosure of extensive personal information.

A final note on the issue of when to disclose pertains to the patient's need for power in the relationship. There is no doubt that therapist self-disclosure, particularly in response to a direct request from the patient, increases the patients's feelings of power and self-efficacy. For the most part this represents a therapeutic effect. However, if the therapist at any time feels that the patient is asking him to disclose for the purpose of gaining the upper hand, the therapist should by all means refuse the disclosure and deal with the power issue. I consider such a power move by the patient to be the exception rather than the rule, but it does happen.

It represents a test of the therapist's ability to maintain his legitimate power and control. Failure on the part of the therapist to pass this test results in the patient's perception of the therapist as weak and easily manipulated.

The only guideline I can provide for determining whether a patient has such motivations when making a direct request is the therapist's intuitive response. If he feels that his patient is attempting to control him and perceives this without feeling defensive or threatened, then his perceptions are probably accurate and he should behave accordingly. Another way to tell if the patient is sincere is by waiting to see if he brings it up again. Specific power moves are usually short-lived. If the patient persists in wanting to gain power over his therapist, he will typically try different tactics and will not become symptomatic if he fails. This is in contrast to the patient's genuine request for disclosure that will most often be repeated in the same form and will result in a symptomatic response pattern if denied.

How to Disclose the Countertransference

Ideally, disclosure of the countertransference will be as natural and comfortable for the clinician as any other therapeutic technique. However, mastery of this technique presents a formidable challenge in that it requires a redefinition of the analytic process. In supervising and consulting with other therapists, I have discovered that they sometimes feel guilty when first using the countertransference, primarily because of the relief that it affords them. Somehow they maintain the notion that anything that is really good for the patient must be painful or difficult for them. Sometimes this is true, of course. But it certainly is possible for both therapist and patient to simultaneously experience relief in the treatment. And as therapists see that their relief does not have to be at the patient's expense, the feeling of guilt falls away.

If a therapist has never disclosed the countertransference before, he should start in a small way. He needs to get a feel for how much each individual patient can tolerate, because tolerance for disclosure varies tremendously. He will also need to get a feel for how much he can tolerate. As mentioned previously, most patients start small ("Are you tired today?"), gradually move into riskier questions ("Do you think what I did was wrong?" or "Do you care about me?"), and ultimately move into the larger risks during the termination phase ("Are you happy with your own life?" or "How can you really care about me and still let me go?").

Disclosures of the countertransference should occur gradually, with each party getting a feel for what is comfortable. If a therapist suddenly decides to use a countertransference disclosure with a patient he has been treating for some time, it is important for him to start in a small way because his patient will not understand this change and he might become highly anxious. The change could easily make him fear that his therapist had suddenly lost control, rather than that he had made a conscious choice to change his technique. If a therapist, who has not previously done so, decides to disclose the countertransference because he is involved in a stalemate or some other crisis with his patient, he should prepare his patient for what he is about to do. He can simply inform him that he has been troubled by a problem that exists between them and that he has given it a great deal of thought. As a result, he has decided to respond to what his patient seems to be asking. Then, the therapist should ask his patient how he feels about that prospect. The patient may respond with fear, which should be discussed and analyzed prior to making a decision regarding disclosure. Or the patient may simply say, "It's about time, I've been trying to get you to do this for the past six months!" Discussing the countertransference disclosure in this manner lets the patient see that his therapist is not out of control and that he will only disclose it if it is mutually acceptable.

The therapist and his patients will educate each other about what language is acceptable, how much feeling is appropriate or tolerable, and how much information is useful. As with all types of interventions, the simpler and briefer it is, the more likely the patient will be to make good use of it. Also, it should be remembered that it can be easy to make the mistake of believing that what works well with one patient will work well with everyone. I have found that even when two patients ask the same question at about the same point in their treatments, there can be vast differences in what kind of answers they need and will benefit from. Very intense, emotional patients tend to need more affect from the therapist, for example, while more contained, easily overwhelmed patients require very little. Some patients continue to ask questions until they feel they understand the "big picture," while other patients will be satisfied with a simple "yes" or "no" to one question and will proceed to something else. This is why the cardinal rule of disclosure is: "Never tell the patient more than he wants to hear." And never assume that you know what that is. Always let him tell you.

Dealing with Specific Countertransference Reactions

Different patients will stimulate different reactions in their therapists. As the treatment progresses and the drama unfolds the patient will attempt to stimulate feelings in his therapist that correspond with the feelings that he believes he stimulated in his early relationships. The more that his therapist emotionally resembles the patient's family members, the more likely and easily the patient will succeed in stimulating his therapist in the desired fashion. However, even if the therapist is quite dissimilar to early figures in the patient's life, the patient will still need to stimulate the therapist in ways that enable him to re-enact the past. (Sometimes patients must leave a certain therapist because they instinctively know that they will never succeed in stimulating that therapist in the way they need to, which is a vital aspect of the "match" between therapist and patient.) I have learned that my role is *not* to refuse to be stimulated in this way. My role is to help the patient understand what he is doing and, toward this end, allow myself to be incorporated into his historical play by being responsive. The therapeutic objective is *not* necessarily for the therapist to feel differently from the others; it is for the therapist to handle his feelings more constructively than did the patient's significant others. Ultimately this enables the patient to be aware of his own feelings and behavior and to take responsibility for both.

We know that our emotional reactions to our patients are potentially destructive and potentially therapeutic. Just as we attempt to educate our patients that there are no "bad" feelings, only destructive behavior, we must remember that this dictum applies equally to us. A therapist who hates his patient is not inherently a bad person or a bad therapist. A bad therapist is a person who cannot tolerate his own ambivalence or his patient's. In this spirit I encourage therapists to weigh all emotions equally and to consider them pertinent to the situation at hand in terms of understanding the truth, rather than wasting time with guilt over sexual or aggressive feelings toward patients. Along the same lines I urge therapists not to become complacent with a patient they like or enjoy. Any state between therapist and patient that threatens the dynamic conflict in the relationship and its resolution, either through persistent pleasure and peace, or through intolerable explosive conflict, threatens to undermine and abort the analytic process.

In the interests of maintaining the productive cycle between patient and therapist, it is important that the therapist be in control of his emotions when expressing them. An out-of-control therapist will only terrify his patient into flight or submission. If a therapist knows that he is not capable of remaining in control when expressing himself, he should not make a disclosure. Rather, he should do whatever is necessary outside of the hour to get control over what he is feeling so that he can express it constructively to his patient. If a patient is *im*patient, the therapist should acknowledge his patient's feelings and observations, but he should also tell him that, as his therapist, he is not yet ready to reveal much—

the patient will simply have to wait. Then the patient's response to this can be processed, with the understanding that he may be less than pleased.

A final note on control: it is not advisable to be so controlled that you strip your disclosure of its intensity and veritable life-blood. Many of the clinicians I talk to about countertransference disclosures say that when making them they are always very cool, calm and controlled. But by being like this, they destroy the essence of their disclosures. For example, a therapist who acknowledges his anger by telling his patient placidly, "Yes, I am angry with you" is not only failing to express affect, but is giving the patient a double message. His voice tone and facial expression say that he feels little if anything, but his verbal message says he is angry. What is the patient supposed to do with this? The point of disclosure is to rationally *demonstrate affect*, not to intellectualize. Therapist intellectualizations are usually met by the patient accusing the therapist of being lifeless, mechanical, overly intellectual or non-responsive.

Patients who are being provocative because they badly need an affective response from their therapists are likely to "up the ante" when they do not get what they need. Continued or intensified provocative behavior from a patient is a sure sign that the requisite affective response from the therapist has not been effectively communicated. Very often this failure will be due to insufficient affective expression by the therapist, regardless of the verbal content of the message.

As a general rule of thumb, countertransference disclosures that contain too much affect, or are ill-timed, or are made by a therapist who is not comfortable and reasonably in control of his emotions, will generate high anxiety in the patient or produce a state of overstimulation. Depending upon the patient's degree of impulse control, overstimulation may result in out-of-control behaviors. Disclosures that are insufficiently genuine and emotional, or miss the mark in some way, will induce a patient's frustration and anger and will usually be followed by a depression on his part. With a patient who cannot express his anger, he will immediately become withdrawn and depressed. If these indications of a failed countertransference intervention present themselves the therapist must essentially start over again, following the guidelines presented here. However, it is important to talk first to the patient about how he is feeling, so that both parties understand what has happened. This is most artfully accomplished if the therapist keeps in mind that the patient is his consultant, and treats him accordingly.

The following technical considerations are presented with the hope that therapists will implement them prudently and to the benefit of their patients. In all cases I would urge any therapist who is not accustomed to disclosing the countertransference to start in a small way and to practice. Just as with any other type of intervention, it takes time to develop skill and finesse, as well as to integrate techniques into a personal style. Authenticity and genuineness are critical to the success of counter-transference disclosures, so do not try to say anything that does not feel natural. If an example given here seems to apply to a situation that you are facing with one of your own patients, some internal rehearsing in your own words might help. Remember that there is *no single right way* to say anything. Whatever is honest, direct, non-judgmental and coming from the heart will be the most effective.

One of the guiding principles of this approach is that the therapist does not have to be perfect and should not even try to be. It will only make him try too hard and seem too wooden. Rather, he should content himself with being thoughtful and feeling reasonably in control of himself and the situation before making any disclosure, then proceed as naturally as possible. If he misses the mark, his patient will let him know, and he can keep struggling until he makes himself understood. Sometimes this struggle is exactly what is therapeutic about a disclosure, so it need not be thought of as a sign of inadequacy or failure to communicate. The patient may not understand everything that his therapist is saying, or he may be ambivalent about any emotional message being sent, which may result in only partial understanding. If the therapist remembers that being engaged in a mutual struggle to understand and be understood is what the process is all about, then he will not need to resist it.

In the next section I go through the major affective countertransference reactions, along with examples of each as they may be expressed to the patient. Remember that these are only examples and any personal statements should be in a form that suits your own personality and verbal style. Within each example, I describe the most common reactions, including what the patient might say and feel in response to your disclosure. In some instances it will be obvious what your reply should be; for others I make suggestions. The intention is to give the reader a feel for the type of interaction that occurs and the dialog that ensues from a countertransference disclosure.

Specific Affective Countertransference Reactions

Anger and Hatred

The feelings that present the most difficulty for us as therapists are the same as those that present the most difficulty for our patients: anger and hatred. So I will begin by addressing them. Patients provoke anger in their therapists in one of two ways, either actively (or directly) or passively (or indirectly). Actively, they provoke their therapists' anger through direct verbal or threatened physical abuse. They yell, insult, threaten to hit, or consistently criticize or nag the therapist. Passively, they might excessively idealize others while showing little regard for the therapist (common to those with narcissistic personalities), or they whine, cling, make unreasonable demands to be comforted or loved, come late to sessions, come to the sessions high on alcohol or drugs, abuse themselves outside of sessions, do not pay their bills on time, recount stories of how they let others take advantage of them while showing no emotion, intrude emotionally or physically on the therapist (which includes excessive calls to the therapist), remain removed and aloof no matter what the therapist does to reach them, or tease the therapist sexually. No doubt I have left out some other stimuli, but all the above situations may provoke anger in the therapist. I also believe that patients, like most people, often communicate indirectly and passively rather than directly and actively.

As an example, Sally provoked my anger passively by declaring repeatedly that she was hopeless and so was the treatment. In the first two years of treatment I tolerated her despair quite well, wanting to understand how she came to feel this way as well as wanting her to know that I could accept her as she was. However, once she responded to treatment—she became less socially isolated, and more sexually active, assertive and self-aware—I noticed that I became much less accepting of her feelings of futility. I *knew* from the progress that she had made that she was *not* hopeless and I began to resent it when she fell into her old and comfortable litany of gloom. I saw her behavior as an expression of her fear of failure and her need to give up on herself. Eventually I became angry at her, which I did not immediately disclose. But she sensed it, and became even more remote, disparaging, and self-pitying. She would refuse to look at me, which only increased my frustration and sense of defeat. I soon realized that while Sally was expressing her own fears, she was also inviting me to feel as hopeless, defeated, frustrated and martyred as she did. This communication through projective identification was very effective, and I finally had to show her my anger and disgust. I told her that I was getting tired of her self-pity and that most of what she said was not true. I added that I knew she was afraid—particularly of trying new things—but so is everyone, and that if they indulged those fears the whole human race would be as paralyzed as she. I told her that I knew she was capable of more and that I expected her to take some risks.

In Sally's case I was pretty much on my own because she had not directly asked me for a disclosure. I had to decide what she could tolerate, based on my previous years' experience with her. As I proceeded with my confrontation I noticed that she re-established eye contact with me and perked up considerably. This was obviously a positive response and it encouraged me to continue. When I finished she began to cry, telling me how she hated herself when she was so removed and pessimistic, but at the same time she was unable to alter her position.

During the encounters when I "broke through" her barrier of negative verbiage and isolation, it became clear to me that no one in her early life had ever done so. Her highly educated parents had been over-protective and non-confrontive to a fault. The dependency they subtly encouraged had undermined her self-esteem and, when she became despondent and withdrawn, they simply left her alone. She knew she had frustrated and angered them, but they had never expressed this to her. I experienced the same anger toward her in the sessions but, *unlike her parents*, I was able to confront her with her behavior and express my feelings about it. When I did so, she always responded with a flood of tears and expressed her fears and doubts to me, showing all the emotion that had been bottled up. Correspondingly, after each of my confrontations she would almost immediately take some risk or action on her own behalf and would come to her next session with the report of some new success. It proved to be a very successful treatment, which I attribute to my show of strong feelings to Sally that her parents and others had suppressed out of fear of hurting her. My success in breaking through her painful self-imposed isolation was clearly therapeutic.

In the interests of presenting a balanced picture, and of demonstrating that mistakes will occur but need not be fatal, I would also like to describe a time when I acted impulsively and sadistically expressed my counter-transference to Sally. One day when she was particularly unreachable, despondent and negative, I became quite frustrated and honestly did not feel like hearing any more of her usual litany. She kept saying that there was nothing she could do to make her life better, and when I pointed out something that she *could* do, I received the expected "yes . . . but" reply, followed by even more expressions of hopelessness. Sally was still a virgin and she was very sensitive about it, believing it was just cause for humiliation. When I had heard all the "yes . . . buts" that I could stand, I angrily said, "Well, I guess you *could* just hang around and do nothing, since you're so convinced that nothing will do any good, and just wait around to become the world's oldest virgin." She responded with shock and hurt and immediately burst into tears. She looked at me with disbelief and asked how I could possibly say such an insensitive and cruel thing to her. I instantly felt regret and shame for my sadistic behavior toward her and was confused by it myself, since I am not typically sadistic toward my patients. I apologized, telling her I wasnt't sure what had come over me, but I knew that what I had said was terrible and I was deeply sorry. She continued to cry, but she also came out with statements that she had never made before. She told me how difficult it was for her to trust anyone—how she had wanted to trust me but had feared that I would do something like this to hurt her. At this point I feared that I had really ruined things between us, but Sally kept on talking about wanting to be closer to me and not hiding so much, which made me realize that something quite positive was happening. We continued to talk with each other until the end of the session, at which time I repeated how sorry I was for what I had said to her. As she got up to leave she spontaneously hugged me, something that had never happened before, and did not again. At that point I was still a bit shaken by what had happened, but I also realized that the situation had been salvaged.

Certainly, I am not advocating making sadistic remarks to patients and I do feel strongly that what I had said was cruel and potentially very destructive. What saved the situation was my immediate heartfelt apology and genuine remorse. And at that moment in treatment, I realized how important the expression of my affect was to breaking through to Sally and patients like her. Sadism was preferable to my "neutrality." Just as important, I learned that making a mistake with the countertransference was not the end of the world, especially if I was open to admitting that I had been wrong or had behaved badly. Mistakes in disclosing the countertransferences are inevitable, as they are with any approach. I think that therapists should not be so worried and fearful of making a mistake that they avoid any and all use of the countertransference.

Let us look at another example of countertransference anger, this one provided by a *direct* expression of patient anger. Jennifer, a patient with a narcissistic personality disorder, tended to interpret all of my behavior as a sign that I did not love or respect her. She made fantastic interpretations regarding what she felt my hidden motives were, then insisted that she was correct. She railed at me for being heartless and rejecting. At one point during one of these occasions I told her point blank that she was wrong. She angrily said, "No I'm not. I know what you meant." I repeated, "No, you don't. I feel sure that your interpretation is wrong. I was feeling nothing of the kind." At that point she became angrier with me, screaming at me that she was right. Because she was hysterical, I immediately tried to calm her down. But I also told her how angry it made me for her to insist repeatedly that she absolutely knew my thoughts and feelings better than I did (which was an attitude that she inflicted on the population at large). I told her that she molded me into what she feared, and she subsequently became so committed to her scenario that when I or anyone else told her she was wrong, she felt that all of her emotions were being negated. Thus the need to fight to the death. The fact that there was always some empathic failure involved in stimulating this scene was less important than confronting Jennifer with her terribly aggressive and alienating behavior. I told her how much I hated her changing my words around and forcing them back on me, how violent this felt to me, and how angry I became in response. At first she was fearful when I became angry, but as we discussed the situation and she realized that I was not going to destroy or eject her from the session, she began to tolerate her fear and to gain insight from what I said to her.

The chief countertransference error in dealing with the above situation was one that I made with Jennifer more than once during her treatment. I waited to act until I was extremely angry with her and then I came on so strong that I frightened her. (At these times she would look scared and ask me if I wanted her to terminate, or if I was completely fed up with her.) When this happened with Jennifer, the immediate issue had to take a back seat and the new issue became one of restoring the equilibrium in our relationship. At that point, Jennifer needed to be reassured that, while I was angry, I was not angry enough to want to end the relationship ("No, I don't have any intentions of ending the treatment. I still want to work with you—I'm just angry.") Waiting too long and subsequently having difficulty controlling the intensity of the countertransference can be a major problem. Once this happens, the therapist has no choice but to focus on restoring the relationship, and discussion concerning the original issue may have to be delayed until the next session. If the patient is significantly fearful, the therapist should apologize for frightening him, acknowledging that he waited too long and should have said something earlier. This not only reassures him that his therapist is still with him, but also demonstrates that he has regained control, has a healthy perspective on the situation, and is willing to take responsibility for his mistakes. (As with all mistakes, a little goes a long way. If a therapist makes many mistakes, he will undoubtedly destroy the patient's sense of safety and ruin the treatment. However, a therapist's failure to express his anger at all also undermines the treatment and promotes rage or depression in the patient. Suppressing anger is also likely to lead a therapist to eventual withdrawal and emotional abandonment of the patient. As stated previously, anger and hatred are particularly troublesome issues for most people, and as such require caution and restraint.)

Sexual Feelings

Gorkin (1985, 1987) notes that the sexualized countertransference is probably the most neglected, both in practice and in the literature. He does not advocate disclosure because of the high level of anxiety that it usually provokes in the patient. In the earlier discussion of this topic I said that I basically agree with his position, but I also feel that there are exceptions to everything. Langs (1974), Stolorow and Lachmann (1984/1985), Atwood, Stolorow and Trop (1989), and Eber (1990) all emphasize that erotic transferences, particularly those that are intense and long-term, do not persist without the cooperation of the therapist. That is, the therapist somehow promotes the erotization of the relationship, usually through frustrating the patient in his pursuit of some more general affirmation of himself, or through subtle seductive or sadomasochistic behaviors that sexually stimulate the patient. Sometimes just being gratified by a patient's intense interest is sufficient to encourage an erotic transference, particularly with a patient who needs to have his sexual desirability confirmed. When an intense erotic transference persists, the therapist did have a role in promoting it, and at some level the patient knows it. But the question remains: when the patient accurately perceives his therapist's erotic interest in him, is it ever therapeutic to acknowledge that he is correct? Or will the therapist only be adding coal to a fire that is already too hot? Atwood, Stolorow and Trop (1989) reported a case of an impasse which resulted from the patient's acute need to have her male therapist admit that he found her sexually attractive. The patient, Alice, was a 36-year-old Oriental woman, an only child who had been totally ignored by her father because he had wanted a boy. She developed a strong erotic attachment to her therapist and, toward the end of the second year of transference, demanded that he acknowledge that he found her attractive and sexually exciting. Atwood describes the situation between them:

> Her demands for a concrete affirmation of her sexual self became increasingly strident. The therapist, feeling enormous pressure, finally did acknowledge that she was an attractive woman whom many men would find appealing. The patient became furious at what she felt was a lukewarm response. She continued to demand that he simply acknowledge that he felt sexually excited by her. She reiterated her awareness that they would actually never do anything sexually, but she still wanted him to demonstrate that he was interested and excited. In reaction to her increasing demand, the therapist became more emotionally disengaged and adopted a more intellectual stance, inquiring into why she was feeling so needy at this time. The patient became even more incensed and felt that he was abandoning her and that she should leave him. It was at this point that the therapist sought consultation in an attempt to understand what had happened between them. (p. 562)

The above situation follows the classic impasse pattern noted earlier and it clearly calls for an affective response from the therapist. Here, Alice is focusing on her therapist's sexual interest in her, with the importance of her attractiveness being over-determined by her history. Her conviction that her therapist is sexually attracted to her is rooted in reality, since Alice is not psychotic. (As I have stated previously, when a non-psychotic patient persistently confronts a therapist regarding his feelings, the patient is taking an accurate reading.) Alice is very probably correct in her belief that her therapist is sexually attracted to her and she is telling him in no uncertain terms that she needs confirmation. Atwood and colleagues provide a good description of the case, yet even so, it is impossible from the information given to ascertain whether Alice's fixation on obtaining the admission of sexual arousal from her therapist is based solely on her need for affirmation of her female sexuality or whether it also represents a displacement of some other emotional response that she believes her therapist has withheld. As I mentioned in the earlier discussion on disclosure, intense sexual preoccupations by patients can result from reaction formation or excessive frustration and inequality in the relationship. When a patient is as frustrated and as focused on erotic aspects of the therapy relationship as Alice was, I would certainly want to consider seriously that there were underlying contributing factors and that the erotic attachment might well be serving as a defense against hostility or other repressed material.

Regardless of what underlies it, once a crisis and impasse of this intensity exists, the patient needs a personal and emotional response to it. Before disclosing something as potentially anxiety-producing as sexual arousal, I would definitely discuss the impasse with the patient and attempt to discover any and all meanings that it has (as the therapist in this case eventually did with some success). Telling the patient that you know the situation is critical and he obviously needs something from you that he is not getting responds to the patient's needs and feelings, and begins transforming the impasse into a joint effort at resolution. The two of you can discuss the situation and attempt to understand what the patient really needs.

However, if the therapist does not respond as needed the patient will soon feel falsely placated, become frustrated and angry anew, thereby reinstating the impasse. In Alice's case, the therapist initially was defensive and distant, which enraged her and intensified the impasse. Following consultation he was able to discuss the impasse with her, explaining that he wanted to be responsive to her, but was not professionally comfortable with directly answering her questions. Atwood and colleagues report that Alice reluctantly accepted her therapist's position, which she viewed as her contribution to re-establishing the relationship. But as I read the case I wondered how long her acceptance would last. Would Alice really be able to accede to her therapist's refusal to answer her questions or would the impasse take hold again later?

If Alice renewed her demands for her therapist to admit his sexual interest in her, I believe he would have had no choice but to do so. Alice had already stated that she knew that their professional relationship did not allow any acting out of sexual feelings and that she had, in fact, accepted this limitation. She simply wanted him to admit what he felt anyway. Undoubtedly such a disclosure from her therapist could be highly sexually stimulating to Alice, but I believe this would pass if the therapist was not being seductive. Furthermore, the problem of sexually stimulating the patient is less severe than frustrating him to the point of dealing with a lengthy impasse or, worse still, a premature termination.

I believe that Alice may have been one of the uncommon patients who actually needed to hear from her therapist that he found her attractive. Though I advise caution and encourage thorough exploration of the meaning of requests such as Alice's, when a patient repeatedly demands to know the truth regarding the therapist's feelings, *no matter what the truth is*, I think he has a right to be treated respectfully and given an answer. (Under *no* circumstances, however, is *acting on sexual feelings* toward a patient appropriate or part of the countertransference techniques advocated here.)

Love and Affection

The topic of love and affection follows the above discussion naturally, in that patients are likely to ask repeatedly, or to even demand, to have their perceptions of the therapist's liking or loving of them affirmed. Most patients are much more concerned with this issue than they are with sexual feelings and I have often been confronted regarding the nature or lack of my affections for my patients. When patients persist in wanting to have their intuition or observations regarding affection confirmed, I do so—even if it means admitting that I *do not* feel much love for them, which is a far less comfortable (but at least as therapeutic) situation than admitting to fond feelings.

Cindy, a young woman who had an almost loveless childhood and expectable difficulties establishing and maintaining relationships with both sexes, asked me how I felt about her. I asked her what she thought. She said she perceived me to be appropriately concerned about her from a professional standpoint, that I was generally kind and positive about working with her. But even after four sessions a week over eighteen months she said that she could not detect any real personal warmth from me and wanted to know if she was right. She said that she feared her lack of early experience had damned her to isolation and that she simply was incapable of inspiring affection in anyone. She considered me, who had not seemed to develop a real attachment to her, to be living proof of her fears. I avoided responding directly to her questions but discussed the general issue with her at length, exploring her anger at her parents and her feelings of hopelessness.

This went quite well and I assumed the issue had been settled, at least for the moment. However, she began her next day's session by demanding an answer to the previous day's question. Yes, everything we discussed yesterday was important, but so was the answer to her question. And she was not about to move on until I answered it. So I did, even though the answer was painful for her. I had to admit that she was right about my lack of affection for her, but I went on to explain that my lack of feelings was because she showed so little emotion, and that this was the key to inspiring feeling in others. I reconfirmed my commitment to helping her to express the intense feelings we both knew she felt but could not show, and I refused to accept her determination that she was hopeless. Simply telling Cindy she was right in her perception that I was not that attached to her could have been quite destructive; she needed to know that her accurate perceptions did not mean she was incurable.

I find it less difficult to express strong affection or love for a patient, but I consider it equally demanding in its own right. One of the first persons I treated after receiving my doctoral training was a young student who, though multi-talented and quite attractive, suffered from serious doubts about both her ability and lovableness. After a year of treatment she asked me one day how I felt about her. In reality I thought the world of her and had come to love her, which she unconsciously knew. As a relative neophyte, I was quite taken aback by her demand to know how I felt. (No-one had ever discussed such things, other than the importance of being "neutral," with me in my training.) I responded to her question by saying that I liked her. Her response was to blush with shame and look away from me. I was shaken by her obvious narcissistic injury and tried to talk to her about it, but she withdrew immediately and remained so until the session ended. Two days later she called to inform me that she would not be able to attend her next session because she was ill with a 103 degree fever. She was quite sick for several days and did not return to therapy until the following week. I was upset by this and feared that her "falling ill" was related to the narcissistic injury that she had received from me. (This was later confirmed by two other such incidents during the course of the transference. And I have observed this same "falling ill" phenomenon, usually accompanied by high fevers, in other narcissistic personalities following severe blows to their self-esteem.)

Upon her return I tried to discuss what had happened with her, but she was very removed and uncooperative. I asked her if her mood was the result of our last encounter and she said "yes," but would go no further. I then asked if it was because of the way I had answered the question. She said "yes," again going no further. I told her that she seemed hurt and humiliated by my answer—was this true? She said "yes." I asked her again to tell me more about it, but she refused. Finally I said that I was very sorry to have hurt her so. She perked up a bit at this and looked at me, but still said nothing. Then I said that I thought that she was so mortified because my answer did not match what she had perceived to be true and that this made her ashamed. She began to come out of her narcissistic withdrawal, maintaining eye contact with me and becoming visibly brighter and more alive. Encouraged by this response, I continued. I told her that she had expected me to say that I loved her—because I did.

At this point she really came alive, but not in the way you might expect. She looked hurt and angry and sarcastically asked me why I hadn't given her that answer two weeks ago. I said that I had no excuse other than that my training had forbidden me to say such things to a patient. She found this to be a rather feeble excuse and was clearly contemptuous of my inability to act on her behalf. I was able to answer her again at a later date with a much better result, but unfortunately for her and for me, my problems in this area continued.

This early in my career I was simply not prepared to deal with someone as emotionally complex and demanding of skill as she was. I continued to stall in my responses to her, but in spite of helping her in many ways, I failed her in others and she terminated prematurely after two years of treatment. I found that my training had actually hindered me in my efforts to address her needs in the therapy relationship. Though someone like her would present a formidable challenge to any neophyte, had I been able to confront my countertransference with her more directly, including some idealization of her, the outcome of her therapy might have been different. (She also wanted some physical comfort from me when she cried, and I will continue the discussion of this case in the section on physical contact that follows later.)

In general, a therapist should not have too much difficulty when his patient wants to know whether his therapist likes him, is attached to him, or cares about him. When his patient wants to know whether his therapist "loves" him, however, the therapist may have problems because "love" has so many different meanings. I believe in using the word "love" sparingly, because it has the potential for being interpreted by the patient as an erotic response, or as an over-investment on the therapist's part. As such, it may stimulate both relief and anxiety in the patient. Luckily, few patients actually use this word themselves, since it does not apply to the relationship often. If a therapist tells his patient that he does, in fact, love him, the therapist needs to be prepared to elucidate exactly what he means and does not mean by it. The distinction between platonic love and erotic love should be clear to the patient so that he understands that his therapist is not "in love" with him. For some time I tried to circumvent this problem by not using the word "love." Instead I used replacements like "care deeply" or "very fond of." This worked, and was even preferred, by some patients. But others considered it a "cop-out" and were annoyed or hurt by my reluctance to use the word "love."

Was I ashamed of it? Why couldn't I use it? Didn't I really feel that strongly? So I abandoned my attempt at simplicity and now use the word love when applicable, always prepared to explain what I mean by it so that the patient does not confuse my expression of deep affection with a declaration of romantic love.

In the event that it is not obvious from previous discussion, I almost never tell a patient how I feel about him until he has told me what he perceives to be true and only after asking him if he really wants me to answer his question directly. Sometimes patients will say "No, I'm not ready to hear that now" but will return to the issue weeks or months later, this time wanting an answer.

As a last note on expressing countertransference love or affection, I have never experienced an occasion when the patient's request for it was indirect—i.e. hinted at or stimulated by projective identification. The one time I thought that this was occurring—the patient went on tearfully for a long time about how she knew I would never love her, just as no one had ever really loved her—I was wrong. I told the patient that I *did* love her, which was true, but she responded with skepticism and high anxiety. There was no question in my mind that I had made a major therapeutic error and that I had done so because I was relieving myself of the pain I had felt during her long tearful expression of never having been loved. I finally couldn't take it anymore and unintentionally rejected her pain and hopelessness by attempting to reassure and comfort her. This incident convinced me that it was unwise to assume the patient wanted or needed to hear about my feelings. Besides, I had broken my own rule by not asking her first if she wanted to know the truth. The negative outcome taught me something I needed to know.

Fears of Abandonment, Rejection, or Engulfment

It seems to me that we are very reluctant to admit to our fears of being abandoned by our patients. It hurts our pride and makes us feel insecure or "insufficiently analyzed." Since we are not supposed to need our patients, how can we possibly fear losing them? But I believe that a certain degree of abandonment fear comes with attachment, even in a therapeutic relationship. Susceptibility to this fear varies from therapist to therapist, of course, and if you never really become emotionally involved with your patients you obviously will never suffer from fear of rejection or abandonment by them.

The symbiotic phase of treatment leaves both patient and therapist particularly vulnerable to threats of emotional or physical abandonment, and such threats may be used by either party as a defense against intimacy or as a punishment for some disappointment or hurt. Many patients test the therapist's response to such a threat, wanting to know that the therapist is adequately attached and committed to the treatment but not so much so that the patient will be denied autonomy and eventual physical separation (i.e. termination). Patients test the degree of a therapist's involvement because they intuitively know that if the therapist is insufficiently involved or merged, then they are not safe. On the other hand, too much involvement on the part of the therapist means potential loss of self for the patient and foreshadows life-long dependency.

Though I consider it to be a universal issue, the threat of abandonment is particularly prominent with borderline personalities. Some remain aloof for years out of fear of engulfment, others clamor wildly for symbiosis. Again, how a patient reacts will depend on his history. The same may be said for the therapist's fear of engulfment, but I hasten to add that a therapist does not have to be suffering from a borderline personality disorder to have some fear of engulfment. Patients who are very intrusive and demanding will ultimately trigger feelings of violation and fears of engulfment in their therapists.

Disclosure of countertransference responses concerning fears of abandonment or engulfment can help the patient to establish a healthy distance and to develop an appreciation for the power he has in the relationship. For example, Susan, who was prone to believing that she was not capable of maintaining any relationship and was therefore doomed to ruining her treatment, would frequently say that she felt like just giving up and leaving. My response was to say that I hoped that she would not do that but that it was, after all, her choice. There was nothing obviously unacceptable about this response, in that it was not inherently too hot or too cold. But Susan couldn't help but notice a slight distancing and matter-of-factness in my voice and manner as I responded to her. She confronted me about this and said that she thought that I distanced from her to defend against the hurt of her threatened abandonment. She pressed me and I had to admit that her observation was correct. I ended up telling her that I had had patients terminate prematurely a few times and, though it did not happen often, it did hurt. I emphasized that it was not their leaving *per se*, but rather the precipitous rupture of the relationship, that was hurtful and disconcerting. This type of ending leaves both parties without satisfaction or closure.

She was clearly pleased by my response. She said that she was glad to know that I could be affected by whether someone stayed, and she was glad to know that she was not the only one who was vulnerable in the relationship. She said that she needed to know things like this so that she could tolerate the asymmetry in the relationship which she found to be difficult because it encouraged her to think of herself as less than me. It was important for her to know that she would have an impact on me if she left and that she could hurt me. In fact, I think that her knowledge of my vulnerability enabled her to stay in the relationship and ultimately to have a successful treatment.

Regarding a therapist's fear of engulfment, a countertransference disclosure usually entails some limit-setting that the patient is seeking. The literature offers two excellent examples of this by noted clinicians. Stewart (1989), in his discussion of technique at the "basic fault," cites an example of a woman patient who demanded to be able to be with him at his house, asking why she had to be different from his wife and children. Stewart says:

> It was not until I spelled out to her that I chose to have my family staying in the house and that I did not choose to have her staying, that she was satisfied and understood what I was talking about, and after this we had no further trouble on this score. (p. 228)

A similar experience is related by Searles (1973), who says:

> I shall never forget the sense of achieved inner freedom which enabled me to tell a hebephrenic woman, in relation to whom I had been enmeshed in anguished symbiotic relatedness for years, that I would never allow her to visit my home—as she had yearned to do—even if my refusal meant that she would stay in a mental hospital all her life. (pp. 251–252)

The analytic tradition has tended to underestimate the strength of the patient, particularly when dealt with honestly and directly, and thus has not encouraged confrontations like those just cited. Yet both of these patients not only tolerated knowing their therapists' true feelings, but also benefited from these disclosures, as did their therapists. The patients were not crushed or disabled in any way by the truth, in spite of their rather high level of pathology.

Less dramatic or intense confrontations can occur over other boundary issues that threaten the therapist, such as frequency and length of phone contacts, requests for extra sessions, or unwelcome requests for affection, comfort or personal information about the therapist. For me, the simplest and most honest reason for not giving the patient what he wants is also the most human one: I don't want to. Learning that every person has his own limits, understanding that individual limits are arbitrary, and being capable of accepting and respecting these limits, is critical to many analytic treatments and can only be facilitated by adequate disclosure from the therapist.

Hopelessness and Depression

Ironically, when we as therapists respond empathically to our patients' feelings of hopelessness or depression, we may inadvertently abandon them on an emotional level. This countertransference response may be particularly evident during the symbiotic phase of treatment, when we intensely share our patients' emotions. And, to the extent that this mutual sharing stimulates recollections of our own pessimism or despair, we will withdraw from our patients.

On the surface, this may seem like one of those situations that we cannot handle effectively. If we keep enough distance so that we do not completely feel our patients' depression, we run the risk of rejecting and alienating them. However, if we are so close to them that we feel their powerful affect, we may be catapulted into another form of distancing that can prove to be equally deleterious.

Not surprisingly, I advocate dealing with these kinds of situations through disclosure of the countertransference. But first, let me acknowledge that some patients can observe their therapist's feelings of hopelessness or despair and experience them in an empathic fashion. Those patients will not be concerned about the therapist's countenance and will leave their sessions at peace and feeling understood or even loved. In these cases, naturally, no problem exists and no disclosure should be made.

However, other patients will notice their therapist's feelings and may feel guilty for having "made" the therapist depressed. Other patients may be fearful—the last thing a despairing patient wants is a therapist who is likewise overwhelmed. Still other patients will directly respond to their therapists' withdrawal and will try to elicit feelings as a way of reconnecting to them. In this case, expression of the countertransference is essential to reassure the patient of the therapist's ability to handle strong emotions, relieving the patient of unnecessary anxiety and guilt.

For example, John, a man in his late thirties with an obsessive-compulsive personality, sought treatment for a variety of reasons including ego-dystonic fetishism. He occasionally despaired over his lot in life. Very much wanting to be "normal," he would sometimes tire of the good fight and become temporarily despondent, expressing suicidal ideation. He was very bright and articulate, as well as highly verbal; he could easily spend an entire session expounding on how hopeless life was in general and how hopeless he was because of his fetish. He felt that no treatment could ever restore him to any semblance of normality. As he said, "What's the point in living?" After one session, in which he articulated these sentiments, not with self-pity so much as with the deep sadness and despair of a good person who tries hard, but fears that he does so against all odds, I felt overwhelmed and wondered if he wasn't right.

At the end of the session, John looked hard at me to take a "reading" of my feelings, and he accurately observed that I looked as though I felt hopeless, too. He seemed to find this both relieving and disturbing. On the one hand, he felt understood and that I had been with him the whole hour, even though he had talked continuously. On the other hand, he sensed the impact that he had had on me and felt that I might be giving up on him. He asked me if he had depressed me and if I now thought he was hopeless and untreatable. I simply said that I didn't, even though I had been moved by his intense feelings and he had taken me back to times in my own life when I had felt despair. Then I added that I had never thought he was hopeless and still didn't, but I did understand that he felt this way sometimes and that he shouldn't worry about expressing it to me. My response was satisfying to him and he never hesitated to express his hopelessness when he felt it. Sometimes he would check to make sure that I still felt the same way. And once he knew that I did, he was satisfied. (Incidentally, John never asked me anything at all about what things in my life had led me to feeling hopeless at times, and I never said anything about them. He did not want or need that information, nor was I particularly interested in giving it to him. He only needed to know how and what I was feeling with him and how that affected our relationship. And he needed to talk with me before he left the session so that we did not end the session as if we were two ships anchored next to each other in deep fog.)

If the therapist's depression is unrelated to the patient yet its presence is accurately perceived by him, the same guidelines apply. For example, a patient says, "Gee, you seem down today. Are you?" I will usually say, "Yes, something is bothering me." The patient needs some reassurance that I will not be burdened by working with him, and I provide it by saying that I am all right and that I am capable of being responsive to him.

This typically ends the issue unless, of course, my depression *is* related to the patient and some aspect of our ongoing relationship, or the patient *fears* that this is so. If this is the case, then more discussion will be initiated by the patient. For example, a patient might say, "Are you depressed because I gave you a hard time yesterday?" I say whatever is true. If I'm not, I might say, "No, my feelings are unrelated to you. But I'd like to know what you mean. Why would I be depressed over yesterday's session?" The patient might then say, "Well, I was complaining about not getting better fast enough. So when I saw you felt bad today, I thought maybe I had hurt your feelings or made you feel like you weren't a good therapist." A traditionally trained analytic clinician might be tempted to make a genetic interpretation, saying, for example, how the patient's response is similar to the way he responded to his mother's depression. Even if the therapist believes this to be true, which it may well be, *he should not say it*. If he and the patient have discussed this issue in the past and both of them are aware of this historical material, the therapist's interpretation will be gratuitous and distracting. If the patient is *not* aware of how it is a repetition, he is not likely to gain this insight by having the flow interrupted. Completing the interaction is more likely to lead to insight. Then, the patient may make the genetic connection himself or the therapist may stimulate it by asking the patient if the situation seems familiar. If he is receptive, the discussion can continue. If not, I would wait for another time, letting it pass at the moment.

Returning to the scene at hand, the patient has just asked if he is responsible for my depression. At different times I have given each of the following responses, depending on what is true:

1. "As a matter of fact, my feelings were hurt yesterday when you said I was a lousy therapist, but I don't think that's contributing to my feeling depressed today. I am feeling bad over a situation in my personal life, rather than in response to you. How do you feel about that?"
2. "No, that's okay. I wasn't hurt by your comments. I knew you were just frustrated because you want to change your life and it's been quite a struggle lately. My depression doesn't have to do with you. Not to worry."
3. "Actually, I do feel lousy because of yesterday's session. But it's not just that session. It's how things have been going lately. This is the third time in two weeks that you have railed at me and told me what a lousy therapist I am, and even when we talk about it I still feel unsure about what's going on and why you feel this way. This difficulty in us coming to some kind of understanding about what is really wrong and resolving it is starting to get to me."

The last response is by far the most infrequently used and the most difficult. But the patient may respond to any of them with relief, satisfaction, confusion, anger, hurt, disappointment or even triumph, depending on what dynamics were involved in reaching the impasse. The therapist should wait for the patient's response and follow his lead. Wherever he goes is where you go. If a private theory of your own is at odds with the direction the patient is taking, do your best to put it aside, even if it is the product of a consultation and you and your consultant have congratulated yourselves on the brilliance of your psychodynamic formulation. It is easy to try to subtly squeeze the patient into a particular mold, but it will only be met by resistance. Ideally, the above scenario can be played out to the satisfaction of both patient and therapist so that it facilitates insight or at least clears away an obstacle to addressing the material that is most important to the patient.

Fear and Anxiety

A therapist's *fear*, here defined as a reality-based reaction to a real and immediate danger, is most likely to be stimulated by a threat of physical harm from a patient. While such threats occur infrequently in analytic treatments, they can happen, particularly with patients with the diagnoses of antisocial personality disorder or paranoid schizophrenia. Some patients with borderline personalities are fond of making threats as well, even though they are not as likely to act on them. Maintaining a cool, untouched exterior and never giving in to the expression of fear can be wise when confronted by antisocial or schizophrenic patients, since they feed on fear and are best controlled by a firm, non-emotional response. Many of these patients have the potential for doing physical harm and will only respond to any expression of the therapist's vulnerability with newly fueled aggression.

Most outpatients in analytic treatment, however, are not of this ilk. They have mostly anxiety, mood or personality disorders that do not include the inclination to physically threaten their therapists unless they are extremely frustrated and out of control. Such feelings can often stem from a particular response, or lack of one, from the therapist. As an example, Kernberg (1987) reports a case in which a patient threatened him with violence because of something that he thought Kernberg had done. The patient had made the acquaintance of a woman who worked at the mental health complex with which Kernberg was associated. Upon dating this woman, the patient inquired whether she knew Kernberg and he became aggressively inquisitory on this subject. His date was understandably put off by his behavior and suggested that they "cool" the relationship. The patient, whom Kernberg describes as paranoid with borderline organization, confronted Kernberg with his belief that Kernberg had turned this woman against him, and Kernberg refused either to admit or deny the truth of his patient's allegation. The patient became extremely frustrated and angry, threatening to harm Kernberg if he didn't tell him the truth. Finally, out of fear, Kernberg broke down and admitted that he knew the woman in question but had not spoken to her since his patient had begun dating her. Kernberg discusses how his show of fear, much to his surprise, was therapeutic:

> The patient grew visibly more relaxed, and said he believed I was not lying. He added that, for some strange reason, all of a sudden the whole issue seemed less important to him; he felt good that I had been afraid and had confessed as much to him. (p. 813)

Kernberg reports an ensuing long silence, during which time he processed the following reaction:

> I had a sense of relief because the patient was no longer attacking me, a feeling of shame because I had shown him my fears of being physically assaulted, anger because of what I perceived as his sadistic enjoyment of

my fear without any compunction over that enjoyment, and intolerance of his enjoyment of that sadistic acting out. *I also felt that the whole relationship with the woman seemed, all of a sudden, less important, which I found puzzling but could not explain to myself further.* (p. 813) [Emphasis mine.]

This case illustrates the importance of communicating affect, including fear, to the provocative patient. Although Kernberg attributes the therapeutic value of this interaction to his setting of limits by asking the patient to provide assurances that he would not become violent, from my point of view the therapeutic benefit was derived primarily from his countertransference disclosure. My idea is supported by the "falling away" of the surface issue regarding the patient's relationship with the woman, revealing the critical importance of the underlying issue—i.e. the interpersonal relationship between Kernberg and his patient.

In my opinion, Kernberg ultimately did the right thing with his patient, even though he might disagree with me about why it was therapeutic. I also believe that the threat of violence could have possibly been averted by simply answering the patient's question in the first place. But as I am fond of saying, none of us always does the right thing at the right time, and with certain patients an emotional situation can quickly escalate out of control. A patient who threatens a therapist with physical harm, litigation, non-payment, termination, or suicide is a person who feels frustrated and thwarted, and is desperate for some sense of strength and power in the relationship. That such intense frustration and feelings of powerlessness are always rooted in the past does not in any way diminish the need to address them in the present, *with affect.*

A therapist's anxiety is likely to be stimulated by a patient's suicide threats or confrontations regarding a therapist's motivations and feelings, because anxiety (as opposed to fear) has unconscious determinants and as such threatens the therapist's reality-testing. He will probably not be able to fully assess the situation nor will he know whether to disclose his anxiety to his patient. Anxiety is almost never what a patient is seeking, since the net effect is often one of temporarily disabling the therapist.

A therapist feels anxiety when a patient needs a particular response and, in provoking the desired response, he accidentally threatens the therapist, overwhelming his defenses. For example, a patient may threaten suicide because he wants to know that the therapist cares about what happens to him, but in making this threat he may send the therapist into an anxiety state that is related to guilt and liability. When this happens the therapist is not in a good position to respond well to the patient.

Ideally, the therapist only experiences anxiety transiently in a session and is able to recover his equilibrium through insight, thereby gaining a perspective on the true situation. But this is not always the case, and

I think an overwhelmed therapist should usually lay low until he has recovered from the anxiety experience. But this advice applies only if the therapist's anxiety is short-lived. If the patient is particularly aggressive in demanding a response and insists on knowing what the therapist is feeling, the best route is simply to admit to being thrown off and needing time to understand and express your response to your patient's provocations. If the situation is critical, as in the suicide example, then a personal response is needed at the moment. A patient who is threatening suicide may actually need to know that his therapist *is* thrown off balance and made anxious by this situation, particularly if the patient has a borderline personality disorder. In cases where the patient perceives the therapist to be too superior to him, or too omnipotent, he may feel the need to disturb the therapist's equilibrium as a way of having an impact on the therapist and demonstrating that even the therapist is vulnerable. On such occasions the therapist has no choice but to admit to being upset by the patient's threats and to then discuss what the patient intends or does not intend to do with regard to harming himself.

Envy

A therapist's envy is one of the most important emotions to be addressed in treatment. Even in successful treatments the therapist's envy can be great and, ironically, may interfere with facilitating an equally successful termination. The case reported by Silverman and discussed earlier (see Chapter 3) is an excellent example of an impasse created when the patient knows he has stimulated his therapist's envy and fears retribution because of it. Envy is also important because it is such an integral part of the psychodynamics of intergenerational competition. Because of the importance and complexity of countertransference envy, which seems to come to the fore especially during termination, I will discuss it at length in Chapter 6.

Other Countertransference Issues

Physical Contact

Physical contact between patient and therapist is so controversial that it is rarely discussed, especially when *writing* about doing therapy. In analytic circles, touching is taboo because it violates the classical notion of analytic treatment as an intrapsychic rather than interpersonal experience. Perhaps the relatively recent emphasis on the interpersonal aspects of analytic treatment will produce further discussion on this much-neglected topic.

Goodman and Teicher (1988) provide an excellent review of the literature on physical contact, noting that Balint, Winnicott, and Little have all advocated it at certain times. They also note that the traditional consensus regarding physical contact is that it represents therapist acting-out and is counterproductive. The chief cautions against physical contact concern stimulating the patient sexually, provoking potentially destabilizing levels of regression and dependency, and encouraging discharge of tension rather than facilitating insight. Reasons to provide physical contact include maintaining the patient's vital connection to the therapist, providing needed reassurance during difficult periods, minimizing pain, and helping the patient to control himself. While Goodman and Teicher warn against physical contact with regressed patients, they believe it can work with the *undifferentiated patient*:

> It seems clear in our review that touching, used over the course of therapy, is often seen as necessary and useful during the course of work with patients who basically have failed to achieve differentiation and integration as separate, related and autonomous human beings. (p. 495)

I admire Goodman and Teicher's attempt to delineate when physical contact is likely to be therapeutic. I agree with the basic idea that physical contact can be therapeutic if used at the right time with the right patient, but I am confused by their distinction between the regressed and the undifferentiated patient.

Stewart (1989) reports experimenting with physical contact, but not with very good results. He says:

> I have noted, and so have some colleagues, that after allowing hand- or finger-holding, even though it is late in the analysis, the patient will have a dream, frightening or otherwise, of being raped or sexually assaulted. (p. 226)

I have had both good and bad outcomes as a result of touching patients. The types of touching I have used include hand-holding and a hand on the shoulder. I have also accepted, but *not initiated*, hugs. I generally am not enthusiastic about hugging, but have found that the narcissistic injury involved in refusing the spontaneous gesture of a patient's hug can have a far worse outcome than accepting it. My preferred type of physical contact is touching the hand of the patient.

I agree with Stewart that if the patient responds to physical contact with dreams of sexual assault or, for that matter, any intense anxiety or experience of intrusion, then the physical contact was inappropriate and harmful. And I have had patients respond in this way. But I have also had patients respond the opposite way. Rather than feeling violated, they have responded with dreams of finally having found a safe and secure place, and have been able to establish a new level of trust heretofore unknown to them. In my mind there is no question that physical contact can be very therapeutic. And my experience is that patients will quickly let you know whether touching them was good for them. The problem, of course, is to predict with some degree of accuracy when physical contact will be therapeutic, when it will be colluding with the patient to avoid pain, or when it will be an independent act of gratification on the therapist's part.

I think that any therapist using physical contact would be wise to use the most minimal contact possible and watch carefully for the patient's reaction, both immediate and in the next few sessions that follow. If the patient seems anxious, confused, withdrawn or depressed, or if he makes references to sexual fears, rape or being taken advantage of, then the physical contact was probably a mistake. Physical contact is *not* beneficial if it results in the patient clamoring for more contact either in or out of the usual session times, or coming to sessions dressed in a sexually provocative way.

On the other hand, if the patient seems more at peace, clearer in expressions of thought or feeling, is more open or responds with some new insight, then I think it is reasonably safe to consider that the physical contact was beneficial. In my experience patients do not pursue greater amounts of physical contact if the touch was therapeutic. Rather they express feelings of relief and contentment and often report dreams that contain themes of safety, soothing or a general sense of well-being following the contact.

In spite of the fact that physical contact is fraught with dangers, including the potential for abuse of the patient and unseemly gratification for the therapist, I have nonetheless made the decision to use it, albeit sparingly, in my approach to treatment. My reasons for this decision stem from a case I made reference to earlier in this chapter involving a patient who terminated prematurely, largely because of my inability to respond to her. I was a neophyte at the time and believed that I should not reveal any of my feelings toward her and should most definitely never touch her. She was 19 years old at the time of the treatment, but in many ways she was a very little girl who stimulated strong protective and maternal feelings in me. This was especially true when she would sob uncontrollably as she recalled her unhappy childhood. When she let me know that her parents and her older brother had all used her as a favorite "plaything" and had all made inappropriate physical contact with her, I felt prepared for her to expect, and to attempt to elicit, the same from me. At the time

I felt confident that touching her would unquestionably be a re-enactment of past harm and that I was doing the right thing, *the only thing*, by not providing any physical comfort—no matter how hard she cried or for how long. Naturally this was painful for me, but I considered it to be part of the price one must pay for being a good analytic clinician. I believed that touching her in any way would have been both destructive and self-indulgent on my part. So I did not.

Finally, she asked me why I didn't touch her and I tried to explain. She said that she understood, but it was plain to see that she only understood intellectually. So she asked if perhaps I could just come over and sit next to her on the couch when she cried so hard. Would that be all right? I gently said that I was sorry and that while I understood how much she wanted me to comfort her, I thought it better for me to remain in my chair. She resigned herself to this, but was very pained by my refusal to touch her. She said that it made her feel too alone and unloved.

After she terminated prematurely I rethought much of what I had done with her and came to the conclusion that one of the ways in which I had erred was in my refusal to touch her. It could be said that I merely failed to interpret and respond adequately to her desire to be touched. But I do not think that is true. When she sat or laid on the couch sobbing, it was one of the most wrenching events I have ever witnessed. At the time it seemed absolutely inhuman not to provide some minimal physical comfort, but I put my faith in the analytic process. Once she terminated, I vowed that I would never go against my own reactions so dramatically again—no matter what I had been taught. Then I set about trying to understand how it might have been helpful to provide some physical comfort to her. After all, there was still the issue of the inappropriate quasi-sexual contact with several members of her family. How could I have touched her without contributing to this pathological history? What would keep me from being seen by her as another narcissistic caretaker who cared more for my own gratification than for her welfare?

It was in the contemplation of this case that I first hit upon the notion of how a patient repeats the past, *up to a point*, and then seeks to make the outcome different. My young patient was reliving her painful childhood with me, including intense episodes of deep sadness, loneliness, and a longing for physical comfort. What she received from her family was physical contact *when they wanted it* and *how they wanted to give it*. It was not in response to her healthy needs and it left her feeling used and abused, as well as abandoned. My role was to respond with physical contact in a way that was not sexual or abusive but that was responsive to her pain. In this way she could then repeat the past and create a new, healthy outcome. Unfortunately, I was too caught up in my duty *not* to allow anything to happen that resembled past horrors, and I subsequently lost sight of what my patient needed. And I did not know enough to listen to my own heart to understand what was right for her.

I have kept the promise I made to myself some years ago and have never let a patient sob unrelentingly without providing the touch of a hand. My office is set up so that I sit in a chair and my patients either sit up or lie down on the couch. So I either go and sit next to them, or move my chair closer and extend my hand. The guideline that I use in determining when to provide physical comfort is whether it seems inhuman not to. And I have met with good results.

I have tried experimenting with physical contact prior to the patient reaching the point of seeming almost desperately in need of it, but I made too many errors; I was intrusive and stimulated anxiety or sexual feelings. I rely on the patient's body language to let me know when physical contact is needed. When a patient is crying hard, begins shifting nervously, and tries to hide his head in shame, I move next to him so that I am not "observing" him. Sometimes the patient will extend a hand, or start groping on the couch or end table, as if that hand had nowhere to go. This is usually an indication of wanting physical contact. Sometimes, although not often, a patient will directly ask me to take his hand. The intensity of the moment pre-empts verbalization, which is a part of what makes it difficult to know when a patient needs physical contact.

As with other interventions, if I have reason to seriously question whether touching will be helpful, I will ask the patient. I say something like, "I would like to come and sit next to you, would that be all right?" If the patient says, "No," "I don't know," or does not answer, then I remain in my chair.

Up to now, all of my references to physical contact center on comforting a crying patient. Is this the only time I provide physical comfort? The answer to this question is a qualified yes, in that I will also touch a patient who has finished crying and is in a kind of twilight, disoriented state.

Physical contact is one of the most difficult issues for me. Though I no longer believe that some minimal, comforting contact is incompatible with the analytic process, knowing how and when to touch requires a great deal of sensitivity and a strong relationship between patient and therapist. Because touching is an integral part of our interpersonal repertoires outside of treatment, I believe it does have its place within treatment as well. The problem lies in the enormous potential for therapist self-indulgence, patient abuse, and well-meaning blunders. Given the difficulties inherent in knowing when the patient needs to be touched, my only recommendation is to use non-sexual physical contact sparingly in the aforementioned context, and to consult the patient if you are seriously conflicted on the issue. I look forward to seeing more published reports on the use of physical contact in analytic treatment so that some true sense of what is helpful and therapeutic can be established.

Disclosure of Personal Values and Opinions

I recently read an article in a newspaper that said that therapists promote a certain amorality when they attempt to establish a state of neutrality or unconditional positive regard between themselves and their patients. The article stated that people are turning to religion in the hope of finding some moral and spiritual direction that psychotherapy does not provide. Many of my patients, particularly the younger ones who are still defining themselves, eventually inquire about my personal values or philosophy of life. And they typically do not ask rhetorical questions. When they ask me point blank what I think or feel or believe about something, they want an answer. Naturally, I almost always ask them what they think and why they are asking me. Once this has been explored, if they still want an answer, I give it. Patients who are weak in their own beliefs and are seeking to emulate me do not push to know my opinions. Once they have explored their own, they are content. When patients are stronger they sometimes *do* push, either to help define their own philosophy or morality through discussion, to show me that they are different from me, or to show that we are similar. Whatever the reason, I always answer if the patient insists. I consider it disrespectful not to. When I disclose my personal values or opinions I let my patients know that what I am expressing is only an opinion and that they are free to agree or disagree. In my experience, disclosure of values can help the patient in building a healthy superego.

Disclosure of personal values and opinions can also come into play with patients who feel shame over past behavior. The case of Janet is a perfect example of this. She came for therapy after returning to school to complete her bachelor's degree. At age 35 and with two adolescent children, she longed to build an independent life for herself. Though she had significant marital and other problems, there was no subject that produced more profound emotion in her than discussing her early physical abuse of her son. In recalling how she slapped around her helpless infant because she was frustrated and out of control, she effectively depicted herself as the consummate bad mother. She sobbed, then looked at me and said , "Wasn't that a horrible thing to do?" I was reluctant to agree with her; I tried to focus instead on how she was reliving the past and how she had gone for counseling, as well as telling her mother and husband that she had abused her son. She poignantly told me how impossible it had been to find anyone who would help her to stop. I also said I understood how ashamed she was. All of this worked fairly well, especially when I mentioned her shame. Yet I couldn't help but notice that she kept reliving this period of her life with regularity in the treatment. Every few weeks she would return to this issue and re-experience her grief and shame. And every time she relived it she would turn to me and ask the same thing: "Wasn't that horrible of me?"

Believing as I do that patients keep returning to the same topic in the same form until they get the response they need, I asked myself what I was not giving to Janet. The only conclusion I could come to was that I did not acknowledge that I agreed with her that she had done a terrible thing. The more I thought about it the more I realized that I was like her mother and husband—I listened to her but never really responded personally. I remember her telling me how she had wanted them to be outraged and to tell her to stop hitting her son. But they didn't: they acted as if they never really heard her, because they didn't want to know. What she needed from me was to confirm the reality of the event and still to be compassionate toward her *while taking in the horror of what she had done*. Having seen the light, I was prepared for our next encounter. And when she said "Wasn't what I did horrible?" I said "Yes, it was. It was a terrible thing for a mother to do to a helpless infant." In saying this to her I not only confirmed the truth about her actions but also provided her with the empathy she was unconsciously seeking as the helpless victim of *her* "bad mother." Her response was to sob uncontrollably, ending just in time to gather herself together to leave at the end of her session. When she later made reference to the abuse of her son, she was able to talk about it without the deep shame she had shown previously, and even to show some compassion for herself, acknowledging that her own difficult childhood had not prepared her for motherhood.

Janet needed me to express the truth of my feelings and thoughts about what she had done, knowing full well what my response was likely to be. At other times patients have asked me the same question and I have honestly answered that I *didn't* think what they had done was so terrible. Whether you agree with the patient is not as important as being willing to answer and be seen as a real person with real values, who is also able to accept differing opinions and values in others.

The classical position is that the analytic therapist does not reveal personal opinions for fear of having an untoward effect on the patient. But I believe that negative consequences only result when the therapist's position is volunteered, rather than sought by the patient. A patient who is not ready to use the therapist's opinions constructively in the treatment will not press the therapist to reveal them.

In Summary

Revelation and analysis of the countertransference are useful additions to the repertoire of analytic techniques, particularly during therapeutic impasses and when used in response to a patient's expressed need. Patients communicate their needs for countertransference interventions both directly and indirectly. Indirectly, the patient commonly uses projective identification, which results in a strong affective response from the therapist. Therapists' intense emotions, when managed intelligently, have the potential for completing the much-needed cycle of affective communication between patient and therapist. Therapists are encouraged to develop countertransference techniques that suit their own personality style, using the guidelines provided in this chapter. Failure to express or analyze the countertransference, particularly at critical moments in the treatment process, can result in long impasses, untimely terminations, and treatments that run their course dominated not by the transference, but by the countertransference. The techniques presented here are meant to facilitate productive cycles of dynamic conflict in treatment and to provide both patient and therapist with the awareness and insight pertaining to the transference–countertransference interplay.

CHAPTER 6

Countertransference Issues at Termination

Over the years I have been struck by how many of my patients describe their parents as having been quite good with them when they were young and dependent. I used to wonder how accurate these descriptions were, given the blissful ignorance that characterizes early childhood and latency. But as I worked with them, they would often substantiate their experiences by describing similar positive interactions between their parents and their younger siblings, children of friends or neighbors, and grandchildren. Watching their parents as they played, loved, and responded to infants and young children, my patients reported feeling envious and nostalgic for that period of good parenting.

The likelihood that their parents actually had done a decent job with them when they were young is supported in patients who present with a high degree of integration and ego strength in spite of their tales of childhood hurts or neglect and current presenting symptoms. It is evident that they *did* receive a measure of adequate caretaking and affection in their early lives, or they could not possibly be as healthy as they are.

Just as the earliest stages of life can be the most blissful, the same can often be said of the earliest stage of analytic treatment. The period of exploration and understanding is intellectually stimulating and emotionally gratifying. During this time, most patients are not terribly difficult; they are in pain and are seeking to be known by me. Very often, they present a moving scene as they spill out the unhappiness of their lives. They are gratifying to work with because they are so relieved and grateful when I, as the therapist, seem to understand and know how to help them. Symptom relief begins almost immediately and both of us feel optimistic and pleased with our partnership. Though I do not wish to equate my patients with infants and young children in any literal sense, the blissful beginning of treatment seems much like the "good" early relationship that exists between most parents and children. (Obviously near-psychotic and psychotic families are exempt from this discussion.)

To carry the analogy further, I have often found that these same patients who I am so enamored with in the early stages of treatment are strangely transformed into people who drive me to distraction and frustrate my desire to feel competent and helpful at later stages. This, of course, is due to the transition from an early positive transference to the period of active conflict in the middle stages of treatment. But I also believe that the transformation arises from the inevitable surfacing of developmental issues that are perhaps just as troubling to the therapist as they may have been to the original caretaker. The therapist may find herself saying, "What happened to that incredibly talented and interesting patient who used to entertain and adore me, and who suffered so nobly when we first met?" and "Who is this competitive, ungrateful, incessantly dissatisfied, and wretched soul who has taken his place?" No matter how many people I treat and what I intellectually expect to occur, I never cease to be emotionally surprised by this transformation.

Like the parent who is emotionally surprised by the child who stomps his foot for the first time and screams "No!" in response to a simple request, I am taken aback by my patients' need to oppose me. On a bad day I may think "I am trying so hard and I am such a nice person, how can they treat me this way?" And I think that my martyrdom is akin to what many parents feel on a difficult day with an uncooperative child. What reasonably healthy parents *and* therapists know, however, is that the person we are confronting is not trying to ruin our day. Rather, our patients are trying to assert their feelings and autonomy as best they can. And it is incumbent upon us to respond to these self-assertive efforts, especially if the parents did not.

The only problem with this scenario is that, even though our responses are moderated by our professional training, we are subject to the same emotions and pressures as the parents. But of course, our reactions are not likely to be as intense and potentially unmanageable. We are generally not as ego-involved with our patients as parents are with their children, nor do we have to spend unending hours at a time with them when they are being difficult. Yet because we are human we *are* susceptible to being hurt and to feelings of pride, abandonment, resentment, envy and competition. I make the analogy here between parents and therapists because related growth processes, as well as the repetition of the past, create fertile ground for comparable interpersonal struggles and inter-generational conflicts.

As our patients suffer and grow they are both sad and delighted as they come to need us less. Rather than being solely devoted to us, they begin to tell us of the new people they have met whom they respect and admire. They stop telling us how important we are and begin telling us of their renewed love for their spouses and children, or of a budding new romance that has captivated their hearts and minds. They do better at work, often achieving promotions and higher incomes. Or they go from underachieving in school to making excellent grades. They can become quite high on life and jubilant in their new-found freedom, which sometimes leads not only to "I don't really need you very much anymore" but also to "and you're really not so hot anyway." Narcissistic patients in particular may shamelessly compete with us, rubbing in the fact that they are more talented or successful than we are. This competition usually stimulates countertransference envy and resentment. And in the case of the patient who is too important to the therapist, there may be an unwillingness to allow the patient to grow up and leave.

Dr P was such a therapist. When she first began treating Connie, a talented woman ten years her junior, Dr P was quite effective. She understood Connie and responded well to her in the first phase in treatment, in part because she shared Connie's neediness and narcissistic vulnerability. Over time, Connie became lovingly dependent on Dr P and was extremely sensitive and attentive to her. She always inquired if Dr P seemed tired, ill or upset and was very tender and solicitous toward Dr P, especially if she was needy. Connie also admired Dr P and did not hesitate to express her close attachment and respect for the therapist who was so responsive to her. As the treatment continued and Connie improved, the two of them were increasingly drawn into an idealized and gratifying relationship.

This early and seemingly blissful relationship (that did in fact produce genuine improvement and growth in Connie) was unfortunately soon undermined by Dr P's difficulty in allowing Connie to mature. As Connie became more independent, Dr P made remarks indicating that she envied Connie's youth and potential, noting that she herself was "getting old." These comments were quite destructive to the therapy, especially since Dr P would not overtly acknowledge her feelings of envy, even when confronted by Connie. For her part, Connie repeated the past by basing her self-worth on how much she could give to Dr P; this ultimately ending in failure because she could not restore and transform Dr P.

Eventually, Connie was forced to seek treatment elsewhere because Dr P sabotaged her attempts to be independent. For example, Connie was invited to present a paper at a professional meeting. This meant a great deal to Connie, for it signified recognition from her peers. She was scheduled to present her paper very early in the morning, which she related to her analyst with no comment. Dr P's response was "Don't be upset if no-one comes." Similar comments and behaviors continued until Connie felt forced to terminate. She did so with hesitancy and guilt, remembering how gentle, loving and understanding Dr P had been earlier in her treatment.

Because of her strong attachment and wish to restore Dr P so that the treatment could continue and end successfully, Connie stayed long after Dr P was no longer able to treat her. Singer (1971) has labeled behavior like Connie's (i.e. her attempts to stay with Dr P and save her) as the "compassionate sacrifice." Hirsch (1980–81) points out that this sacrificial behavior is akin to Searles' propositions regarding patients' needs to provide their families with whatever they need, an attitude that is easily transferred to the therapist. As mentioned in earlier chapters, patients attempt to heal their therapists for the same reasons they attempt to heal their families—so that the therapist can give them what they need. And as Hirsch also says:

> In general, individuals limit their growth for fear that it will put them too far beyond their family and lead to two broad consequences, i.e. a frightening sense of cutoffness and aloneness, and a deep injury toward those loved family members who cannot tolerate the others' development and figurative abandonment. (p. 122)

In Connie's case, it had been very difficult for her to leave her parents and hometown, and she had done so only after years of struggle. She felt guilty and frighteningly alone as she contemplated her independence, feeling that separation was the end of the world. Even though she knew she was too tied to her family, much of what she experienced with them was pleasurable and reassuring, which only increased her ambivalence. Because she desperately wanted her freedom, she won the struggle and set out on her own. But unresolved issues, including dependency needs and separation and loss, ultimately led her to seek psychoanalysis.

In replicating the past, Connie established a loving and close relationship with her analyst, only to find that it resulted in a new dependency relationship from which she had to similarly and painfully extricate herself. Dr P acted like Connie's family: she denied her envy, dependence and fear of losing Connie because Connie made her feel good. Instead, she admitted only to positive feelings toward Connie and subtly sabotaged her whenever she made too much progress. Connie forced the issue of termination, set a date, and left, but not without incessant conflict, guilt and anger, following a long period of "compassionate sacrifice" in which she desperately tried to transform Dr P. Why hadn't her analyst loved her enough to support her growth and development? How did the relationship become so enmeshed and destructive when the early years had been so good? As Connie asked herself these questions her answers reflected self-blame and a feeling that she had done something wrong or had been found by her analyst to be unworthy.

Had Dr P been more aware of her countertransference envy and dependence, and her anger at Connie for wanting to leave, Connie's treatment might have ended differently. But Dr P could not work through these issues with Connie because, in part, she felt it was "wrong" for her to feel the way she did. Her shame over needing Connie and being so envious of her led her to destructive behavior toward her "favorite patient." Saying goodbye would never have been easy for these two, but it could have been less traumatic for Connie if Dr P had accepted the inevitable conflicts and losses that accompany the end of the symbiotic phase of treatment and the beginning of termination.

Hirsch (1980–81) emphasizes the importance of the analyst's acceptance of negative reactions to termination as normal:

> The corollary to the patient's compassionate sacrifice is the analyst's anxiety about being surpassed by his or her patient in important ways. The degree of resolution of issues of competition, jealousy and envy are important here. Nonetheless, it is rare not to experience those feelings in the context of an intense relationship. Our patients are often younger, smarter, in better health, better looking, have more potential, have more excitement in their lives, have better relationships with their loved ones, have more money, and on and on. Analysts who are unable to acknowledge both the fact of such differences and ensuing jealousy or competitiveness run the risk of acting unconsciously to stifle the patient. (p. 127)

Racker (1968) brought to light the repercussions for intergenerational competition on the analytic process:

> The desire to bind the patient also corresponds to the desire of parents not to "let go of" their children. As the liberation of the patient from the infantile dependence and its transference equivalent is the core of analytical treatment, we must admit that this desire on the analyst's part acts as a tendency *not* to cure the patient. Thus together with the desire to cure (which likewise has deep roots in the unconscious) we find tendencies in the analyst in the opposite direction. (p. 108)

For the most part, therapists do not acknowledge these tendencies. We emphasize our desire to heal and understand. We deny any wish to keep a patient down or to keep a patient dependent because we perceive these attitudes as shameful. In the context of larger society, the same can be said for parenting. When was the last time you heard parents admit that they did not want to let their children go? Or were so envious of their youth and potential that they found themselves actively competing with and trying to defeat their own children? Yet we know that this happens with some regularity. These attitudes are considered unacceptable for parents, teachers or therapists, in spite of the fact that, up to a point, they are normal and are part of the reality of any relationship.

Therapists hide their envy and resentment because they are afraid that disclosing such feelings will be destructive to the patient and the treatment. They assume that the patient will not know of their envy unless they admit to it and that the patient is not capable of dealing directly with their ambivalence. They also patronizingly assume that confronting what is going on in the here-and-now robs the patient of the opportunity to deal with his intrapsychic experience and the history that determined it. But I think that the therapist's refusal to acknowledge her envy is a defensive maneuver that denies both reality and responsibility in the relationship. This can be seen in Silverman's case study reported earlier. His patient most certainly knew he was stimulating Silverman's envy when he repeatedly threw up to Silverman that his home was far more grand than Silverman's and that he made much more money than Silverman did. He did not want Silverman to attempt to denigrate his achievements, as he felt his father had—he simply wanted Silverman to admit he was envious. When Silverman wouldn't do this, his patient resorted to infantile provocations and, failing to achieve the desired result, fell into depression.

Authority figures who feel envious of and competitive with those whom they are charged to nurture and teach are not malicious or petty so much as they are reluctant to lose a gratifying relationship and, as they age, to face their own mortality. The growth and separation of our children, pupils, supervisees and patients force us to face the reality of their extended and exciting futures compared with our increasingly subdued and routine lives. As they leave us they are often embarking on new relationships and career opportunities, while we go on with business-as-usual. And our pride and feelings may be sorely hurt by those who seem to have quickly forgotten how much they needed and relied on us at one time. The termination phase is characterized by the de-idealization of the therapist, which is part of decathecting the relationship. Now, most of the patient's libidinal energy is directed toward new relationships and activities and toward himself. One day the therapist realizes that a certain "charge" is gone and she is no longer the "loved one." (The patient's withdrawal of love, libido and dependency from the therapist may or may not coincide with the therapist's withdrawal from the patient, with the timing of the withdrawal related to the extent of mutuality in the termination phase. This is discussed in more detail below.)

Discussions of termination issues in the literature are largely devoted to determining when a treatment should end. Shane and Shane (1984) cite the patient's overall emotional health, symptomatic improvement, structural change, increased autonomy, capacity for introspection and self-analysis, self-continuity, and developmental attainments as indicators of readiness for termination. It seems that there is no such thing as a "complete" treatment (i.e. the patient is never fully "cured") and, for the most part, "success" as it relates to treatment is a relative term.

Nonetheless, it seems to me that we should come to some consensus regarding criteria for a successfully completed treatment, not only to recognize the path that leads naturally to termination, but also as a way of measuring our ability to facilitate good treatments. Certainly, however, this should not be confused with unilaterally dictating when a treatment is over and when it is not.

As I read the literature, I often get the impression that *the analyst has the power* to decide when and if the treatment is over. Yet the irrefutable reality is that the treatment is over when either the therapist *or* the patient is no longer interested in continuing the relationship. When a patient decides that he wants to set a termination date and leave, no therapist whom I have ever talked to would seriously consider saying, "But you aren't ready to leave. You haven't really developed a strong capacity for self-analysis." Even if the therapist is right, the patient would not stay for this purpose beyond a token time to pacify the therapist. Patients leave when they feel the relationship no longer offers the opportunity for continued growth and development, no matter what the reason. This may be the limitations of either person, or the limitations of the relationship as a psychodynamic entity. In the best of all possible worlds the decision to end the relationship is coincident with meeting the goals of treatment established mutually at the beginning of treatment, but this is not necessarily so. (Novick (1982) points out that the regular failure of therapists to set treatment goals contributes to the problem of deciding when to terminate.)

It often seems that once termination is a possibility, both therapist and patient scramble to offer reasons why it is a good and timely thing to do. My own view of termination is that it occurs when patient and therapist are "done" with each other. What I mean by this is that the relationship has either failed to evolve productively, has evolved to the point of conflict and has stalemated owing to countertransference dominance, or has evolved to the point of dynamic conflict and been resolved *to the extent that a particular therapist-patient pair were able to do so*—which we call success. Inherent in my view is the recognition of the limits of any therapeutic relationship as well as of the process itself.

As an example, when therapist and patient meet in a treatment setting it is hoped that a certain amount of libidinal investment will take place, and that a basic trust will be established, so that the transference may be enacted actively and emotionally in the present. In this therapeutic relationship, there are cycles of conflicts, resolutions of these conflicts, and achievement of insights that occur between the patient and therapist. When these two people are "done" with each other it is because the tension in the relationship that precipitated the conflict has been lost. And, it was lost because it diminished productively through constant interaction and working through, or it escalated out of control, prohibiting closure. A favorite analogy of many analytic clinicians is the dramatic stage play. The drama in the consulting room can be likened to the action in a well-written play: Early in the play, the characters and premise are revealed; this is followed by building and resolving the conflict within the play, which usually ends with the attainment of insight or acceptance of reality by the protagonist. As with a good analytic treatment, the ideal amount of tension in a play keeps the audience involved and interested but not overwhelmed. The ending is neither precipitous nor too drawn out, but rather gives the audience the opportunity to process what has happened between the characters and what it means, allowing a sense of closure.

Analytic treatment approached from this interpersonal perspective places the ideal time for beginning termination at the hypothetical point where the patient has achieved all that he needs. It is at this point that termination begins, whether the process is conscious in the minds of either patient or therapist. Whether it is timely, whether the goals of treatment have been met, or whether each person in the therapeutic dyad is satisfied with the results are all basically irrelevant. Once the idea crystallizes for either patient or therapist that there is not much more to be gained in spending time together, then termination has begun. (A major factor for many patients in making this decision is how much they must sacrifice in terms of time and money. I find that patients who pay a considerable amount of the fee out-of-pocket tend to stay less time than patients whose insurance covers most of the cost.)

The decision to end a treatment may or may not be mutual, but the more mutual it is, the smoother the termination phase will be. Unsurprisingly, mutuality in the earlier stages of treatment is likely to carry over into the termination phase, providing a smooth transition toward the end. I believe that more authoritarian and "troubled" treatments present more problems at termination. These kinds of relationships do not prepare either party for the autonomous atmosphere that is characteristic of a successful termination.

Yet even mutual and otherwise successful treatments may break down at the point of beginning the termination phase. I doubt that there is any such thing as a good end to a bad treatment, but a good treatment can be wrecked by a failure to address important termination issues. For example, in the case of Connie and Dr P, the basic tension between them was not resolved because of Dr P's inability to deal with her dependence on and envious resentment of Connie. The tension in the relationship became unbearable and unproductive and Connie felt she had no choice but to terminate. Neither party was truly "done" with the other, yet at the same time they were, in the sense that their situation steadily worsened and was seemingly unresolvable. Needless to say, the termination was a destructive and unhealthy event for them; each was forced to separate psychologically from the other after the relationship had ended rather than working it through together in the termination phase.

Aborted endings are also evident when the therapist cannot participate in the grieving process; i.e. she avoids acute pain in the present and squashes her patient's necessary grieving. And if the termination is excessively prolonged, such a therapist is likely to use the patient as a self-object, rewarding him for his responsive or entertaining personality and encouraging an endlessly friendly relationship. Any of these counter-transference obstacles, singly or in combination, temporary or long-term, must be addressed with the patient to achieve a successful termination.

At this point I can imagine the reader saying: "Of course—the things you say are obvious. And for those therapists who have such counter-transference difficulties, a remedy already exists. Consultation, self-analysis and, if necessary, a return to personal analysis are the methods for dealing with these troubling situations. Analysis and psychoanalytic psychotherapy have long been practiced in this way, and to my way of thinking, quite successfully. Your suggestions of dragging the patient into the therapist's neuroticism or character pathology seem highly inappropriate and an invitation to an emotional free-for-all."

My answer to this is primarily a repetition of what I have been saying throughout this book. First of all, I think we greatly underestimate how frequently countertransference problems arise. Second, I do not believe that the conventional analytic method is as consistently effective as expressing the countertransference. Third, the countertransference is only expressed in response to the patient *who is already aware of a counter-transference problem and is seeking to discuss this openly*. In the case of Connie, for example, she confronted Dr P with her inability to let go, which Dr P denied. Instead, Dr P focused on Connie's fears of leaving and on her grandiose wish that Dr P needed to keep her. Though Dr P was accurate in her assessment of Connie's feelings, by denying the countertransference that Connie was well aware of, she blocked the opportunity for the two of them to talk out and resolve their mutual dependency and fear of separation.

The notion that Dr P represents an exceptional case seems to me to deny the regularity of significant countertransference enactments in the therapeutic relationship. And, to disregard the patient's desire to know the truth and to refuse to engage in resolving transference–countertransference problems is arrogant and disrespectful, as well as a gross underestimation of the patient's ability to help resolve such difficulties.

For those readers who are skeptical regarding the likelihood of failed and poorly terminated treatments, or about the need for awareness and admission of possible therapeutic blind-spots, I cite a recent pilot study of Kantrowitz *et al.* (1989) suggesting that many analysts significantly overestimate the positive effects and outcomes of their treatments and are entirely unaware of the psychodynamics that they have in common with their patients. Kantrowitz and colleagues studied the patient–analyst match, noting when patient and analyst had certain issues in common. They found five analytic cases in which patient and therapist had the same narcissistic issues:

> Neither patients nor analysts expressed awareness of the central problems in themselves or in the other. Four of these five analysts viewed their patients as having successfully entered into and benefited from psychoanalytic treatment. They believed a transference neurosis had been established and at least partially resolved. The fifth analyst was less positive about the patient's ability to enter into psychoanalytic work without the use of some parameters, and was more actively gratifying to this patient than would be usual with standard psychoanalytic technique. *According to psychological test findings, these five cases showed little or no improvement following psychoanalysis.* (p. 908) [Emphasis mine.]

Granted, these findings are based on small samples and cannot be considered conclusive. Yet they do support the concept of the analyst as a potential hindrance to the analytic process, particularly when narcissistic issues are at the forefront. (This preliminary report also supports the ideas of Finell (1985), cited earlier, concerning consequences of the analyst's narcissism.)

Kantrowitz and colleagues also note that countertransference issues seem more important than any other factor pertaining to a poor outcome:

> While some errors may be due to limited skill, we believe that what may be perceived as "poor technique" leading to a disruption of the analytic work may frequently be the consequence of dynamic interplay between the patient's difficulties and some quality, characteristic, or conflict of the analyst. (p. 915)

Countertransference problems not only lead to premature terminations but also contribute to the lackluster endings of many analytic treatments. According to Glover (1955), the majority of analyses are discontinued rather than terminated:

> They never pass through a terminal stage and most are, strictly speaking, stalemate analyses. I, too, would suggest that many analyses that end under what seem to be mutually agreed-upon terms are in fact premature terminations brought about by either the patient or the analyst. (p. 331)

The need to confront the countertransference to achieve a successful termination is underscored by Buxbaum (1950), who says , "to resolve the countertransference becomes a major part of the analytic process of termination" (p. 190). As I previously indicated, dealing with the countertransference at termination in a way that does not provoke an emotional free-for-all is accomplished by adhering to the guideline of following the patient's lead. Determining the degree of countertransference revelation and analysis depends on its strength and on the patient's capacity for confronting it. Most patients seem to ask for more counter-transference disclosure during the termination phase, but the frequency of their requests at this stage correlates with the frequency of requests at earlier stages. Some patients ask only for certain information such as "Is it really okay for me to go?" or "Will you remember me and think of me from time to time?" Others demand a more comprehensive revelation and understanding of the transference–countertransference dynamics. They want and need to know what the nature of the therapeutic relationship has been, how the therapist contributed to conflicts, what areas were difficult for the therapist to address because of her own limitations, and how each feels about the pending separation and loss. Little (1951) discussed how the literature reflects the difficulty many analysts have with facing these vital termination issues *with the patient*:

> Analysts writing about the final stages of analysis and its termination speak over and over again of the way in which patients reach a certain point, and then either slip away and break off the analysis just at the moment when to continue is vital for its ultimate success, or else slip again into another of their interminable repetitions, instead of analysing the anxiety situations. Countertransference may perhaps be the deciding factor at this point, and the analyst's willingness to deal with it may be the all-important thing. (p. 38)

Separation and Loss

Critical to resolution of the countertransference, in addition to the aforementioned issues of narcissistic gratification, envy and competitiveness on the therapist's part, are the issues of separation and loss. Firestein (1982), in his study of termination in psychoanalysis, reported that:

> . . . analysts experienced not only varying degrees of anxiety over terminating with their patients, but gradation of what, for want of a better description, could be called grief. They referred to regrets about ending the collaboration with an interesting, witty, or gifted individual; a patient who "worked well" in analysis; or one who was responsible for an especially instructive learning experience for the analyst. It was apparent that an analyst's gratifications from conducting an analysis consist of more than the functional satisfaction of doing one's job well. Separation reactions are experienced by both members of the dyad. (p. 215)

More recently, Klauber (1986), in an exploration of the elements of the psychoanalytic relationship, noted the following:

> It is strange . . . that there seems to be no discussion of the effects on the analyst of forming relationship after relationship of the deepest and most intimate kind with patient after patient, and mourning which at some level must be involved for each one of them. (p. 202)

Traditionally, any grieving at the time of termination has been a one-way street—at least on the surface. I think that most therapists will acknowledge the sadness inherent in saying goodbye to someone with whom they have worked for years. But few seem to consider the possibility that *mutual grieving* might be therapeutic. Standard practice and theory require the analytic therapist to contain and process her grief internally, rather than burdening the patient with feelings that may make him feel guilty about leaving. Yet patients who are in the process of leaving invariably seek answers to questions like "Will you miss me after I leave?", "Will you still think of me after I am gone?", "Will you be sad to see me go?"; or, while still in the midst of grieving the loss, "If you really care about me, how can you let me go?" Such questions present poignant moments in the treatment and, from my perspective, provide a unique opportunity for the therapist to respond with feeling, while still acknowledging the reality of and the necessity for termination.

Naturally, every situation with every patient is unique. With some patients there may be relief that a difficult treatment is over. With others the therapist may feel deep sadness. Ambivalence often prevails, of course, either because the therapist is ambivalent toward the patient or about the termination. If the patient has done well the clinician is typically pleased and proud of the progress he has made and happy that he is no longer in need of treatment. Yet the patients it is easiest to be happy for, the ones who have truly grown and irrevocably altered their lives, may also be the ones it is hardest to lose.

Regarding termination and countertransference grief, how much should the therapist express to the patient? To what extent should a therapist reveal his feelings, and to what end? As with all other countertransference reactions, I believe it is best to follow the patient's lead. For some patients, mutual grieving might be too overwhelming. They may have enough trouble dealing with their own grief and the prospect of mutual grieving may be frightening. These patients, however, do not attempt to elicit their therapist's feelings. They are content to grieve alone, with the therapist as compassionate witness to their experience. Mutuality is comfortably achieved through silently noting the therapist's sad expression or slightly depressed mood as the termination date approaches. Patients who do not wish to know any more about what their therapists are feeling do not ask for it.

Other patients, however, not only seek to know what their therapists are feeling, they cannot rest until they stimulate some affective expression on the therapist's part. Since patients in the termination phase use little or no projective identification to stimulate their therapists, most requests for disclosure of the countertransference are quite direct and straightforward. Nothing can be clearer or simpler than "Will you miss me?" And most patients are quite satisfied with the simplest of responses, such as "Yes, I will."

But, you may ask, what if the truth is that you will *not* miss your patient? What if the answer is "No"? My own experience is that this rarely happens. Instead, patients who have been quite difficult to work with will cry and will say that they wished things could have been easier so that I *would* miss them. If a patient who I would *not* miss insists on an answer to his question, I assume that he needs to know the truth and I tell it to him as gently as possible.

When a patient who knows that I care very much about him says, "How can you care about me and still let me go?", the only answer I can give is "I am letting you go because I *do* care about you." We must give our patients credit for understanding that it is in their best interests to leave one day. Even patients who have desperately wanted me to be their mothers or lovers throughout much of their treatment have always understood that the fulfillment of any of these fantasies would be destructive. So when I tell them that I am letting them go because I care about them, they understand and appreciate my response. Patients who have been held emotional hostage by hostile dependent parents are especially moved by the acknowledgement of my genuine caring as something that promotes their autonomy and personal freedom rather than being "the tie that binds."

At times I have been moved to tears by a patient who is grieving the end of our relationship. Granted, the tears I shed are also for past losses in my own life, just as this is so for my patient. Yet for each of us the pain is also real in the present. And the times when I have been moved to tears have proven to be therapeutic for my patients in that they report feeling very good afterward, experiencing equality and respect. Again, though, I want to emphasize that I do not match my patients' affect. While they may be sobbing, my own expression of grief does not go beyond a tear or light weeping, which accurately reflects the depth of my feeling. In this way the patient very clearly sees to what extent we share feelings without feeling overwhelmed or concerned that I need to be taken care of. A therapist who breaks down sobbing when she expresses grief is obviously someone who has insufficiently grieved past losses and needs to take care of this problem in a personal analysis.

Besides seeking to know the extent of their therapist's grief, many patients will also seek assurances that the therapist will be all right without them. Again, patients whose parents trained them to be responsible for their happiness have difficulty believing that their therapist is perfectly capable of taking care of herself. Reassurance, in and of itself, will not respond to this patient's feelings. The patient will only be convinced of the therapist's genuine desire to let go when her mood and responses to increased separation and autonomy are positive.

Sometimes the patient may need to know that the therapist's off-mood or bout of flu or whatever is not connected to the pending termination. If the patient accurately perceives that his therapist seems "down," the question may arise, "Are you depressed because I am leaving you soon?" I think that the therapist should not hesitate to answer the question honestly, so that the patient is clear about what is happening.

You may say that this sounds well and good provided the therapist is upset about something else, but what if the therapist *is* depressed because the patient is leaving? What if the patient is the aforementioned rare person who is bright, talented, interesting, lovable, has made good progress, and in the process has enhanced the life of the therapist? What if, in reality, it is difficult for the therapist to let the patient go?

I prefer to tell the patient the truth. If he is asking the question, then he unconsciously already knows the answer and will not respond well to being put off or distracted. Also, the therapist's ambivalence about separation is likely to be a repetition of the patient's past. The patient's parent probably had trouble letting him go, too, but could not admit it and give him a chance to accept and understand the parent's feelings.

The therapist who can admit her reluctance to having her patient leave can also potentially avert a situation in which the patient stays on for years after the treatment has really ended. Telling a patient that he will be missed, that it is hard to say goodbye, and that it is sad to lose him can provide both patient and therapist with an opportunity to deal with the situation honestly and directly. Invariably, the patient will be concerned or even upset and will probably ask if he should stay. And he may be angry because the therapist is making his leavetaking difficult. But he will probably also be touched that his therapist is so involved with him and is seeking a way to facilitate his autonomy.

Once these feelings are disclosed, the therapist needs to help her patient process his responses, to confront her own dependence on the patient and to let the patient help with the separation process. For example, if a therapist knows that she is not quite ready for one of her patients to leave, *and he asks directly if he should stay longer*, it may be wise to ask for an additional week or two in the interests of facilitating a guilt-free or at least guilt-reduced termination for the patient. Otherwise, the patient will have to guiltily tear himself away from his therapist or, even worse, delay termination while pretending that he is doing so out of his need rather than in response to his therapist's.

Mutual De-idealization and Disappointment

In addition to the difficult issues of envy, competition, and separation and loss that characterize the termination phase of treatment, there are the issues of de-idealization and disappointment. As the treatment winds down both parties confront all that they could not accomplish and the extent to which they could not transform or be transformed. I recommend caution as a therapist deals with countertransference disappointments, such as "blaming" the patient for not having improved more or for failing to fulfill some of her fantasies. Because the therapist's disappointment with her patient usually has more to do with disappointments in her own life, and because disclosing disappointment is often demoralizing to the patient, I think it should not be disclosed. If the patient accurately picks up on the therapist's disappointment, *and confronts the therapist with it*, the therapist has an obligation to take responsibility for her feelings and to say no more than "Yes, I am disappointed, but in myself, not you. I usually think I should be able to do more, or be more than I can be, and I am prone to being hard on myself when I fall short. But I really believe that you've accomplished a lot here."

Regardless of countertransference issues, at the termination phase the patient has emerged from symbiosis with his therapist, has improved his reality-testing, is much more direct in communicating feeling, and is seeking to affirm all of these accomplishments with his therapist. In this phase the patient is much more likely to hypothesize regarding the therapist's psychodynamics, and often cites numerous instances of the therapist's behavior throughout the treatment as supportive evidence. The patient is likely to solicit or even demand disclosure of the transference-countertransference as well as its analysis. In the interests of understanding and closure, the patient may ask about the psychodynamic sources of the therapist's earlier countertransference disclosures. The patient can then see clearly how his therapist's psychodynamics either mirrors or complements his own, giving him a deeper understanding and appreciation for the transference–countertransference exchanges that have determined the nature and character of this very important and long-term relationship.

For example, I had a patient who accurately noted how much I hated it when she blamed me for everything that went on in her life. Even when I said nothing she could tell by looking at my face that I was suppressing anger. During the termination phase she asked me why I had lost my patience so easily when she blamed me, saying that I had seemed particularly sensitive on this issue. Understanding that her blaming behavior would be seen as undesirable and unappealing to anyone, she wondered if she was right in thinking that this had bothered me more than the average person. I told her she was right. I informed her that I grew up with family members who often made me the scapegoat for anything that upset them and, after growing up under this psychological oppression, I tended to studiously avoid people who were prone to blaming me and I was no doubt less tolerant of it than most. We also discussed how she had assessed this vulnerability of mine rather early in the treatment, knowing how to get to me when she wanted to.

For her to understand why I reacted as I did, along with why she needed to blame others and frequently wished to provoke anger in others, is what I call analysis of the transference–countertransference (as defined in Chapter 5). It is an overall view of how, what and why things happen in the treatment relationship. It acknowledges the role of past experience and the unconscious in both patient and analyst, and helps the patient to understand how transference reactions can be managed, if not eliminated.

Had I used this patient's inquiry as the basis for some long diatribe about the misfortunes of my childhood, I would have been misusing her therapy hour to indulge myself. She merely asked me to verify her observation that I was vulnerable in a particular area and to give a general explanation of why this was so. I gave her the most parsimonious but complete answer that I could. And I would not say any more unless she asked. There is no doubt, particularly during the termination phase when the patient is less in need of seeing the therapist as invulnerable, that one question can lead to another. If I think some questions are getting too far afield, I ask the patient if they are really necessary. At this point the patient usually backs off and admits that curiosity has taken over. If the patient is clearly still working on understanding something, and says that he needs a bit more information, I will provide it unless I have personal reasons for not wishing to do so.

Following the analogy between normal psychological development and the analytic process, the termination phase is one of autonomy and equality. It is a time for being free of attachment to irrational authority and for achieving separation and individuation without guilt. Just as adolescents compete with their parents and even gloat when they discover that they are stronger, faster, better-looking, or smarter than their parents, so do our patients compete with us. Like the growing adolescent, a patient's stimulation of our envy represents both a wish and a fear. If he succeeds he fears being struck down by the still-powerful parent, yet if he fails to inspire envy then how good can he be? The late adolescent looks forward to leaving home and having an independent life, yet still wishes to return to the parents for admiration and approval.

Once independence is achieved, the growing young adult seeks to know his parents as individuals in the world. He wants to understand how and why his relations with them worked. And, more confident, strong and independent, he needs to know about their weaknesses as a part of really knowing and accepting them as separate human beings. It seems only natural that we accord our adult patients their comparable needs and wants arising from a similar growth process—the analytic treatment. To the extent that their own parents failed in according them equal status, I think it even more critical that we do not make the same mistake.

Termination is the last opportunity to facilitate true and healthy separation, something usually accompanied by grief and envy. When the patient is ready and able to confront the countertransference, I believe it should be disclosed and analyzed, both in the interest of respecting him as another competent adult and giving him the freedom to continue to use and build his strength in the world.

Conclusion

Disclosure and analysis of the countertransference provide a means for the analytic clinician to maximize the interpersonal encounters inherent in any treatment. I have outlined the techniques for using the countertransference to heighten and enhance the analytic experience, but urge therapists to understand and appreciate their own talents, limitations and interpersonal style when implementing these techniques.

My response to those who fear that disclosure of the countertransference, even when done conservatively and at the patient's behest, will lead necessarily to "wild analysis" and unseemly gratification of the therapist's personal needs, is simply this: more damage is done when the therapist hides than when he or she is direct and honest. I believe that more harm is done to patients by well-meaning therapists who do not want to "burden" their patients than by honest, straightforward clinicians who admit to the realities of doing therapy.

Under no circumstances should the guidelines for disclosure of therapist affect, opinions and values advocated in this book be confused with advocating dismissal of boundaries in the therapeutic relationship. In fact, part of the aim of this book is to offer alternatives for therapists who have identified a need to express themselves so that the integrity of the analytic situation can truly be maintained. It is my belief that a therapist's inhibition of affect actually lends itself to therapist acting-out because the need to express oneself in an intense interpersonal situation is so basic and inescapable.

It is my hope that clinicians reading this book will be able to use the countertransference techniques successfully in the spirit of responding to a patient's genuine need in a responsible and compassionate manner. However, no matter how a therapist feels about any given patient, the boundaries that define the analytic situation and ensure the safety of the patient must be maintained. It is not my intent, nor would I ever condone, disclosure of the countertransference for the purpose of establishing a personal or social relationship with the patient beyond the treatment setting, or engaging in physical contact, sexual or otherwise, at any time.

The point of disclosing therapist affect is not to act on it, but rather to acknowledge the reality of the interpersonal relationship that exists, and often to provide the needed pre-verbal response to the patient's pre-verbal communication. Finally, I hope that this book will aid therapists who understand the importance of affect and who wish to be actively involved in a more mutual and non-authoritarian analytic relationship.

References

Abend, S. M. (1986). 'Countertransference, empathy, and the analytic ideal: the impact of life stresses on analytic capability', *Psychoanalytic Quarterly*, **55**, 563-575.

Abend, S. M. (1989). 'Countertransference and psychoanalytic technique', *Psychoanalytic Quarterly*, **58**, 374-395.

Arlow, J. (1985). 'Some technical problems of countertransference', *Psychoanalytic Quarterly*, **54**, 164-174.

Atwood, G. E., Stolorow, R. D., and Trop, J. L. (1989). 'Impasses in psychoanalytic therapy: a royal road', *Contemporary Psychoanalysis*, **25**, 554-573.

Balint, M. (1968). *The Basic Fault*. Tavistock, London.

Benedek, T. (1953). 'Dynamics of the countertransference', *Bulletin of the Menninger Clinic*, **17**, 201-208.

Bion, W. R. (1959). *Second Thoughts*, Heinemann, London.

Bion, W. R. (1962). *Learning from Experience*, Heinemann, London.

Bion, W. R. (1967). 'Notes on memory and desire', *Psychoanalytic Forum*, **2**, 271-280.

Bird, B. (1972). 'Notes on transference: universal phenomenon and hardest part of analysis', *Journal of the American Psychoanalytic Association*, **20**, 267-301.

Bollas, C. (1983). 'Expressive uses of the countertransference', *Contemporary Psychoanalysis*, **19**, 1-34.

Bollas, C. (1986). 'The transformational object', in *The British School of Psychoanalysis: The Independent Tradition* (Ed. G. Kohon), pp. 83-100. Free Association Books, London.

Bollas, C. (1987). *The Shadow of the Object: Psychoanalysis of the Unthought Known*. Columbia University Press, New York.

Brenman-Pick, I. (1985). 'Working through in the countertransference', *International Journal of Psycho-Analysis*, **66**, 157-166.

Brenner, C. (1985). 'Countertransference as a compromise formation', *Psychoanalytic Quarterly*, **54**, 155-163.

Buxbaum, E. (1950). 'Technique of terminating analysis', *International Journal of Psycho-Analysis*, **31**, 184-190.

Compton, A. (1975). 'Aspects of psychoanalytic intervention', in *Kris Study Group Monograph VI* (Ed. B. Fine and H. F. Waldhorn), pp. 23-97.

Compton, A. (1988). 'Psychoanalytic cure', *Psychoanalytic Review*, **75**, 217-229.

Dahl, H., Keller, V., Moss, D., and Trujillo, M. (1978). 'Countertransference examples of the syntactic expression of warded-off contents', *Psychoanalytic Quarterly*, **47**, 339-363.

Eber, M. (1990). 'Erotized transference reconsidered: expanding the counter-transference dimension', *Psychoanalytic Review*, **77**, 25-39.

Finell, J. S. (1985). 'Narcissistic problems in analysts', *International Journal of Psycho-Analysis*, **66**, 433-445.

Finell, J. S. (1986). 'The merits and problems with the concept of projective identification', *Psychoanalytic Review*, **73**, 103-120.

Firestein, S. K. (1982). *Termination in Psychoanalysis*. International Universities Press, New York.

Fromm, E. (1956). *The Art of Loving*. Harper and Row, New York.

Gedo, J. (1989). 'An epistemology of transference', *Annual of Psychoanalysis*, **17**, 3-15.

Gill, M. (1979). 'The analysis of the transference', *Journal of the American Psychoanalytic Association (Supplement)*, **27**, 263-288.

Gill, M. (1982). *Analysis of Transference*, Vol. I. International Universities Press, New York.

Gill, M. (1984-1985). 'The range of applicability of psychoanalytic technique', *International Journal of Psychoanalytic Psychotherapy*, **10**, 109-116.

Giovacchini, P. L. (1972). 'Interpretation and definition of the analytic setting', in *Tactics and Techniques in Psychoanalytic Therapy*, Vol. I (Ed. P. L. Giovacchini), pp. 291-304. Science House, New York.

Gitelson, M. (1952). 'The emotional position of the analyst in the psychoanalytic situation', *International Journal of Psycho-Analysis*, **33**, 1-10.

Glover, E. (1955). 'The terminal phase', in *The Technique of Psychoanalysis*, pp. 138-164. International Universities Press, New York.

Goodman, M., and Teicher, A. (1988). 'To touch or not to touch', *Psychotherapy*, **25**, 492-500.

Gorkin, M. (1985). 'Varieties of sexualized countertransference', *Psychoanalytic Review*, **72**, 421-440.

Gorkin, M. (1987). *The Uses of Countertransference*. Aronson, Northvale, New Jersey.

Greenberg, J. (1986). 'The problems of analytic neutrality', *Contemporary Psychoanalysis*, **22**, 76-85.

Greenson, R. R. (1965). 'The working alliance and the transference neurosis', *Psychoanalytic Quarterly*, **34**, 155-181.

Greenson, R. R. (1967). *The Technique and Practice of Psychoanalysis*. International Universities Press, New York.

Greenson, R. R. (1971). 'The "real" relationship between the patient and the psychoanalyst', in *The Unconscious Today* (Ed. M. Kanzer), pp. 213-232. International Universities Press, New York.

Greenson, R. R. (1974). 'Loving, hating, and indifference towards the patient', *International Review of Psycho-Analysis*, **1**, 259-266.

Grotstein, J. S. (1987). 'Making the best of a bad deal: a discussion of Boris's "Bion Revisited"', *Contemporary Psychoanalysis*, **23**, 60-76.

Heimann, P. (1950). 'On countertransference', *International Journal of Psychoanalysis*, **31**, 81-84.

Hirsch, I. (1980-1981). 'Authoritarian aspects of the psychoanalytic relationship', *Review of Existential Psychology and Psychiatry*, **17**, 105-133.

Kantrowitz, J. L., Katz, A. L., Greenman, D. A., Morris, H., Paolitto, F., Sashin, J., and Solomon, L. (1989). 'The patient-analyst match and the outcome of psychoanalysis: a pilot study', *Journal of the American Psychoanalytic Association*, **37**, 893-919.

Kasin, E. (1986). 'Roots and branches', *Contemporary Psychoanalysis*, **22**, 452-458.

Kernberg, O. (1965). 'Notes on countertransference', *Journal of the American Psychoanalytic Association*, **13**, 38–56.

Kernberg, O. (1975). *Borderline Conditions and Pathological Narcissism*. Aronson, New York.

Kernberg, O. (1987). 'Projection and projective identification: developmental and clinical aspects', *Journal of the American Psychoanalytic Association*, **35**, 795–819.

Klauber, J. (1986). 'Elements of the psychoanalytic relationship and their therapeutic implications', in *The British School of Psychoanalysis: The Independent Tradition* (Ed. G. Kohon), pp. 200–213. Free Association Books, London.

Kohut, H. (1971). *The Analysis of the Self*. International Universities Press, New York.

Kohut, H. (1977). *The Restoration of the Self*. International Universities Press, New York.

Langs, R. J. (1974). *The Technique of Personality*, Vol. II. Aronson, New York.

Langs, R. J. (1975). 'The patient's unconscious perception of the therapist's errors', in *Tactics and Techniques in Psychoanalytic Therapy*, Vol. II (Ed. P. L. Giovacchini), pp. 230–250. Aronson, New York.

Langs, R. J. (1976). *The Bi-Personal Field*. Aronson, New York.

Langs, R. J. (1978). *The Listening Process*. Aronson, New York.

Lipton, S. D. (1977) 'The advantages of Freud's technique as shown in his analysis of the rat man', *International Journal of Psycho-Analysis*, **58**, 255–274.

Little, M. (1951). 'Countertransference and the patient's response to it', *International Journal of Psycho-Analysis*, **32**, 32–40.

Little, M. (1957). '"R"—The analyst's total response to his patient's needs', *International Journal of Psycho-Analysis*, **38**, 240–254.

Little, M. (1981). *Transference Neurosis and Transference Psychosis*. Aronson, New York.

Lomas, P. (1987). *The Limits of Interpretation: What's Wrong with Psychoanalysis?* Penguin, New York.

Malin, A., and Grotstein, J. (1966). 'Projective identification in the therapeutic process', *International Journal of Psycho-Analysis*, **47**, 26–31.

McLaughlin, J. T. (1981). 'Transference, psychic reality and countertransference', *Psychoanalytic Quarterly*, **50**, 639–664.

Miller, A. (1981). *Prisoners of Childhood: The Drama of the Gifted Child*. Basic Books, New York.

Money-Kyrle, R. E. (1956). 'Normal countertransference and some of its deviations', *International Journal of Psycho-Analysis*, **37**, 360–366.

Moses, I. (1988). 'The misuse of empathy in psychoanalysis', *Contemporary Psychoanalysis*, **24**, 577–594.

Namnun, A. (1976). 'Activity and personal involvement in psychoanalytic technique', *Bulletin of the Menninger Clinic*, **40**, 105–117.

Novick, J. (1982). 'Termination themes and issues', *Psychoanalytic Inquiry*, **2**, 329–365.

Pierloot, R. A. (1987). 'The analysand as a character in search of an author', *International Review of Psychoanalysis*, **14**, 221–230.

Racker, H. (1968). *Transference and Countertransference*. International Universities Press, New York.

Reich, A. (1950). 'On the termination of analysis', in *Psychoanalytic Contributions*, pp. 121–135. International Universities Press, New York.

Reich, A. (1960). 'Further remarks on countertransference', *International Journal of Psycho-Analysis*, **32**, 25-31.

Sandler, J. (1976). 'Countertransference and role-responsiveness', *International Review of Psychoanalysis*, **3**, 43-47.

Schafer, R. (1976). *A New Language for Psychoanalysis*. Yale University Press, New Haven.

Schafer, R. (1983). *The Analytic Attitude*. Basic Books, New York.

Schlessinger, N., and Robbins, F. (1983). *A Developmental View of the Psychoanalytic Process: Follow-up Studies and Their Consequences*. International Universities Press, New York.

Searles, H. F. (1973). 'Concerning therapeutic symbiosis', *Annual of Psychoanalysis*, **1**, 247-262.

Searles, H. F. (1975). 'The patient as therapist to his analyst', in *Tactics and Techniques in Psychoanalytic Therapy*, Vol. II (Ed. P.L. Giovacchini), pp. 95-151, Aronson, New York.

Searles, H. F. (1979). *Countertransference and Related Subjects*. International Universities Press, New York.

Shane, M., and Shane, E. (1984). 'The end phase of analysis: indicators, functions, and tasks of termination', *Journal of the American Psychoanalytic Association*, **32**, 739-777.

Silverman, M. A. (1985). 'Countertransference and the analyzed analyst', *Psychoanalytic Quarterly*, **54**, 175-199.

Singer, E. (1971). 'The patient and the analyst: some clinical and theoretical observations', in *In the Name of Life* (Eds. B. Landis and E. S. Tauber), pp. 56-68. Holt, Rinehart and Winston, New York.

Slakter, E. (Ed.) (1987). *Countertransference*, Aronson, New York.

Stein, M. (1988). 'Writing about psychoanalysis', *Journal of the American Psychoanalytic Association*, **36**, 393-408.

Stern, D. B. (1988). 'Not misusing empathy', *Contemporary Psychoanalysis*, **24**, 598-609.

Stern, D. B. (1989). 'The analyst's unformulated experience of the patient', *Contemporary Psychoanalysis*, **25**, 1-33.

Stewart, H. (1989). 'Technique at the basic fault/regression', *International Journal of Psycho-Analysis*, **70**, 221-230.

Stolorow, R. D., Brandchaft, B., and Atwood, G. E. (1987). *Psychoanalytic Treatment: An Intersubjective Approach*. Analytic Press, Hillsdale, New Jersey.

Stolorow, R. D., and Lachman, F. (1984/1985). 'Transference: the future of an illusion', *Annual of Psychoanalysis*, **12/13**, 19-37.

Strachey, J. (1934). 'The nature of the therapeutic action of psychoanalysis', *International Journal of Psycho-Analysis*, **15**, 117-126.

Sullivan, H. S. (1953). *The Interpersonal Theory of Psychiatry*. Norton, New York.

Szasz, T. (1963). 'The concept of transference', *International Journal of Psycho-Analysis*, **44**, 432-443.

Tansey, M. J., and Burke, W. F. (1989). *Understanding Countertransference: From Projective Identification to Empathy*. Analytic Press, Hillsdale, New Jersey.

Tauber, E. S. (1954). 'Exploring the therapeutic use of countertransference data', *Psychiatry*, **17**, 331-336.

Tower, L. (1956). 'Countertransference', *Journal of the American Psychoanalytic Association*, **4**, 224-255.

Tyson, R. L. (1986). 'Countertransference evolution in theory and practice', *Journal of the American Psychoanalytic Association*, **34**, 251-274.

Wachtel, P. (1986). 'On the limits of therapeutic neutrality', *Contemporary Psychoanalysis*, **22**, 60-70.

Wallerstein, R. S. (1988). 'One psychoanalysis too many?', *International Journal of Psycho-Analysis*, **69**, 5-21.

Whipple, D. (1986). 'Discussion of "The merits and problems with the concept of projective identification by Janet Finell"', *Psychoanalytic Review*, **73**, 121-128.

Winnicott, D. W. (1949). 'Hate in the countertransference', *International Journal of Psycho-Analysis*, **30**, 69-74.

Zetzel, E. (1956). 'Current concepts of transference', *International Journal of Psycho-Analysis*, **37**, 369-376.

Index

$\langle \Phi | + \# \rangle = \#$